Psychoanalytic Studies of the Work of Adam Smith

T0304170

Psychoanalytic Studies of the Work of Adam Smith blends the rich intellectual herit-age of the hermeneutic tradition with the methods and concepts of psychoa-nalysis, in order to examine the seminal works of Adam Smith. This is the first book on Smith to analyze the works of the ground-breaking moral theorist and founding father of economics from a psychoanalytic perspective, whilst also examining the human capacities and skills that are necessary to put Smith's ideas into practice.

Starting with a detailed discussion of the psychological difficulties that afflicted Smith, Özler and Gabrinetti examine the influence that Smith's life had on the ideas that are found in his major works. The authors explore the sympathetic process in Smith's *The Theory of Moral Sentiments (TMS)* from an intersubjectivist perspective and use ideas from developmental psychology to argue that sympathy leads to morality. This book contains a thorough analy-sis of the defenses that are used to create Smith's moral system in the *TMS* and explores how Smith's ideas were precursors to concepts later developed by Freud. The authors show that Smith's attitude toward women was at best ambivalent and consider the reciprocal interaction between markets and moral-ity from an evolutionary psychology perspective.

Covering an impressive range of topics, this book will appeal to academics and postgraduate students with an interest in psychoanalysis, moral philosophy, history of thought and the social sciences. The book should also be of interest to more advanced undergraduate students.

Şule Özler is Associate Professor of Economics at UCLA, and a research psy-choanalyst at the New Center for Psychoanalysis. She also maintains a private practice. Her research interests include psychoanalytic examination of philo-sophical, history of thought and history of economic thought texts.

Paul Gabrinetti is a member of the C.G. Jung Institute of Los Angeles and a former Professor of Clinical Psychology at Pacifica Graduate Institute. He maintains a private practice, and his research interests include the use of the analytic psychologies in human and historical proceedings, and the role of myth in psychological change.

Psychoanalytic Explorations

Books in this series:

Psychoanalytic Studies of the Work of Adam Smith

Towards a Theory of Moral Development and Social Relations

Şule Özler and Paul Gabrinetti

Routledge
Taylor & Francis Group

LONDON AND NEW YORK

First published 2018 by Routledge

2 Park Square, Milton Park, Abingdon, Oxfordshire OX14 4RN
52 Vanderbilt Avenue, New York, NY 10017

Routledge is an imprint of the Taylor & Francis Group, an informa business

First issued in paperback 2018

British Library Cataloguing-in-Publication Data
A catalogue record for this book is available from the British
Library

Library of Congress Cataloging-in-Publication Data
A catalog record for this book has been requested

ISBN: 978-1-138-95562-2 (hbk)
ISBN: 978-0-367-14101-1 (pbk)

Typeset in Bembo
by Apex CoVantage, LLC

To our families

Contents

Abbreviations

TMS: *The theory of moral sentiments.* 2009. K. Haakonssen (ed). Cambridge: Cambridge University Press.

WN: *The wealth of nations.* 1981. R.H. Campbell, and A.S. Skinner (ed.) Indianapolis: Liberty Fund.

LJ: *Lecture on jurisprudence.* 1978. R.L. Meek, D.D. Raphael, P.G. Stein (ed). Indianapolis: Liberty Fund.

Acknowledgments

We thank Allan Compton, James Fisher, Charles L. Griswold, Joseph Natterson, J. Mark Thompson and especially Joyce O. Appleby for helpful comments. Şule Özler thanks Peter Loewenberg for being instrumental in her training in psychoanalysis, without which this book would not have been possible. J. Mark Thompson was always there for her as a sounding board for the ideas in this book.

We also thank Routledge for the permission to use the earlier material in this book. Earlier versions of the following papers were published in the *Psychoanalytic Review*: "Defenses and morality: Adam Smith, Sigmund Freud, and contemporary psychoanalysis", and "Adam Smith and dependency". "A known world: An analysis of defenses in Adam Smith's *The Theory of Moral Sentiments*" was published in the *Adam Smith Review*.

Chapter 1

Introduction

Adam Smith (1723–1790) is considered the father of modern economics, an influential moral philosopher of the 18th century and was a key member of the Scottish Enlightenment. We will provide a brief biographical summary at the conclusion of this chapter.

This book introduces a range of psychoanalytic perspectives on the work of Adam Smith to illuminate the important psychological content embedded in his work, identify the salient issues within this content and evaluate their significance to the structure of morality and social relations. The primary source material that we will be examining is *The Theory of Moral Sentiments* (TMS). It has been recognized that while Smith was not writing as a psychologist, there are several important applied psychological processes embedded in his philosophical writing. Given that the first laboratory of experimental psychology and the first work in psychoanalysis were not to begin for over a hundred years after Smith's time, he could not have known that in addition to establishing a moral philosophy, he was also giving rise to a moral psychology based on interpersonal interactions.

Through a psychoanalytic examination of Smith's work, we attempt to uncover the psychological concepts that are present but not at the forefront of Smith's work. While looking at the psychological processes that are active in his work, we put together a critique of the strengths and limitations of the psychological concepts that are implied in his theory and suggest an expansion of the understanding of his work from a psychoanalytic perspective. This book seeks to bring into explicit awareness not only the conscious intent of Smith's work but also the unconscious implications of his theory, including its application. The unconscious meanings from Smith's work are examined using the Hermeneutic tradition. The Hermeneutic tradition has a special significance for psychoanalysis (Loewenberg, 2000). As in philosophical Hermeneutics, in psychoanalysis several possible interpretations and multiple meanings are considered and integrated. In so doing we look to expand the understanding, the pragmatic application and the strengths and limitations of this ground-breaking work.

To accomplish this, we look at Smith's theory from several different psychoanalytic perspectives. We examine Smith's attitude and understanding of the instincts (what Smith calls passions or sentiments) and his antipathy to them. We assert the perspective that instincts are the reason for a moral theory and that they are more than just a force to be disliked and worked against; they serve an important purpose for human kind, not the least of which is procreation and the capacity to develop and defend our integrity. Further, we study the foundational interactive basis of Smith's theory and the possibilities that this interactive process potentiates. We examine the necessity for ego capacity that Smith highlighted in his pivotal assertion of the primacy of self-command. Integral to individual function, we then go into the evolution of defensive styles and the potential for the integration of defenses, which allow for a greater humanization of defensive processes that facilitate a more genuine self that grows out of ongoing interactions. This humanization is facilitated by the incorporation of the sympathetic/empathic process. While it is tempting to simply contrast a more contemporary view with an older view and proclaim the more modern one to be better, once again, we endeavor to point out the foundational strength of Smith's work and its limitations.

The TMS was originally published in 1759, and was translated to both French and German soon after its publication. Smith revised it six times, the last being in 1790. Smith became so well-known after the publication of this book that many wealthy students left their schools in other countries to enroll at Glasgow to study under Smith. The TMS won him high praise from Hume, Burke and Kant. Smith's system was seen as a giant step forward in moral philosophy. Adam Smith's legacy was tied to the Scottish Enlightenment, and the French and American Enlightenments.

Adam Smith's TMS created a bedrock for his moral and ethical structure. Smith's work is a promulgation of the great themes of the Enlightenment. His work on the TMS puts forward ideas about freeing us from war and faction, repression and especially religious institutions. His moral philosophy was very explicit about the correct attitudes in human behavior; it took to task what was seen as the prejudicial and dogmatic assumptions about culture, social hierarchy, freedom and religion. He contended that modern liberty requires moral virtue, not wisdom. He personally saw the TMS as a doctrine of moral emotions, not philosophical reason. Smith based his morality and social harmony on "sentiments" (also termed passions). He saw a decent ethical life as based on passions, which displaced the theoretical pursuits of philosophy as a basis for human life. This pragmatism based on sentiments (what psychoanalysis refers to as instinct) moves at least a portion of his work in the direction of what later evolved into psychology and psychoanalysis.

One of the chapters in this book focuses on *The Wealth of Nations* (1776) (WN from this point on). Smith's later work was a precursor to the modern academic discipline of economics, known as homo economicus. In this book, he laid the foundations of the concept that self-interested behavior in a competitive economy would lead to economic prosperity. The division of labor was seen as the basis for growth and prosperity. The book was an instant success, selling out of its first edition in six months. This book was the basis for Smith's notoriety as the father of modern economics. One of our chapters will briefly focus on the WN, and we undertake an analysis of what motivated Smith's work in this area.

In this current book, we do not go into the LJ (1978), however, we refer to it in several chapters of this book. The LJ contains two sets of lecture notes. They were taken from Smith's lectures of the 1760s. It also contains an early draft of the WN. The lectures address his "theory of the rules by which civil government ought to be directed" (LJ, p. 5). According to Smith, the primary purpose of government was to preserve justice, which meant security from injury. He elaborated by saying an individual's rights to his property, social relations, reputation and his person must be protected by the state.

The organization of our book is as follows. Chapter 2 is entitled "An intersubjective interpretation of sympathy". This chapter introduces the interactive understandings that come from the branch of psychoanalytic study that speaks to the mutual interactions between people, and applies these understandings to Smith's sympathetic interactions between the spectator (observer) and the agent (observed). This chapter gives a brief description of sympathy from the TMS and reviews the psychoanalytic literature on intersubjectivity. We then present an integration of sympathy and intersubjectivity. Sympathy that occurs between the agent and the spectator is through imagination. Even though the spectator owes his existence to real spectators of the society, he is internalized and imagined by the agent. The spectator, through imagination, puts himself in the agent's situation, and feels something analogous to what the agent feels. The spectator compares his feelings with those of the agent. To have a concordance of sentiments, both the spectator and the agent work hard. Sympathy is the concordance of sentiments. In the psychoanalytic literature, intersubjectivity is associated with mutual influence, mutual recognition and shared meaning. We argue that the sympathetic process is intersubjective, since all the elements that are identified in the sympathetic process are also described and elaborated upon in the psychoanalytic literature. We also explain why we see sympathy as the forerunner of empathy, which is a crucial element of the intersubjective process. We argue that our perspective differs from the literature on this subject since we see sympathy as the forerunner of empathy.

Chapter 3 is entitled "Sympathy, empathy and empirical evidence from developmental psychology". Sympathy in the TMS has both a cognitive and an affective dimension, as in empathy. As with sympathy, through empathy one imagines being in the other's situation and experiences the other's psychological states. In this chapter, we review the concept of empathy, including Freud's usage of the term. We point out that Freud was familiar with Smith's work. We argue that sympathy is a forerunner of the psychoanalytic and developmental term empathy. Smith's theory to date has not been examined in the light of empirical literature related to empathy. The empirical literature suggests that empathy leads to moral (pro-social) behavior, and as such supports Smith's theory. Specifically, the evidence shows that empathy leads to pro-social behaviors such as sharing, helping and cooperation. These behaviors are evidenced in the first year of life, and as children grow up they show: 1) the cognitive capacity to interpret states of others; b) the emotional capacity to experience, affectively, the states of others; and c) evidence of behavioral repertoire that facilitate attempts to alleviate the discomfort of others.

Chapter 4 is entitled "The impartial spectator, conscience and morality". Here we describe Smith's moral system that serves as the foundation for understanding the following chapters. The main focus of this chapter is the tension between self-command and the instincts (passions as Smith refers to them). This tension comes as the result of the impartial spectator evaluating the behavior or passions of the agent. The spectator's impartiality is crucial for moral judgments. The spectator achieves this by imagining that he is also spectated. Conscience (internalized morality) is the result of cumulative interactions between the spectator and the agent. The agent judges himself as the spectator would, by dividing himself into two: the one part is the spectator and the other is the agent. Morality is created through the dynamic interaction between the spectator and the agent, which replaces the power of the individual with the power of the community, brought about by the spectator and the agent seeking harmony with each other's emotions. The self-command of the agent is necessary for the impartial spectator to go along with the agent's passions. In the section entitled "of the influence and authority of conscience", Smith states that the virtuous man has the "most perfect command of his original and selfish feelings", which has the sympathetic feelings of others (TMS, p. 176). Self-command prospers most under difficult and challenging conditions. Morality is achieved through social coordination and self-command in the sympathetic process. The bedrock of morality for Smith is self-command over passions (instincts). However, we also argue conversely that instincts are more than a process to be devalued. Without instincts, there would be no need for self-command or morality, and instincts provide the foundational energy to drive the dynamic process.

"The role of the Deity in Smith's moral system" is the title of Chapter 5. This descriptive chapter underscores that for Smith, the Deity provides the content of his moral philosophy. He sees the invisible hand of the Deity as the designer and guide of the universe. Morals are an extension of the Deity's design. Impartial spectators who act as the human vicegerents of the Deity implement morality. The sympathetic process is the mechanism through which the design of the Deity is transmitted. Smith sees cooperation with the Deity as acting morally, and Smith sees the Deity as benevolent and protective even through adversity.

Chapter 6 is entitled a "Known world: an analysis of defenses in Adam Smith's *The Theory of Moral Sentiments*". One of the essential elements for the human transition from an instinctually unreflective state to the conscious implementation of a moral structure is a psychological defense system. Defenses are necessary to restrain purely instinctual action. This leads us to analyze the psychological defense system that Adam Smith employs in TMS. The defense structure creates a knowable world, which we have termed as the "known world". By a known world, we mean a world in which consensual rules are implemented and followed by all people, creating a stable system. Thus, the known world is a system that reifies defenses at a social level and allows the implementation of a moral structure. Smith's primary defensive structure is composed of the rationalization of his positions, the moralization of the rightness of his position and the intellectualization of his positions. These are all methods that facilitate the restraint of instinctual affect and allow for morality. In addition, Smith carefully and exactingly displaces anger according to the values of his moral structure on to the "proper objects" of resentment. This type of displacement also requires both repression and suppression of affective impulses in order to accomplish displacement. All of these strategic defensive arrangements make possible the structure of his known world. It is this defensive known world that is conveyed through the intersubjective interactions that communicate the core of morality through the sympathetic/empathetic process. This system of defenses in the TMS, like any other defensive system, has both strengths and limitations. Its strengths facilitate the structure of the moral system that Smith promotes, and its limitations exclude creativity, change, dynamism and spontaneity.

In Chapter 7, entitled "Defenses and morality: Adam Smith, Sigmund Freud and contemporary psychoanalysis", we show the development of a through line from the work of Adam Smith in his TMS on the impartial spectator, through Sigmund Freud's work on the superego. The premise is that Smith's work in the mid-18th century was a predecessor to Freud's work in the early 20th century. While their work had a different primary focus, both Smith and Freud relied on defenses as an integral part in the imposition of any type of moral structure upon instinctual life. We discuss the similarities and differences between Smith's and Freud's approaches. In addition, we discuss how defenses are an integral part in the internalization of a moral structure, and how one's relationship to those defenses ultimately plays a very important role in ongoing individual development. We also look at how the evolving attitudes towards defenses in psychoanalytic theory have made great strides relative to Smith's reliance on a more religious attitude, in humanizing the more sadistic qualities of the superego (impartial spectator). We also highlight the shift from a one-person psychology to a two-person psychology in defenses and moral development as articulated in the contemporary psychoanalytic literature.

Chapter 8 is entitled "An evolutionary psychological and adaptive defenses view of relations between markets and morality". This chapter examines the reciprocal effect of markets on morality and morality on markets, looking at Smith's original ideas in this area, and from the perspective of evolutionary psychology and adaptive defenses. Growing out of evolutionary psychology are the pivotal capacities for delayed gratification and trust in the complex human interactions that make possible the reciprocity between markets and morality. Delayed gratification and the development of trust evolve from the integration of adaptive defenses in relation to the impulsive demands of immediate instinctual needs. Here we examine the reciprocal and intersubjective nature of these interactions with a particular emphasis on the adaptive defenses that facilitate the means for individuals to adopt morality. We apply this set of under-standings to Smith's work and show the relationship between markets and morality that are in his writing along with the significant defensive processes that are necessary to accomplish the application of such a theory. Delayed grati-fication, which is a moral virtue according to Smith, leads to savings furthering growth. Increased trust among participants leads to increased trade in the mar-ket place. Due to the realized benefits of trust in the market place, cooperative morality is enhanced.

"Adam Smith and dependency" is the title of Chapter 9. The focus of this chapter is on the work and life of Adam Smith. Adam Smith is widely recog-nized as the father and founder of contemporary economics. A latent content analysis is applied to his seminal text in economics, WN. The results reveal that Smith considers dependence on others a problem and sees the solution to this problem in impersonalized interdependence. In addition, his views on social dependency and personal dependency reflected in his LJ and the TMS are analyzed. This analysis suggests a central tension between dependence and independence in Smith's writings. The personal dependency patterns he exhib-ited in his life, through a reading of his biographies, which also suggest a tension between dependence and independence in his life, are also identified. Benefit-ting from psychoanalytic literature, it is proposed that developing the ideas in the WN was part of Smith's creative solution to this tension. In particular, his solution to one individual's dependence on another was through a system of impersonalized interdependence. In other words, it is argued that Smith defended against his personal dependence through his economic theorizing.

The title of Chapter 10 is "On friendship". Smith's notion of friendship can be conceptualized from two different perspectives. First, there is evidence in his writings that would characterize his attitude towards friendship as being based on its usefulness in gaining sympathy. This perspective views friendship as prescriptive and is based on an evaluative thought process to gain the approval of the other. This position is not based on the need for intimate interaction or feeling states, rather it is objectified to alleviate the potential of personal dread. Second, Smith observes that where love and friendship motivate people, society flourishes and is happy. In our reading, the bulk of his arguments in this area show a stronger emphasis on the first. There is also a debate about whether Smith saw commercial societies as conducive to "warm" friendships or leading to "cool" interactions. Our view is that commercial societies are not conducive to warm friendships but led to cool relations. This is consistent with our argu-ment in Chapter 9 that for Smith interactions among individuals took the form of impersonalized interdependencies. We then examine friendship in Smith's writing from a psychoanalytic perspective. Smith speaks of friendship and love from an idealized point of view. On the one hand, he has an optimistic perspec-tive on friendships. Yet within his structure there is no real accommodation of the difficulties that come from human interactions. His idealization takes the form of seeing interactions from a good/bad, inclusive/exclusive and right/wrong point of view. Those who live up to these ideals are included and those who do not are excluded. For example, Smith does not include the interactions of love, guilt and reparation, which are ongoing dynamics in human relationships. Smith does not have a mechanism to accommodate the positive and negative feelings that exist within friendship. In addition, mature dependence is not present in Smith's approach because there are no accommodations for differences. Mature dependence implies dependence of some sort, which Smith defended against in his writings.

"A Jungian interpretation of the place of women in Smith's works" is the title of Chapter 11. This chapter brings in the work of C.G. Jung as we take up the issues of instinct, women and self-command in Smith's work. In the TMS, the WN and the LJ, Smith's attitude towards women is at best ambivalent and at times devaluing of women. His ambivalence reflects his ambivalence between the instinctual nature that all human beings are born with that he mostly identified with women, and self-command that he sees as the primary domain of men. Smith characterizes this as the difference between humanity, which women have the capacity for because it comes from the instinct, and generosity, which requires the development of "self-command" and is generally the possession of men. He views men as having the necessary self-command for the achievement of generosity and of a virtuous moral structure. There is a premium of self-command over instincts because instinctual life requires no exercise of effort and self-command. He considers moral virtue, which is largely founded on self-command, as a great advancement over basic humanity, and values this achievement over instinctual life. To outline the cultural attitudes about women during Smith's time, we review the feminist approaches of the time, the works of Rousseau and Hume. We conclude that Smith's ambivalent attitude towards women, as manifested in his writings, mirrored the cultural attitudes of the time. Smith's personal unconscious was deeply affected by the cultural unconscious of his time (the unconscious manifested through the culture). From a Jungian perspective, we examine the cultural attitudes towards gender and capacity, and his non-gendered perspective on development. Jung viewed instinct and the capacity for self-command (ego capacity) as being present in both genders. While these capacities were culturally seen as being different in biological men and women, Jung saw them as being equally present in both men and women, and capable of being developed. Further, Jung's perspective views men and women as both having the capacity for development or "individuation" that is not gendered when it comes to the development of self-command in relation to instincts. We again conclude that Smith placed a premium on self-command over instincts. In contrast, we also assert that without instincts, there would be no need for or energy to fund self-command.

Our concluding remarks follow in Chapter 12.

Biographical information

Smith was born in Kirkcaldy, Scotland in January 1723. Smith's father, the senior Adam Smith, died about six months prior to Smith's birth. Smith senior had been a customs officer at Kirkcaldy. Smith's father left several of his friends to be guardians of the young Adam Smith. These men, who included merchants and professionals, were participants in the early stages of the Scottish Enlightenment, to which Adam Smith became a major contributor.

The elder Smith died a fairly rich man, leaving a large income and some property to his wife and child. His family could afford good accommodations for the young Adam Smith throughout his years of schooling. Smith's dependence on income from his family continued through his teens and adulthood. Throughout his life, Smith was frequently dependent on wealthy businessmen, gentry, intellectuals and aristocrats for teaching positions, his pension and ultimately his appointment as a customs officer.

Smith's father married Margaret Douglas in 1720. She was descended from a powerful, landowning family. Not much is known about her character. What we do know about her is that she was a Stoic woman with firm religious values. As a Stoic woman, she believed in controlling one's emotions through self-command, a personal discipline that she clearly passed on to Smith.[1] Based on her portrait by C. Metz (Kirkcaldy Museum of Art) (Ross, 1995, p. 310), Ross states that she appears as an "austere and dignified figure [and that her] . . . face seems to be [that] of a woman with strong character, with dark, heavy-lidded eyes under dark eye brows" (p. 309). Following his interpretation of the portrait, Ross states that "when Smith writes in *WN* of the two systems of morality, on the one hand the liberal and on the other the strict and austere (v.i.g.10), it is perhaps appropriate to think of his mother as upholding the values of the second" (p. 309).

At 14, Smith entered University of Glasgow and studied moral philosophy. He was a graduate scholar at Balliol College, Oxford; however, he left before his scholarship expired in 1747, having suffered from the symptoms of a nervous breakdown. The following year he began giving public lectures in Edinburgh sponsored by the Philosophical Society of Edinburgh. In 1750 he met the philosopher David Hume. He earned a professorship in 1751 at Glasgow University, where he taught logic courses. In that same year he was elected to be a member of the Philosophical Society of Edinburgh. In 1762 he was conferred the title of Doctor of Laws at the University of Glasgow. In 1764 Smith went to France as a tutor and stayed under the hospitality of David Hume. After 18 months in Toulouse, he moved on to Geneva, and then to London in 1766, continuing his work as a tutor. In 1767 he returned to Kirkcaldy with his mother and cousin. In 1773 he returned to London and continued with his writing and was also admitted to the Royal Society of London. In 1778 he was appointed as commissioner of customs in Scotland and went to live with his mother in Edinburgh. He had an honorary position of Lord Rector of the

University of Glasgow from 1787 to 1789. He died in 1790 after an agonizing illness and expressed disappointment that he had not achieved more.

Note

1 Smith himself placed a great value on the regulation of emotions, reflecting his upbringing with Stoic morals. Smith writes, "Self-command is not only itself a great virtue, but from it all the other virtues seem to derive their principle luster" (*TMS*, p. 284). Smith saw early childhood as a period of overwhelming emotions "when an indulgent ... parent must pit one violent feeling in the child against another ... to restore their charge's even temper" (Ross, 1995, p. 21). However, he believed there was no such indulgent partiality at school and that the school years were therefore crucial in character formation.

References

Loewenberg, P., 2000. Psychoanalysis as a hermeneutic science. In Brooks, P. and A. Woloch, eds. *Whose Freud? The place of psychoanalysis in contemporary culture.* New Haven, CT: Yale University Press. pp. 96–115.

Ross, I.S., 1995. *The life of Adam Smith.* Oxford: Clarendon Press.

Chapter 2

An intersubjective interpretation of sympathy

I. Introduction

Different psychoanalysts emphasize different aspects of intersubjectivity. 1) Stolorow and his collaborators (Stolorow, Atwood and Brandchaft, 1994; Stolorow and Atwood, 1979) view intersubjectivity as *mutual influence*, which starts at birth. 2) *Mutual recognition*, which develops later in infancy is the focus of Stern (1985; Stern et al., 1998), Ogden (1985; 1992a, 1992b) and Benjamin (1988; 1990). 3) Stern (1985) and Ogden (1992a; 1992b) highlight the creation of *shared meaning* in intersubjective process, an achievement of a later development in infancy. In our view, these different approaches are not opposed to each other. Rather they describe different overlying properties that are present in intersubjectivity along developmental lines.

We are going to elucidate the active intersubjective processes that are operative within Smith's understanding of sympathy and their implications for the transmission of morality. While Smith was not necessarily thinking in terms of the intricate interpersonal consequences that have been researched by contemporary psychoanalysts, we are going to point out important intersubjective products that are the result of Smithian sympathy. Sympathy is the foundation of Smith's moral system in the TMS; Villiez (2006) has referred to it as the "the backbone of Smith's theory". In his descriptions of sympathy, Smith gives an account of the intersubjectivity that encompasses all the above-mentioned dimensions.

Sympathy has two meanings for Smith. The first meaning is pity "for the misery of others". According to Smith, sympathy is a fundamental principle of human nature:

> How selfish soever man may be supposed, there are evidently some principles in his nature, which interest him in the fortune of others, and render their happiness necessary to him, though he derives nothing from it except the pleasure of seeing it.[1]

(TMS, p. 11)

The second meaning of sympathy is "fellow- feeling" with any passion, and it is this meaning of sympathy that is predominantly used by Smith:

> Pity and compassion are words appropriated to signify our fellow-feeling with the sorrow of others. Sympathy, though its meaning was, perhaps, originally the same, may now, however, without much impropriety, be made use of to denote our fellow-feeling with any passion whatever.
>
> (TMS, p. 13)[2]

The sympathetic process occurs between a spectator and an agent. A spectator is not an actual bystander but is a creation of the agent's imagination, though the imagined spectator owes its existence to real spectators that have been experienced throughout life. The impartiality of spectators is crucial. This is achieved by spectators imagining they are spectated by others. According to Smith, we are each other's spectators, who mitigate our self-interest when we imagine that other spectators observe us at a distance.

The spectator, through an imaginative process, puts himself in the agent's situation and forms an idea about how the agent is affected in a given situation, and "an analogous emotion springs up, at the thought of his situation" (TMS, p. 13), though the spectator might have the experience in a weaker degree. The spectator compares his own feelings to the feelings he imagines the agent has. Sympathy is a similar feeling to that of the agent and it gives pleasure. It is a concordance between the actual feelings of the agent and the imagined feelings of the actor by the spectator. Sympathy is not a passion. The spectator can sympathize with the feelings, motives and actions of the agent. If there is not a concordance of sentiments reached by both the actor and the spectator, they work together to achieve it, as we will describe in a later subsection. Sympathy is spectatorial in an interdependent relationship. It is through sympathy that emotions are communicated and understood. They guide judgment.

In a Smithian sense, sympathy is a technical term. For instance, in the face of the agent's anger or joy, the spectator may feel angry or joyful in sympathy with the agent.

> It is perhaps more appropriate, therefore, to think of sympathy as an adverbial modification of a given feeling, in the sense that the term indicates the way that the spectator has the feeling – he has it sympathetically. . . . Smithian sympathy has a kind of universality.
>
> (Brodie, 2006, p. 164)

Through the use of imagination, sympathy engenders both cognitive and emotional experiences between the spectator and agent. It has a cognitive dimension in that the formation of any idea in the agent's experience is an intellectual undertaking. At the same time sympathy also has an emotional dimension because we feel at least similar to what the agent feels.

This dynamic interaction between the spectator and the agent creates a consensual morality. Through the sympathetic process, individuals learn to adjust their passions to live with each other and ultimately in a society. Smith identifies the Deity as the foundational source of his moral philosophy. Smith sees morality as a manifestation of the Deity's design, in which sympathy is the mechanism for the implementation of this design. He sees the resulting structure or principals of morality as directions of an omniscient Deity, and they are disseminated through human vicegerents in the person of the impartial spectator. Smith believed that our sense of right and wrong is based not on reason but feeling: "the first perceptions of right and wrong . . . cannot be the object of reason, but of immediate sense and feeling" (TMS, p. 377).

Smith describes moral psychology when he explains the dynamics in the development of morality through the psychological interactions between the spectator and the agent. This is a prototype for the more everyday interactions between a parent and a child, for example, in which observations and feedback that are shared between individuals create a consensual moral structure over time.

As we state in this chapter and elaborate in Chapter 3, in a more modern lexicon, this description of sympathy is what is referred to as empathy in psychoanalytic and human development vernacular, and as such Smith's sympathy is a forerunner of our more current understanding and use of the term empathy. In broad terms, empathy is apprehending another's conscious and unconscious psychological processes.

Smith's sympathy is an intersubjective one. First, as in the psychoanalytic literature on intersubjectivity, in the sympathetic process there are two subjectivities involved. As in Kohut (1982), Stolorow, Atwood and Brandchaft (1994), and Stolorow and Atwood (1979), in the dynamic interaction between the spectator and the agent while they are adjusting their sentiments there is mutual influence.

Second, the agent and the spectator have a mutual recognition by putting themselves in each other's position as in Ogden, 1994 and Stern, 1985. There is a dialectical interplay between the agent and the spectator. Recognition is possible when the other recognizes us and we recognize them.

Third, morality that is created through the concordance of sentiments in the sympathetic process allows for the creation of a shared meaning as in Stern, 1985, and Ogden, 1992a, 1992b.

In section II we provide a brief description of approaches to intersubjectivity. Section III presents Smith's views on sympathy, mutual sympathy and the dynamic quality of sympathy between the agent and the spectator. In section IV we draw parallels between sympathy and empathy, both of which involve an intersubjective process and compare to the views in the Smith literature. Section V contains an intersubjective interpretation of sympathy. Concluding remarks are in section VI.

II. Intersubjectivity in psychoanalytic literature

Kohut brought in the role of the analyst's subjectivity in a treatment situation in addition to the patient's subjectivity in his self-psychological approach, and as such his approach was a precursor of the intersubjective turn in psychoanalysis (Teicholz, 1999; 2001).[3] A central concept in Kohut's approach is empathy. We will elaborate on Kohut's use of the term in our discussion section; for now it suffices to state that empathy is defined as a "mode of observation attuned to the inner life of a man" (Kohut, 1982, p. 396). Empathy is both a mode of affective responsiveness and bonding as well as a mode of psychological investigation. In his use of empathy, Kohut (1971; 1977) highlighted the analyst's impact on the analytic situation through empathy. In this view the analyst becomes a participant in the analytic situation.[4] The analytic situation is impacted in an unidentifiable but unique way by the analyst; as such the observer is included in the field that is observed, as in the sympathetic process.[5]

Stolorow and collaborators

For Stolorow et al. (1986), intersubjectivity means contextualization, or systemic regulation and *mutual influence* starting at birth.[6] Subjectivity is the individual's unconscious and conscious patterns of organizing experience (Atwood and Stolorow, 1984). Such patterns are always present both in the patient and the analyst. Due to this, analysts must "continually strive to expand their reflective awareness of their own unconscious organizing principles . . . so that the impact of the analytic process can be recognized and itself become the focus of analytic investigation" (Stolorow et al., 1986, p. 6). In this approach, the view that sees subjects as isolated monads is inaccurate (Stolorow and Atwood, 1992). Stolorow (2002) describes intersubjectivity as "contextual precondition for having any experience at all" (p. 330). Individuality can only be brought about from the "interplay of two subjectivities" (Orange, Atwood and Stolorow, 1997, p. 15). A patient's experience can only be understood in the *co-created* intersubjective field. Psychological phenomena are a product of the "interface of reciprocally interacting worlds of experience", not a product of isolated intrapsychic mechanisms (Stolorow, 2002, p. 330).

Ogden

For Ogden's intersubjectivity, *recognition of minds* is central, which is an achievement that occurs later in infancy. Ogden (1994; 2004) highlights that the analysand and the analyst are not separate subjects. He conceptualizes intersubjectivity as dialectical and emphasizes the interdependence of subject and object, as opposed to viewing the analyst and the analysand as separate subjects. As in Winnicott's analysis of the mother-child relationship, there is a dynamic tension between the analysand and the analyst as they coexist simultaneously in their separateness. The analyst's idiosyncratic ideas, feelings or recollections are seen as the creation of an experience "that has not previously existed in the form it was now taking" rather than individually determined (2004, p. 18). The analyst's reverie transforms all aspects of the experience and it becomes a manifestation of the unconscious interplay of analytical subjects. The product of the unconscious interplay is termed the "analytic third". The third subjectivity is generated by the analysand and the analyst, and is created by the interaction of the two participants. It is an independent dynamic unit of the intersubjective event.

Central to the first establishment of subjectivity is language with the separation of symbolized and symbol, which requires a recognition of a separate mind in one's self and the other (Ogden, 1992a; 1992b). Infants becomes able to interpret their experience once they understand the word and the "thing" are not identical, opening a space between symbol and symbolized. A parallel space takes shape in the realm between mother and child in concert with the symbol and symbolized. In this way an "intersubjective third" is created in the relationship.

Coinciding with the first attainment of language, intersubjectivity makes shared meaning possible.[7] Ogden (1985) states meaning arises from difference. There is neither any meaning in a completely homogeneous field nor recognition of the existence of the homogeneous field, because of lack of any terms other than itself to attribute to it.

Stern

According to Stern (1985) and Stern et al. (1998), intersubjectivity is about *recognition of the mind* of the self and the other, which emerges towards the end of age one. In this approach an infant can recognize the separateness of mind in self and other only after the subjective self has been established. The ability for this recognition requires prior development along linguistic, relational, cognitive and affective paths as well as mutual regulations between the infant and primary care takers.

According to Stern there is a core or physical sense of self before the subjective sense of self and long before the infant can recognize his mind and the other's mind. Even though the infant can make distinctions between actions that result from the other's body and his own body, he does not yet recognize intentionality, or the presence of minds. The capacity for recognition requires that the primary care takers regulate the infant well enough overtime. Through this regulation some sense of predictability about what might emerge from the other and the infant is yielded. As a result, between seven and nine months, the subjective self emerges, which is built upon the core self. The infant's simultaneous recognition that the other has a separate and unique and a parallel inner life is tied to the development of the subjective self. Stern calls this recognition intersubjective relatedness. The acquisition of language also makes it possible to have shared meaning: "the acquisition of language is potent in the service of union and togetherness. In fact, every word learned is the by-product of uniting two mentalities in a common symbol system, a forging of shared meaning" (Stern, 1985, p. 172).

Benjamin

Benjamin (1988; 2004; 2011) defines intersubjectivity as *mutual recognition*, which occurs later in infancy. Recognition is possible only if we concurrently and first recognize the other. The other has to recognize us. Otherwise, the recognition we have will be worthless. Recognition is part of human development. She introduces the notion of intersubjective mental space co-created by both subjects, which she calls the "third". There is an affirmation that human beings are linked by a third in the reciprocal affirmation of the other. That the suffering of humans matters independent of their origins or status is contained in the third. Similar to transitional space in Winnicott, it means being able to perceive things from the other's perspective. The possibility of mutual recognition and mental space for thought is due to the shared third. Two people have a common third. They surrender to this and have dialogical relationship and then they are able to reflect on their interactions. When Benjamin talks about this form of moral thirds, she states that it is based on the essence of intersubjectivity itself and is a consequence of mutual recognition.

III. Sympathetic process as an intersubjective process

Sympathy

Prior to giving an intersubjective interpretation of the sympathetic process, let us describe sympathy, mutual sympathy and the dynamic quality of the sympathetic process as Smith does.

Imagination is at the root of the sympathetic process. It is through imagination that we are able to change situations and capture the sentiments of the other.[8] Smith states, "we transport ourselves in fancy to the scenes of those distant and forgotten adventures, imagine ourselves acting out the part . . ." (TMS, p. 87).[9] Through imagination, we get inside the experience of others, joining to their world, and the gap between the individuals is bridged. Sympathy can only be the result of imagination, since our knowledge is limited by our experiences.[10] The spectator imagines how he would feel and act if he were in the agent's situation, and asks himself whether he would be motivated by the agent's circumstances to feel and act in the same way. The spectator's assessment has a cognitive and emotional dimension.

Brown (1994) characterizes the sympathetic process as "seeing" or "vision". The author notes that "In the TMS the activities of watching, seeing and observing all constitute forms of moral judgment" (p. 60). Similarly, Rothschild (2010) states:

> The image of moral experience, in the book, is of looking or glimpsing, at oneself or at others. . . . To have moral sentiments is to have looked, in as clear a light as possible, at the outside events of life, and to have imagined the life within.
>
> (p. 27)

Griswold (2010) points out that Smith uses both visual and auditory metaphors to convey the comprehension of the other's experience.[11]

Smith emphasizes entering into another's situation, not simply entering the feelings of the other.[12] According to Smith, sympathy arises not "so much from the view of the passions, as from that of the situation which excites it" (TMS, p. 15). The spectator responds to what he imagines the actor's situation is. The degree we sympathize depends on our knowledge of the situation.

> General lamentations, which express nothing but the anguish of the sufferer, create rather a curiosity to inquire into his situation, along with some disposition to sympathize with him, than any actual sympathy that is very sensible. The first question which we ask is, what has befallen you? Till this be answered, though we are uneasy both from the vague idea of his misfortune, and still more from torturing ourselves with conjectures about what it may be, yet our fellow-feeling is not very considerable.
>
> (TMS 14–15)

What does entering in the other's situation mean? Earlier in the text Smith emphasizes that entering into the other's situation is considering what our own feelings would be in the same situation, which is referred to as imagining being X in the literature, which we discuss in the discussion section. He states that:

> As we have no immediate experience of what other men feel, we can form no idea of the manner in which they are affected, but by conceiving what we ourselves should feel in the like situation. Though our brother is upon the rack, as long as we ourselves are at our ease, our senses will never inform us of what he suffers. They never did, and never can, carry us beyond our own person, and it is by the imagination only that we can form any conception of what are his sensations. Neither can that faculty help us to this any other way, than by representing to us what would be our own, if we were in his case. *It is the impressions of our own senses only, not those of his, which our imaginations copy.*
>
> (TMS, pp. 11–12)[13] (emphasis added)

Smith, later in the TMS, emphasizes that sympathy is not about what we would feel as ourselves in the other's situation, but what we would feel if we were the other person (in the literature this is referred to as imagining being X in X's situation):

> But though sympathy is very properly said to arise from an imaginary change of situations with the person principally concerned, yet this imaginary change is not supposed to happen to me in my own person and character, but in that of the person with whom I sympathize. *When I condole with you for the loss of your only son, in order to enter into your grief I do not consider what I, a person of such a character and profession, should suffer, if I had a son, and if that son was unfortunately to die: but I consider what I should suffer if I was really you, and I not only change circumstances with you, but I change persons and characters. My grief, therefore, is entirely upon your account, and not in the least upon my own. It is not, therefore, in the least selfish. . . . A man may sympathize with a woman in child-bed; though it is impossible that he should conceive himself as suffering her pains in his own proper person and character.*
>
> (TMS, p. 374)[14,15] (emphasis added)

It is important to clarify that the second formulation requires the first formulation. In other words, unless we have the capacity to imagine being X, we cannot have the capacity to imagine being X in X's situation. There is no inconsistency in the TMS, rather there is a more complete and complex view, as Smithian sympathy entails both. As we present in the discussion section, empathy also involves both. This is an important reason for us asserting that the process of sympathy in Smith was a forerunner of empathy in the modern psychoanalytic literature.

Freud (1930) also talks about putting ourselves in the other's situation. "We shall always consider other people's distress objectively – that is to place ourselves, with our own wants and sensibilities, in *their* conditions, and then to examine what occasions we should find in them for experiencing happiness or unhappiness" (p. 89). We should note that Freud was familiar with Adam Smith's work, as he indicated in a letter he wrote to Silberstein in August of 1879; he states, "I have some marvelous books to read . . . a great philosopher . . . Adam Smith's fundamental book on the wealth of nations . . ." (p. 174).

The sympathetic process is self-referential because we judge the opinions and actions of others:

> as right, as accurate, as agreeable to truth and reality: and it is evident we attribute those qualities to it for no other reason but because we find that it agrees with our own.
>
> (TMS, p. 25)

At the same time, spectators are also shaped by social experience, and moral culture of the time, as well as their past experiences and sensibilities.

In the sympathetic process, the spectator feels not unlike the agent. Smith tells us the following:

> By the imagination we place ourselves in his situation, we conceive ourselves enduring the same torments, we enter as it were into his body, and become in some measure the same person with him, and thence form some idea of his sensations, and even feel something which, though weaker in degree, is not altogether unlike them.
>
> (TMS, p. 11–12)

Even when the spectator is informed of the situation, the spectator's feelings fall short of the agent's and vary in kind:

> What [spectators] feel, will, indeed, always be, in some respects, different from what he feels, and compassion can never be exactly the same with original sorrow; because the secret consciousness that the change of situations, from which the sympathetic sentiment arises, is but imaginary, not only lowers it in degree, but, in some measure, varies it in kind, and gives it a quite different modification.
>
> (TMS, p. 27)[16]

For Smith, sympathy occurs when the spectator evaluates the reactions of the agent as proper or improper. This approach takes in the totality of the agent by considering the agent's feelings. On this point, Smith states the following:

> When the original passions of the person principally concerned are in perfect concord with the sympathetic emotions of the spectator, they necessarily appear to this last just and proper, and suitable to their objects; and, on the contrary, when, upon bringing the case home to himself, he finds that they do not coincide with what he feels, they necessarily appear to him unjust and improper, and unsuitable to the causes which excite them. To approve of the passions of another, therefore, as suitable to their objects, is the same thing as to observe that we entirely sympathize with them; and not to approve of them as such, is the same thing as to observe that we do not entirely sympathize with them.
>
> (TMS, p. 20)[17,18]

Smith links sympathy to approval:

> If upon bringing the case home to our own beast, we find that the sentiments which it gives occasion to, coincide and tally with our own, we necessarily approve of them as proportioned and suitable to their object; if otherwise, we necessarily disapprove of them, as extravagant and out of proportion.
>
> (TMS, p. 23)

There are some cases, according to Smith, we approve without sympathy. "A little attention, however, will convince us that even in these cases our approbation is ultimately founded upon sympathy . . ." (TMS, p. 21). Smith gives the example that we may approve the laughter of our company even though we do not laugh because we are in a "grave humour". From experience, however, we know that we would laugh in the same situation were we not in a grave humor. We thus approve the laughter.[19]

According to Smith, sympathy is more likely to occur among family, friends or acquaintances than among strangers, they feel little for those with whom "they have no particular connexion" (TMS, p. 100)[20]:

> He is more habituated to sympathize with [his family]. He knows better how everything is likely to affect them, and his sympathy with them is more precise and determinate, than it can be with the greater part of other people. It approaches nearer, in short, to what he feels for himself.
>
> (TMS, p. 257)

Since we expect less sympathy from strangers, we assume more tranquility before them and bring our passions to a pitch they can go along with. "Society and conversation, therefore, are the most powerful remedies for restoring the mind to its tranquility" (TMS, p. 28). Smith argues that there is more sympathy for dependent children than for our parents. Habituation strengthens sympathy. Smith moves to affection from habituated imagination.

> What is called affection, is in reality nothing but habitual sympathy. . . . Relations being usually placed in situations which naturally create this habitual sympathy, it is expected that a suitable degree of affection should take place among them.
>
> (TMS, p. 258)

As such our affection for others increases and sympathy becomes more habituated as social distance shrinks (Peart and Levy, 2005).

Mutual sympathy

Sympathy is pleasurable. Mutual sympathy is the pleasure of having sympathetic feelings:

> But whatever may be the cause of sympathy, or however it may be excited, nothing pleases us more than to observe in other men a fellow-feeling with all the emotions of our own breast; nor are we ever so much shocked as by the appearance of the contrary.
>
> (TMS, p. 17)

Mutual sympathy is another source of satisfaction. It is disagreeable not being able to sympathize. According to Smith any pain we might feel due to the painful feelings of the actor is overweighed by the pleasure derived from the correspondence of feelings. Smith says:

> Sympathy, however, enlivens joy and alleviates grief. It enlivens joy by presenting another source of satisfaction; and it alleviates grief by insinuating into the heart almost the only agreeable sensation which it is at that time capable of receiving.
>
> (TMS, p. 18)

It is the concord of passions that gives mutual sympathy, which is a disinterested pleasure in the sense of having pleasure from one's own private wellbeing.

On the issue of whether sympathy is always pleasurable or not, Smith states the following:

> in the sentiment of approbation there are two things to be taken notice of; first, the sympathetic passions of the spectator; and, secondly, the emotion which arises from his observing perfect coincidence between his sympathetic passion in himself, and the original passion in the person principally concerned. This last emotion, in which the sentiment of approbation properly consists, is always agreeable and delightful. The other may either be agreeable of disagreeable, according to the nature of the original passion, whose feature it must always, in some measure, retain.
>
> (TMS, p. 56, note a)[21]

Heath (1995) argues that Smith considered pleasure associated with sympathy being due to his recognition of the effort that would have to be made to see whether an agreement could be secured or whether an agreement would be possible.

Mutual sympathy is a foundational element of Smith's moral structure. The mirroring process between two people, which affirms mutual experiences in the modern psychoanalytic language, could be likened to mutual sympathy. Smith's depiction therefore embodies a psychological process.

The dynamic quality of sympathy

Sympathy takes place in a dynamic context. In the larger context of human culture, we are all spectators and actors working together to form a consensual morality. Sympathy is not "automatic, passive and mindless" (Radner, 1980) because both the actor and the spectator work hard to reach a concordance of sentiments through the sympathetic process.

In the chapter with the title "of the pleasure of mutual sympathy", Smith asserts that human beings derive pleasure from sympathy. He asserts that both the spectator and the agent yearn for mutual sympathy. In their mutual desire, both the spectator and the agent work hard to reach a concordance of sentiments.

The spectator must work hard at putting himself in the agent's position and pay attention to every detail, and he must undertake that imaginary change of situation as perfectly as possible.

> the spectator must, first of all, endeavour, as much as he can, to put himself in the situation of the other, and to bring home to himself every little circumstance of distress which can possible occur to the sufferer. He must adopt the whole case of his companion with all its minutest incidents; and strive to render as perfect as possible, that imaginary change of situation upon which his sympathy is founded.
>
> (TMS, p. 26)

The spectator has the will to sympathize with the agent even if he is not naturally inclined to do so. If he does not initially sympathize he works at ironing out differences. The spectator attempts to change his perspective and feelings.[22]

Even after all this effort the spectator might still not be able to conceive the sufferer's emotions to the extent the sufferer does. The change of places is imaginary, through which the spectator understands the agent well enough to form "some idea of his sensations". Since a spectator never really becomes one with the agent and never loses sight of his separateness, a spectator's understanding can never be perfect.[23]

The agent desires a more complete sympathy and works hard to gain it. Griswold (1999) gives the following reasons. The agent has more invested in the situation, thus has more at stake than the spectator. While the spectator's emotions are imaginary, the actor's emotions are related to the real situation. The agent also wants to avoid the pain of solitude: "The horror of solitude drives him back into society" (TMS, p. 99). An additional factor motivating the agent for concordance of sentiments is his yearning for approbation. Towards this end the agent adjusts his passions. He does this under the critical eye of the spectator.

Smith argues for the role of Nature in reaching a concord of sentiments:

> In order to produce concord [of sentiments], as nature teaches the spectators to assume the circumstances of the person principally concerned, so she teaches this last in some measure to assume those of the spectators.
>
> (TMS, p. 27)

Sympathy is a social practice in which ordinary people encounter one another and moral life is a social practice. Essentially, human beings are social (Fricke, 2013). People are

> constrained by their selfishness, are nevertheless capable of coordinating with others and producing morality together without the artificial machinations of political coercion, philosophy, religion or formal education.
>
> (Forman-Brazilai, 2010, p. 62)

It is a social process according to Smith:

> This natural disposition to accommodate and to assimilate, as much as we
> can, our own sentiments, principles, and feelings, to those which we see
> fixed and rooted in the persons whom we are obliged to live and converse
> a great deal with, is the cause of the contagious effects of both good and
> bad company.
>
> (TMS, p. 263)

Sympathy has a socializing feature as well as a character constituting feature.[24]
Sympathy socializes both the agent and the spectator, since the first would like
to be the object of sympathy and the second would like to sympathize. Moral
exchanges therefore create sociality.

IV. Theory of mind, sympathy, empathy

We have argued that Smith's sympathetic process is an intersubjective one
that is very similar to what is described in the psychoanalytic literature.
In the literature on Smith, Brown (2012) also argues that the sympathetic
process is intersubjective.[25] The author makes this point by describing the
sympathetic process, without any reference to the psychoanalytic literature
on intersubjectivity. According to her, the argument that the sympathetic
process is intersubjective raises two questions. The first is how it is that the
spectator has access to the other's feelings and how it is achieved. Brown
argues that Smith has a theory of mind. She refers to two approaches. First
is the theory-theory of mind ("folk psychology", see for example Stich and
Nichols, 1992). Second is simulation theory (see for example Gordon, 1995).
There is, of course, a similarity between our approach and Brown's approach
on this issue. Were it not possible to access others' minds, sympathy would
not be possible.

In theory-theory of mind we have a theory of the workings of other minds,
which might be innate or a result of social acculturation of the young. Through
theory of mind we have an ability to understand others' mental states. It is a
human capacity through which we explain and predict the mental state and
behavior of others. Theory-theory of mind has primarily focused on inten-
tional states that reflect an individual's desires and beliefs. Through theory-
theory of mind, individuals are better able to comprehend and represent the
environment around them.

According to simulation theory we access other minds through imagination.
It is about transporting ourselves in the other's temporal and spatial location.
Our ability to read other minds is based on our ability to simulate their situation, using the mind of the observer as a model. It refers to decision making
within a pretend context. The simulation is not theory driven rather it is process driven.

An important mechanism to have access to other minds is not considered by Brown (2012). This mechanism is the process of mentalization, a term coined by Fonagy and Target (1996), as described in the psychoanalytic literature (see for example Fonagy, 1999; Fonagy et al., 2015). Mentalization is

> the capacity to understand and interpret human behavior in terms of the putative mental states underpinning it as it arises through the experiences of having been so understood in the context of an attachment relationship.
> (Fonagy, 1999, p. 13)

Mentalization involves both an interpersonal component and a self-reflective component. In infancy, through his mirroring process, the infant's awareness of his own feelings and thoughts and his ability to distinguish the thoughts and feelings of others the infant develops the capacity to mentalize. The capacity for empathy is deeply rooted in mentalization. It is indeed considered to be a form of mentalization (Frith and Frith, 2004).

It is the second issue Brown discusses that we disagree with. The author makes a distinction between (1) the spectator's imagination of what the spectator would feel if he were X in X's situation (imagining being X in X's situation), and (2) the spectator's imagining what X would feel in X's situation (imagining being X), calling the former sympathy and the latter empathy. The author further suggests that "it is the other's feelings that are experienced in the spectator's imaginative episode" in the case of empathy, and in the case of sympathy, "it is the spectator's feelings that are experienced in the spectator's imaginative episode" (p. 257). In our view this is a false distinction.

Gordon (1995) also makes the same distinction, and instead of "imagines feeling" he uses "imagines being". Darwall (1998) interprets sympathy as "projective empathy". With this the author means that first, the spectator unselfconsciously projects himself into X's situation. Second, using X's perspective, he responds to this. Third, this response of the spectator is attributed to X. As such it is a hybrid of the above two distinctions meaning "imagining myself being X in X's situation". The author argues that Smith's empathy "already involves sympathy" (p. 267). Finally, Nanay (2010) argues that the two interpretations above are interchangeable. The author asserts that "imagining being X in X's situation is a special case of imagining being X" (p. 90).

Our view is similar to Darwall (1998) in that empathy already involves sympathy. Specifically, we argue that empathy or Smith's sympathy entails both (1) and (2). Empathy means apprehending another's experience and feelings. Empathy would not be possible without both self-referencing to what we would feel in our situation, and without imagining being the other in the other's situation. These two aspects are inseparable elements of empathy. As to Nanay's approach, we differ in that (1) and (2) are not interchangeable but they are both present. Obviously, we also differ from Brown and Gordon because we argue that both (1) and (2) are present in empathy, not only (2).

In order to clarify our view, let us refer to Kohut (1959), who introduced revolutionary ideas to psychoanalysis, for whom empathy was essential in a treatment situation. The author states:

> The inner world cannot be observed with the aid of our sensory organs. Our thoughts, wishes, feelings, and fantasies cannot be seen, smelled, heard, or touched. They have no existence in physical space, and yet they are real, and we can observe them as they occur in time: through introspection in ourselves, and through empathy (i.e., *vicarious introspection*) in others.
>
> (p. 459) (emphasis added)

He then asks:

> But is it yet always true that introspection and empathy are essential constituents of every psychological observation? Are there not psychological facts that we can ascertain by nonintrospective observation of the external world?
>
> (p. 461)

Kohut says that the answer is negative with a couple of examples. One of them is the following:

> We see a person who is unusually tall. It is not to be disputed that this person's unusual size is an important fact for our psychological assessment − without introspection and empathy, however, his size remains simply a physical attribute. Only when we think ourselves into his place [imagine being in X's situation], only when we, by vicarious introspection, begin to feel his unusual size as if it were our own [imagine being X in X's situation] and thus revive inner experiences in which we had been unusual or conspicuous, only then begins there for us an appreciation of the meaning that the unusual size may have for this person and only then have we observed a psychological fact.
>
> (p. 461) (We added the remarks about X in the above quote in [ ] to point out that empathy entails both (1) and (2) above.)

As we have stated earlier, it would not be possible to imagine being X in X's situation without imagining being X. In other words, psychoanalytically, empathy has two components. The first component is what might be called general sympathy (imagining being in X's situation), the second component is being able to wonder about the internal experiences of the other and feel something analogous (imagining being X in X's situation).

V. Intersubjective elements of the sympathetic process

In the comparison between Smith's sympathy and the intersubjective psycho-analysts, we have pointed out the confluence of their work. While Smith was not thinking in terms of the complexities that have been studied by the later psychoanalytic theorists, we have presented material in both areas of study and in conclusion would like to recap the many similarities that have come to light.

Kohut (1982) spoke about there being two subjectivities involved in the analytic dyad, and that through empathy have a mutual effect upon each other. This is the same kind of interaction that Smith elucidated in the sympathetic process between the agent and that of the spectator. He describes the spectator having an impact on the agent and the agent works to find concordance with the spectator. Their subjectivities are interdependent as opposed to being sepa-rate subjects. There is a dynamic, dialectical interaction between these two sub-jectivities, as is referred to in Ogden (1994; 2004), the observer is also observed and there is a mutual recognition of the "inner minds" of the other.

Through the dynamic interaction between the spectator and the agent, they place themselves in each other's situations through imagination. The spectator imagines what the agent would be feeling, the agent imagines how the specta-tor would be responding. In this process, there is the first and necessary recogni-tion that they have separate minds. This is the same process that is elucidated in Ogden (1994; 2004), Stern (1985) and Stern et al. (1998). There is also a mutual recognition (Benjamin, 1988; 2004; 2011, Stern, 1985, Stern et al., 1998) of the other in this process and the potential for reciprocal affirmation (Benjamin, 1988; 2004; 2011). Through this process the agent and the spectator come to recognize their intersubjective relatedness (Stern, 1985, Stern et al., 1998).

As Stolorow (Stolorow et. al., 1987) and his colleagues have elucidated, there are significant mutual influences that occur through the interplay of two sub-jectivities. Once again this is very similar to Smith's agent and the spectator in their desire to have sympathetic influence on each other. They both work hard in the sympathetic process to achieve a satisfactory mutual influence with each other. In this process, the spectator impacts the dynamic interaction between himself and the agent plays a reciprocal role in this interaction (Kohut, 1971). The spectator and agent become participants in the interaction.

For Smith, sympathy creates a shared meaning in the creation of a shared morality. This is identical in process, although the goals may be different, to what goes on between the analyst and the analysand (Ogden, 1985; Emde, 1995). Through the sympathetic process, the agent and the spectator reach a consensual meaning, which brings about a shared morality.

VI. Conclusion

As we have pointed out through several psychoanalytic perspectives, the unfore-seen and the unconscious implications of sympathy as was used by Smith are many. The sympathetic process is the foundation for Smith's theory of morality, and as we outline, the basis for the discovery of many intersubjective processes that have become so important to the understanding and transmission of human experience. Mutual influence, mutual recognition and shared meaning are the more current understandings that have come out of the current literature, and elaborate on the important and influential subtleties that are in the sympathetic process that Smith originally theorized upon to create moral development.

Notes

1 Otteson (2002) attributes three meanings to this statement. First, there is a claim that sympathy is distinctive to human nature. The statement, however, does not necessarily imply that; Smith only states that "it is in his nature". Furthermore, for example de Waal (2012) argues that animals have empathy. We later argue that sympathy is the forerunner of empathy. Otteson's (2002) second argument is that other people's happiness is necessary to human beings. Third, the pleasure of seeing other people's happiness leads us to act out of consideration to their happiness.

2 Otteson (2002) argues that Smith uses sympathy in three different senses. First, "natural fellow-feeling" and pity we have for others, which is a general interest we have about the fortunes of others. Second is the pity we have for others. Third is the correspondence of feelings between the spectator and the actor.

3 See Teicholz, 2001 and Bohleber, 2013 for useful reviews of intersubjectivity in psychoanalytic literature.

4 The same view can be found in Loewald (1988): "The origin of individual psychic life . . . is a transindividual field, represented by the mother/infant matrix, not an individual unconscious and instincts residing in an individual" (pp. 50–51). Similarly, each participant effects the other's experience in a patient-analyst system of mutual interaction (Hoffman, 1983).

5 Similarly, Jung (1968) states that "in psychology the means by which you study the psyche is not the psyche itself. . . . The observer is the observed" (pp. 41–42). (faces in the cloud)

6 Mutual influence and regulation are also central to the writings of Beebe and Lachmann (1988a; 1988b); Lachmann and Beebe (1992; 1996a; 1996b) based on their infant research, and as such these occur at birth.

7 Emde (1995) also refers to intersubjectivity as "shared meaning".

8 In the TMS there is no separate analysis of imagination but a theory of imagination must be deduced from a number of passages. For an analysis of imagination see Griswold (2006).

9 Imagining ourselves before the eyes of other people has been likened to theatricality (Marshall, 1984).

10 Peart and Levy (2005) point out that when we exchange positions we preserve our own consciousness.

11 He argues that the metaphor of vision is useful for Smith for the following reasons. First, it is useful to talk about perspective for Smith's theory of ethics. Second, it suggests a detachment from the object seen. Third, it suggests a model where the spectator's ego is left behind. "The impartial spectator's own perspective-distorting turbulence is also left behind" (p 68). Fourth, seeing is a natural way of talking about the imagination. Fifth, intellectual vision is correctable.

12 Entering into the other's situation is important for three reasons (Griswold, 1999). First it creates a measure of objectivity, to allow for independent evaluation. Second, it requires

a measure of understanding, especially when there is "divided sympathy" as in the case of hatred and resentment, "our sympathy is divided between the person who feels them, and the person who is the object of them" (TMS, p. 41). Third, it explains the situation in which even though the agent does not have the feelings the spectator thinks he does, the spectator sympathizes with the agent, such as in the case of a dead or insane person or with infants. Even when the spectator does not have the same feeling as the agent, the spectator may sympathize with the agent. Smith refers to sympathy with the dead as "illusion".

13 Smith's psychologically minded approach anticipates Freud, as is evident in the following statement: "We shall always consider other people's distress objectively – that is to place ourselves, with our own wants and sensibilities, in *their* conditions, and then to examine what occasions we should find in them for experiencing happiness or unhappiness" (Freud, 1930, p. 89).

14 The above quotation provides a defense against Thomas Reid's criticism that Smith's system is essentially selfish (Stewart-Robertson and Norton, 1980). The criticism is based on the notion that selfishness is how I would feel if *I were in the shoes of the actor's situation*. Yet as in the above quote, Smith says that "I should suffer if I was really you".

15 An important issue is whether Smith's account of sympathy is selfish. Griswold (1999) distinguishes two senses of selfishness: (1) only when it is to our advantage we sympathize with others; (2) not being able to enter into another's situation since we are confined to our senses. He then arranges a spectrum of selfishness based on Smith's examples.

16 Thus, Griswold's (2006) claim that "in a literal sense, the spectator does not feel the actor's feelings *at all*; he or she imagines being in the [agent's] *situation* and responds accordingly" (at all is emphasized by us) is arguable since as in the above quote the spectator feels the agent's feelings though it varies in degree or in kind.

17 Fricke (2013), referring to this passage, argues that Smith makes a distinction between "sympathetic emotion" and "sympathy", which are two different kinds of feelings. Sympathetic emotion is imagined by the spectator. It is the emotion the spectator imagines he would feel. According to the author, sympathy is a second order feeling, it is not imagined. It refers to a concordance of feelings between the spectator and the agent. Moral judgments are based on sympathy. Judgments of the spectator are set by himself, by imagining how he would feel and act.

18 Schliesser (2014) makes four claims. First, the sympathetic process depends on a causal relationship. Second, there is counterfactual reasoning in the sympathetic process. Third, agents belong to a causal order of nature. And finally, "Smithian judgments of propriety are intrinsically judgments about the proportionality of causal relations" (p. 308).

19 There are alternative accounts of this link in the literature. Griswold (1999) states that equating approval with sympathy would destroy the possibility of ethical evaluation. It is also argued that the approval that the imaginative identification constitutes is only partial, which allows disapproval (Sugden, 2002). According to Darwall (1998), it is not possible to have sympathy without approval.

20 According to Freud we empathize more easily with what we are more familiar with (Freud, 1921).

21 This statement, which was originally published in the second edition of the TMS (1761), was a response to a critical letter by Hume which states that sympathy could be disagreeable. Hume criticizes Smith by giving an example where an "ill-humord Fellow . . . throws a Damp on Company, which I suppose wou'd be accounted for by Sympathy; and yet is disagreeable" (Hume 28 July 1759, which is quoted in Greig, 1932, p. 313).

22 Brodie (2006) likens this effort on the part of the spectator to "critique" and "improvement", stating that these two basic concepts of the Enlightenment underly Smith's description of the spectator.

23 Griswold (1999; 2006) discusses separateness arguing that we are physically separate and that we are not able to literally feel each other's sensations. He argues that the sympathetic process does not eliminate the sense of separateness between the two parties. This is appropriate because we are fundamentally separate and it gives the spectator "emotional space" to assist the actor. See also Deigh (1995).

24 "... sympathy in Adam Smith's sense is a socializing agent" (Raphael, 1985, p. 31).

25 Brown (2011), who applies a Prisoners' Dilemma game to the TMS, argues for the importance of intersubjective individuality in three areas: (1) "Social emulation and material self-betterment presuppose intersubjectively constituted individuality" (p. 180), (2) "sympathetic responses to others are constructed in terms of spectatorial relations among intersubjectively constituted in individuals" (p. 180), (3) "morality is made possible by a society since it is society that provides the initial moral looking-glass by which people are able to evaluate themselves" (180).

References

Andrew, G.E., 1998. Anarchic conscience and enlightenment reason. In: Yamamoto, T., ed. *Philosophical designs for a social-cultural transformation (Ecole des Hautes Etudes en Sciences Cultururelles and Rowman and Littlefield)*. Lanham: Rowman & Littlefield. pp. 77–85.

Atwood, G.E. and Stolorow, R.D., 1984. *Structures of subjectivity: Explorations in psychoanalytic phenomenology*. Hillsdale, NJ: The Analytic Press.

Beebe, B. and Lachmann, F. M., 1988a. Mother-infant mutual influence and precursors of psychic structure. In: Goldberg, A., ed. *Frontiers in self psychology: Progress in self psychology*. Hillsdale, NJ: Analytic Press. Vol. 3, pp. 3–25.

———, 1988b. The contribution of mother-infant mutual influence to the origins of self and object representations. *Psychoanalytic Psychology*, 5, pp. 305–337.

Benjamin, J., 1988. *The shadow of the other: Intersubjectivity and gender in psychoanalysis*. New York: Routledge.

———, 1990. An outline of intersubjectivity: The development of recognition. *Psychoanalytic Psychology*, 7(Suppl), pp. 33–46.

———, 2004. Beyond doer and done to: An intersubjective view of thirdness. *Psychoanalytic Quarterly*, 73, pp. 5–46.

———, 2011. Acknowledgment of collective Trauma in light of dissociation and dehumanization. *Psychoanalytic Perspective*, 8, pp. 207–214.

Berry, C., 2003. Sociality and socialization. In: Brodie, A., ed. *Cambridge companion to the Scottish Enlightenment*. Cambridge: Cambridge University Press. pp. 243–257.

Bohleber, W., 2013. The concept of intersubjectivity in psychoanalysis: Taking critical stock. *The International Journal of Psychoanalysis*, 94, pp. 799–823.

Bolstanki, L., 1999. *Distant suffering: Morality, media and politics*. Cambridge: Cambridge University Press.

Brodie, A., 2006. Sympathy and the impartial spectator. In: Haakonssen, K., ed. *The Cambridge companion to Adam Smith*. Cambridge: Cambridge University Press. pp. 158–188.

Brown, V., 1994. *Adam Smith's discourse: Canonicity, commerce and conscience*. New York: London.

———, 2011. The Theory of Moral Sentiments and the prisoners' dilemma. *The Adam Smith Review*, 6, pp. 172–190.

———, 2012. Intersubjectivity and moral judgment in Adam Smith's Theory of Moral Sentiments. In: Fricke, C. and F. Dagfinn, eds. *Intersubjectivity and objectivity in Adam Smith and Edmund Husserl*. Berlin: Ontos.

Carrasco, M.A., 2011. From psychology to moral activity. *Adam smith review, 6*, pp. 9–29.

Campbell, T.D., 1971. *Adam Smith's science and morals*. London: George Allen and Unwin.

Clark, H.C., 1992. Conversation and moderate virtue in Adam Smith's 'Theory of Moral Sentiments'. *Review of Politics, 54*(2), pp. 185–210.

Darwall, S., 1998. Empathy, sympathy, care. *Philosophical Studies, 89*, pp. 261–282.

Deigh, J., 1995. Empathy and universalizability. *Ethics, 105*, pp. 743–763.

De Waal, F. B. M., 2012. Empathy in primates and other mammals. In: Decety, J., ed. *Empathy: From bench to bedside*. Cambridge: MIT Press. pp. 87–106.

Emde, R.M., 1995. Review *Autism and the development of mind. Journal of International Psychoanalysis, 76*, pp. 187–189.

Firth, A., 2007. Adam Smith's moral philosophy as ethical self-formation. In: Firth, A., G. Cockfield and J. Laurent, eds. *New perspectives on Adam Smith's theory of moral sentiments*. Cheltenham: Edward Elgar. pp. 106–123.

Fonagy, P., 1999. Male perpetrators of violence against women: An attachment theory perspective. *Journal of Applied Psychoanalytic Studies, 1*, pp. 7–27.

Fonagy, P. and Target, M., 1996. Playing with reality: I. theory of mind and the normal development of psychic reality. *International Journal of Psychoanalysis, 77*, pp. 217–233.

———, 2003. *Psychoanalytic theories: Perspectives from developmental psychopathology*. New York: Brunner-Routledge.

Forman-Brazilai, F., 2010. *Adam Smith and the circles of sympathy: Cosmopolitanism and moral theory*. Cambridge: Cambridge University Press.

Freud, S., 1921. Group psychology and the analysis of the ego. In: Strachey, J., ed. *The standard edition of the complete psychological works*. London: Hogarth Press. Vol. XVIII, pp. 69–144.

———, 1930. Civilization and its discontents. In: Strachey, J., ed. *The standard edition of the complete psychological works*. London: Hogarth Press. Vol. XXI, pp. 57–146.

———, 1992. Letter from Sigmund Freud to Eduard Silberstein, August 10, 1879. In: Boehlich, W., ed. *The Letter of Sigmund Freud to Eduard Silberstein 1871–1881*. Cambridge: Harvard University Press.

Fricke, C., 2013. Adam Smith: The sympathetic process and the origin and function of conscience. In: Berry, C.J., M.P. Paganelli and C. Smith, eds. *The Oxford handbook of Adam Smith*. Oxford: Oxford University Press. pp. 177–200.

Frith, U. and Frith, C.D., 2004. Development and neurophysiology of mentalizing. In: Frith, C.D. and D.M. Wolpert, eds. *The Neuroscience of social interaction: Decoding, imitating and influencing the actions of others*. Oxford: Oxford University Press. pp. 109–130.

Gordon, R.M., 1995. Sympathy, simulation and the impartial spectator. *Ethics, 105*, pp. 727–742.

Greig, J.Y.T. ed., 1932. *The letters of David Hume*. Oxford: Oxford University Press. Vol. 2.

Griswold, C.L., 1999. *Adam Smith and the virtues of enlightenment*. Cambridge: Cambridge University Press.

———, 2006. Imagination: Morals, science, and arts. In: Haakonssen, K., ed. *The Cambridge companion to Adam Smith*. Cambridge: Cambridge University Press. pp. 22–56.

———, 2010. Smith and Rousseau in dialogue: Sympathy, pitie, spectatorship and narrative. In: Brown, V. and S. Fleischacker, eds. *Adam Smith Review, 5*, pp. 59–84.

———, 1996. *Natural law and moral philosophy: From Grotius to the Scottish enlightenment*. Cambridge: Cambridge University Press.

Heath, E., 1995. The commerce of sympathy: Adam Smith on the emergence of the morals. *Journal of History of Philosophy, 33*, pp. 447–466.

Hoffman, I.Z., 1983. The patient as the interpreter of the analyst's experience. *Contemporary Psychoanalysis, 19,* pp. 389–422.

Hope, V., 1984. Smith's demigod. In: Hope, V., ed. *Philosophers of the Scottish Enlightenment.* Edinburgh: Edinburgh University Press. pp. 157–167.

Jung, C.G., 1968. *Analytic psychology: Its theory and practice.* New York: Pantheon.

Kernberg, O.F., 1987. Projection and projective identification: Developmental and clinical aspects. *Journal of the American Psychoanalytic Association, 35,* pp. 795–819.

Kohut, H., 1959. Introspection, empathy, and psychoanalysis – An examination of the relationship between mode of observation and theory. *Journal of the American Psychoanalytic Association, 7,* pp. 459–483.

———, 1971. *The analysis of the self.* New York: International University Press.

———, 1977. *The restoration of the self.* New York: International Universities Press.

———, 1982. Introspection, empathy, and the semicircle of mental health. *International Journal of Psychoanalysis, 63,* pp. 395–407.

———, 1984. *How does analysis cure?* In: Goldberg, A. and P. E. Stepansky, eds. Chicago: University of Chicago Press.

Lachmann, F.M. and Beebe, B., 1992. Reformulations of early development and transference: Implications for psychic structure formation. In: Barron, J., M. Eagle and D. Wolitzky, eds. *Interface of psychoanalysis and psychology.* Washington, DC: American Psychological Association. pp. 133–153.

———, 1996a. Three principles of salience in the organization of the patient-analyst interaction. *Psychoanalytic Psychology, 13,* pp. 1–22.

———, 1996b. The contribution of self- and mutual regulation to therapeutic action: A case illustration. In: Goldberg, A., ed. *Basic ideas reconsidered: Progr. self psychology.* Hillsdale, NJ: The Analytic Press. Vol. 12, pp. 123–140.

Loewald, H.W., 1988. Psychoanalysis in search of nature: Thoughts on metapsychology, "metaphysics", projection. *Annual of Psychoanalysis, 16,* pp. 49–54.

Marshall, D., 1984. Adam Smith and the theatricality of moral sentiments. *Critical Inquiry, 10*(4), pp. 592–561.

Mossner, E.C. and Ross, I.S., 1977. *The correspondences of Adam Smith.* Oxford: Clarendon Press.

Myers, M.L., 1975. Adam Smith as a critic of ideas. *Journal of History of Ideas, 32*(2), pp. 281–296.

Nanay, B., 2010. Adam Smith's concept of sympathy and its contemporary interpretations. In: Brown, V. and S. Fleischacker, eds. *Adam Smith Review, 5,* pp. 85–105.

Nussbaum, M.C., 1995. *Poetic justice: The literary imagination and public life.* Boston: Beacon.

Ogden, T.H., 1985. On potential space. *International Journal of Psycho-Analysis, 66,* pp. 129–141.

———, 1992a. The dialectically constituted/decentered subject of psychoanalysis. I: The Freudian subject. *International Journal of Psycho-Analysis, 73,* pp. 517–526.

———, 1992b. The dialectically constituted/decentered subject of psychoanalysis. II: The contributions of Klein and Winnicott. *International Journal of Psycho-Analysis, 73,* pp. 613–626.

———, 1994. The analytic third: Working with intersubjective clinical facts. *International Journal of Psycho-Analysis, 75,* pp. 3–19.

———, 2004. The analytic third: Implications for psychoanalytic theory and technique. *Psychoanalytic Quarterly, 73,* pp. 167–195.

Orange, D.M., Atwood, G.E. and Stolorow, R.D., 1997. *Working intersubjectively: Contextualism in psychoanalytic practice.* Hillsdale, NJ: Analytic Press.

Otteson, J.R., 2002. *Adam Smith's market place of life.* Cambridge: Cambridge University Press.

Peart, S.J. and Levy, D.M., 2005. A discipline without sympathy: The happiness of the majority and its demise. *The Canadian Journal of Economics, 38*(3), pp. 937–954.

Peters, J.D., 1995. Publicity and pain: Self abstraction in Adam Smith's theory of moral sentiments. *Public Culture, 7*, pp. 657–684.

Piper, A. M. S., 1991. Impartiality, compassion, and modal imagination. *Ethics, 101*, pp. 726–757.

Preston, S.D. and De Waal, F. B. M., 2002. The communication of emotions and the possibility of empathy in animals. In: Post, S., L.G. Underwood, J.P. Schloss, and W. B. Hurlburt, eds. *Altruistic love: Science, philosophy, and religion in dialogue.* Oxford: Oxford University Press. Ch. 17.

Radner, J.B., 1980. The art of sympathy in eighteen-century British moral thought. *Studies in Eighteenth-Century Culture, 9*, pp. 189–210.

Raphael, D. D. 1985. *Adam Smith.* Oxford: Oxford University Press.

———, 2007. *The impartial spectator: Adam Smith's moral philosophy.* Oxford: Clarendon Press.

Raphael, D.D. and Macfie, A.L. eds., 1976. *Adam Smith: The theory of moral sentiments.* Oxford: Clarendon Press.

Rothschild, E., 2001. *Economic sentiments: Adam Smith, condorcet, and the enlightenment.* Cambridge, MA: Harvard University Press.

———, 2010. The theory of moral sentiments and the inner life. *Adam Smith Review, 5*, pp. 25–36.

Schliesser, E., 2014. Counterfactual causal reasoning in Smithian sympathy. *Revue Internationale de Philosophie, 269*(3), pp. 307–316.

Sen, A., 1987. *On ethics and economics.* Oxford: Basic Blackwell.

Stern, D.N., 1985. *The interpersonal world of the Infant.* New York: Basic Books.

Stern, D.N., Sander, L., Nahum, J., Harrison, A., Lyons-Ruth, K., Morgan, A., Bruschweiler-Stern, N. and Tronick, E., 1998. Noninterpretive mechanisms in psychoanalytic therapy: The "something more" than interpretation. *The International Journal of Psycho-Analysis, 79*, pp. 903–922. (The authors also identify themselves as The Process Study Group.)

Stewart-Robertson, J.C. and Norton, D.F., 1980. Thomas Reid on Adam Smith's theory of morals. *Journal of History of Ideas, 41*, pp. 381–398.

Stich, S. and Nichols, S., 1992. Folk psychology: Simulation or tacit theory? *Mind and Language, 7*(1–2), pp. 35–71.

Stolorow, R.D., 2002. Impasse, affectivity, and intersubjective systems. *Psychoanalytic Review, 89*, pp. 329–337.

Stolorow, R.D. and Atwood, G.E., 1979. *Faces in a cloud: Subjectivity in personality theory.* Northvale, NJ: Aronson.

———, 1986. Reply to R. White, M. Basch, and M. Nissim-Sabat. *Psychoanalytic review, 73*(3), p. 301.

———, 1992. *Contexts of being: The intersubjective foundations of psychological life.* Hillsdale, NJ: Analytic Press.

Stolorow, R.D., Atwood, G.E. and Brandchaft, B., eds., 1994. *The intersubjective perspective.* Northvale, NJ: Aronson.

Stolorow, R., Branchaft, B. and Atwood, G. 1987. *Psychoanalytic treatment: An Intersubjective Approach.* Hillsdale: The Analytic Press.

Sugden, R.D., 2002. Beyond sympathy and empathy: Adam Smith's concept of fellow-feeling. *Economics and Philosophy, 18*, pp. 63–87.

Teicholz, J.G., 1999. *Kohut, Loewald, and the postmoderns: A comparative study of self and relationship.* Hillsdale, NJ: The Analytic Press.

———, 2001. Chapter 2: The many meanings of intersubjectivity and their implications for analyst self-expression and self-disclosure. *Progress in Self Psychology, 17*, pp. 9–42.

Villiez, C.V., 2006. Double standard-naturally! Smith and Rawls: A comparison of methods. In: Montes, L. and E. Schleisser, eds. *New voices on Adam Smith.* London: Routledge. pp. 115–139.

Wolin, S.S., 1960. *Politics and vision: Continuity and innovation in western political thought.* Boston: Little Brown.

Young, T. J., 1997. *Economics as a moral science.* Lyme: Edward Elgar Publishing Limited.

Chapter 3

Sympathy, empathy and evidence from developmental psychology

I. Introduction

This chapter is an attempt to examine a significant component of Smith's moral theory in the light of current research in psychoanalysis and human development. As we described in Chapter 2, sympathy, which is a mechanism to implement the Deity' design, is the cornerstone of Smith's theory of moral development. For Smith, sympathy is the distinctly human capacity that allows people to experience each other. Morality is co-created through an interactive sympathetic process. Sympathy as defined by Smith bears a strong resemblance to what is referred to in current psychoanalytic theory and practice as empathy (Kohut, 1971). With this in mind, we examine the current theory in psychoanalysis and the empirical research in human development that examines the significance of empathy in human interactions. The current literature supports many of Smith's hypotheses about sympathy's (empathy's) significance in human interactions. The findings from developmental psychology indicate that empathy leads to pro-social behavior, providing further support for Smith's arguments.

Numerous definitions of empathy have been put forward with subtle differences depending on the varying parameters in their psychoanalytic frameworks. A general consensus among current writers seems to suggest that empathy has both cognitive and affective components and refers to the experiencing of another's psychological state.[1] Imagining oneself in the other's situation is the cognitive component of empathy. The affective component of empathy refers to the close matching of another's emotional condition and inner experiences that come with this type of imagination.

Empathy therefore is a response that stems from the experiencing of another's situation or state, and often includes significant aspects of the other's emotional conditions. Human empathy occurs in the context of fluid, complex and interdependent social interactions.

Smith's theory to this date has not been examined in the light of empirical literature related to empathy. Smith's theoretical writing on sympathy as the basis for moral behavior is analogous to empathy in both psychoanalytic theory and in the empirical research on the development of moral or pro-social behavior. In particular, the research gives empirical validation to this structural component of Smith's theoretical argument and shows that moral behavior is strongly influenced by empathy.

The first part of our argument, which is contained in the next section, is that Smith's concept of sympathy is a forerunner to the current psychoanalytic and developmental term, empathy. In Section III we present the current literature in psychoanalysis and developmental psychology that shows a strong link between empathy and pro-social behavior or morality. We postulate that the current literature on empathy supports Smith's philosophical speculation on the centrality of sympathy to the development of morality. Section IV contains our conclusions.

II. Sympathy and empathy

Sympathy in the work of Adam Smith has been reviewed comprehensively in Chapter 2 of this book. However, for reader's continuity in this section, we will offer a short description of sympathy in Smith's work before going on to review the literature on empathy. In the sympathetic process the spectator puts himself in the agent's situation through an imaginative process. The spectator then compares what he imagines the agent is feeling with his own feelings. If the spectator can go along with the agent's feelings, there is sympathy. When there is no sympathy, both the actor and the spectator work hard to gain sympathy. This type of sympathetic response is the foundation of Smith's morality: because we are able to experience another in such a direct way, we form the basis for an internalized conscience relative to them. To put it another way, our inherent capacity to experience what another person feels becomes the reflective basis and motive for building moral behavior with another because of our inherent capacity to feel into the other's experience as with ourselves.

Titchener (1909) coined the term empathy (Einfuhlung):

> Not only do I see gravity and modesty and pride and courtesy and stateliness, but I feel and act them in my mind's muscle. That I suppose, is a simple case of empathy, if we may coin that term as rendering of Einfuhlung.
>
> (p. 21)

Empathy is integral to psychoanalysis, and the empirical literature of developmental psychology, particularly as it relates to therapeutic (helpful) human interactions and the development of pro-social/moral behavior. This section will look at empathy in psychoanalysis. The work on empathy in developmental psychology will be covered in the sections that follow.

Freud wrote about empathy (Einfuhlung [feeling in]) to describe the process of consciously or unconsciously putting ourselves in another's position to appreciate their circumstances and to understand their happiness or unhappiness.[2]

Freud's first use of the term empathy (Einfuhlung) is in 1905 in *Jokes and their Relations to Unconscious*.[3] He states:

> Thus we take the producing person's [joking person] psychical state into consideration, put ourselves into it and try to understand it by comparing it with our own.
>
> (p. 186)

Freud uses "putting himself into" (Sichhineinversetzen) and empathy interchangeably. In 1912 Freud states:

> [T]he doctor must put himself in a position to make use of everything he is told for the purposes of interpretation and of recognizing the concealed unconscious material without substituting a censorship of his own for the selection that the patient has forgone. To put it in a formula: he must turn his own unconscious like a receptive organ towards the transmitting unconscious of the patient. He must adjust himself to the patient as a telephone receiver is adjusted to the transmitting microphone. Just as the receiver converts back into sound waves the electric oscillations in the telephone line which were set up by sound waves, so the doctor's unconscious is able, from the derivatives of the unconscious which are communicated to him, to reconstruct that unconscious, which has determined the patient's free associations.
>
> (pp. 115–116)

Freud's most famous remarks about Einfuhlung were made in 1921. He states that identification among the members of a group occurs through a process of empathy. With regards to identification he states:

> We are faced by the process which psychology call "empathy [Einfuhlung]" and which plays the largest part of our understanding of what is inherently foreign to our ego in other people.
>
> (p. 108)

He saw empathy as a way of understanding and/or appreciating the experience of another. This bears a striking resemblance to Smith's statement: "by imagination we place ourselves in his position". Because Freud was in the unique position of empathically "feeling in" to another's experience on a daily basis, he also knew that empathy in immediate interpersonal interactions could bring with it difficulties by inaccurately projecting one's own experience into another's situation, which could contaminate our perceptions of their experience. The first generation of analysts argued these issues and for the most part agreed with Freud's adoption of the neutral attitude of a surgeon, which guards against too great a reliance on empathy and with the concern that there is a potential difficulty in mistaking our experience to be like another's or projecting our experiences into another (Bolognini, 2004).

In 1928 Ferenczi defines empathy as the capacity to put ourselves in the other's shoes. According to him, both feeling and thinking remain active. Fliess (1942) describes empathy as dynamic. According to him, using empathy means introjecting the object temporarily and then projecting back to the object what he has introjected. He can then perceive from within as well as from without.

Projection in sympathetic interactions

Within psychoanalytic theory and practice, projection is the technical term that is used to denote the "projecting" of one's own inner contents upon or into another. This usually occurs when one is trying to understand another's actions from our own frame of reference, which may or may not be accurate (Freud,1921; Kohut, 1971). In more extreme cases one attempts to get rid of unacceptable contents within oneself by "putting them into another" and then identifying them with the other person and disowning their contents within us. This is referred to as projective identification (Kernberg, 1987).

It is important to note here that sympathy has a projective aspect to it, the deciding piece being whether one is conscious of his projection or not. It is part of a sympathetic process if one is conscious. On the other hand, if one is not conscious that he is projecting, then it is not part of sympathy, but simply projection.

There is little doubt that one of the potential difficulties in sympathetic relatedness is the contamination of our emotional or intellectual understanding of the other through some form of projection. That is why, as Smith suggests, it is important to take the full context of the other's situation into consideration, and/or elucidate our premise about their condition interactively with the other, which in many situations allows for clarification. Seeking to address the difficulties that may be engendered by projection is of particular consequence in Smith's work, given that these interactions have the effect of shaping moral behavior. In these interactions, particularly as they relate to moral judgment, a clear understanding of what is being conveyed and understood on the part of both participants allows for the accurate concordance between them. Smith does not elaborate on projection as such. We can't expect it from him since he did not have access to analytic situations as psychoanalysts have had.

Within the literature on Smith, there are different views on whether sympathy is a projection or not. For example, Fleischacker (2004) states that "Even [when there is transfusion] . . . we are really projecting ourselves into other people's situations, rather than merely adopting the emotion they seem to be experiencing" (pp. 9–10). Fleischacker (2004) further argues that consideration of the transfusion view is part of Smith's opposition to sympathy being an imaginative projection theory. Peart and Levy (2005) argue that Smith's treatment of sympathy is one of projection. Griswold (1999) argues that when

Smith speaks about fear of death, it might be called projective identification. On the other hand, "sympathizing with the living . . . would seem to come to more than imagining *oneself* in their situation; otherwise sympathy would collapse into self-centered projection" (p. 90). Darwall (1999) states that the spectator unconsciously projects himself to the agent's standpoint. He refers to Smith's sympathy as "projective empathy".

The current movement in psychoanalytic literature on empathy

As psychoanalytic work has progressed, the recognition of empathetic understanding playing an important role in human development and in psychotherapeutic relationships has grown. Empathy has gained a great deal of support as an integral component in therapy. Indeed, it was demonstrated as a crucial component of effective psychotherapy regardless of theoretical orientation (Truax and Carkhuff, 1967).

Bolognini (2004) laid out an excellent review of the history and development of empathy within the evolution of psychoanalytic theory and practice. He points out that empathy re-emerged in the 1950s, finding support and clinical articulation with the work of both Schafer (1959) and Greenson (1960). Bolognini (2004), in summarizing Greenson's contributions, reported that it was through one's "plentiful supply of personal experiences to draw on . . . [that] make it easier to understand the patient" (Bolognini, 2004, p. 46). Similar to Smith, this points out the need for a concordance of one's own experience with that of the other as a key to sympathy/empathy with the other's experience.

Schafer (1959) uses the term "generative empathy" and states that "Generative empathy may be defined as the inner experience of sharing in and comprehending the momentary psychological state of another person" (p. 350). Olden (1958) views empathy as an identification of oneself with another so as to better understand their needs. According to Greenson (1960), empathy is an emotional knowledge. The analyst enters the patient and undergoes his experiences as if he were the patient. The analyst is mindful of what is going on in himself while undergoing this process. It includes the sharing and experience of the feelings of another. In the empathetic process both closeness and separateness are important. Empathy occurs in a relationship in which objects are separate.

Pao's (1984) description of empathy highlights its dynamic nature clearly. The person who wishes to understand and the person who wants to be understood are involved in the experience. They both play an active part. Step by step, they form interconnected communications, which are composed of mental interactions and continual exchange. This is analogous to Smith's description of the dynamic process in Smith's sympathetic process.

Kleinans and post-Kleinans use the term empathy in only few occasions; however, they have an original and coherent theory of empathy. Hinshelwood (1989) states that empathy is a result of normal projective identification according to Klein. Money-Kyrle (1956) states that the analyst becomes intro-jectively identified with the patient. He understands the patient's inside and reprojects and interprets. Bion's (1967) concept of reverie is very important here. The child's projections and projective identifications are received, con-tained, elaborated, modified, transformed and returned to the child by the mother. This has a constitutive role in the child's mental apparatus, which is an interpersonal event. According to Grotstein (1994), the subject carries out a limited and partial projective identification. The person receives this and accommodates within his own inner reality through introjective identification.

More than anyone within contemporary psychoanalytic work, Kohut (1971, 1977, 1984) proposed the centrality of empathy in psychoanalytic work. He illuminated the importance and usefulness of empathy in human interactions when it comes to conveying the experiences of being seen, valued and/or understood. "No psychology of complex mental states is conceivable without the employment of empathy" (1984, p. 174–175). In particular, whether it is through the conveyance of understanding, or conveying to another that they are "understood, that is, that another person has been able to experience, at least in approximation, what he himself experienced, whether, for example, the experience in question is one of inner emptiness and depression, or of pride and enhanced self-esteem" (Kohut, 1984, p. 176–177). Kohut is particularly articulate in the importance of empathy to healing and to the development of the self.

Our view of empathy is best described by the following quote from Kohut (1959), which we referred to in Chapter 2:

> We see a person who is unusually tall. It is not to be disputed that this per-son's unusual size is an important fact for our psychological assessment – without introspection and empathy, however, his size remains simply a physical attribute. Only when we think ourselves into his place [imagine being in X's situation], only when we, by vicarious introspection, begin to feel his unusual size as if it were our own [imagine being X in X's situation] and thus revive inner experiences in which we had been unusual or con-spicuous, only then begins there for us an appreciation of the meaning that the unusual size may have for this person and only then have we observed a psychological fact.
>
> (p. 461) (We added the remarks about X in the above quote in [ ]
> to point out that empathy entails both (1) and (2) above.)

As we have stated in Chapter 2, it would not be possible to imagine being X in X's situation without imagining being X. In other words, psychoanalytically, empathy has two components. The first component is what might be called general sympathy (imagining being in X's situation), the second component is being able to wonder about the internal experiences of the other and feel something analogous (imagining being X in X's situation).

In psychoanalytic practice the use of empathy is both a means for understanding another's experience and the vehicle for conveying that understanding or experience back to another. The very act of conveying such understanding seems to be integral to the healing process. Similarly, this kind empathic human contact, as will be further revealed in the review of literature on pro-social or moral development, plays as important of a role in human development as it does in interpersonal healing. For the purposes of the present work, we will look into the qualities of empathy that make a difference in the developments of pro-social/moral interactions.

As we stated in Chapter 2 in a more modern lexicon, Smith's description of sympathy is what is referred to as empathy in psychoanalytic and human development vernacular, and as such Smith's sympathy can be seen as a forerunner of our more current understanding and use of the term empathy. In broad terms empathy is apprehending another's conscious and unconscious psychological processes. We should again note that Freud was familiar with Adam Smith's work, as he indicated in a letter he wrote to Silberstein in August 1879; he states, "I have some marvelous books to read . . . a great philosopher and wit, Adam Smith's fundamental book on the wealth of nations . . ." (p. 174). We do not know if Freud read the TMS, where the concept of the impartial spectator is developed; however, given that he read Smith's later work on economics, it would not be surprising if he indeed had read Smith's previous landmark work.

III. Developmental research on empathy in the development of pro-social/moral behavior

Introduction to pro-social behavior

In this section we will refer to the development of pro-social and moral behavior synonymously. In the review of this literature we will be pointing out the links between the development of morality and the key role that empathy plays in both its development and implementation. In the research in human development there is a goldmine of empirical findings linking empathy to the development of pro-social/ethical behavior. Researchers such as Carlo (2006), Hoffman (1982, 2000), Emde and Easterbrooks (1987), and Zahn-Wexler and Radke-Yarrow (1990) have looked into the developmental origins of empathy and its central role in the development of pro-social/moral behavior.

This line of inquiry is intended to support the integral relationship that was first postulated by Smith on the relationship between sympathy (empathy) and the development of moral structure that he laid out in the TMS.

Carlo (2006) refers to pro-social behaviors as altruistic because they are defined by their primary desire to help others. He found that the development of altruistic behavior is closely related to child-rearing practices and that these practices need to be matched with the child's cognitive level and ability. This type of parenting is an empathic attunement in and of itself. Of further importance in the development of altruism in children is in their observation of adults who model sharing, comforting and helping. The growth of this ability to comprehend another's situation is an important condition for pro-social altruistic behavior. Along the same lines, Batson (1991) considers what he calls the "empathy-altruism hypothesis". In this view, empathy is a crucial factor determining altruistic behavior. Altruism in this context means acting on behalf of someone who is in need or distress.

Empathy has also been linked to socio-cognitive correlates of empathy. The capacity for perspective comes as a result of understanding another's situation and the ability to differentiate self and other. There are several types of what Carlo (2006) refers to as perspective taking. Increasing understanding of another's intentions, situation and thoughts would be examples of social (cognitive) perspective taking. The ability to understand another's emotions is affective perspective taking. Finally, the ability to understand the literal visual point of view of another is perceptual perspective taking. As a result, understanding another's feelings and thoughts facilitates other oriented behaviors. It leads to empathy, reduction of aggressive and antisocial forms of behavior, comforting, sharing and volunteering.

Moral reasoning is another link between social cognition and pro-social behaviors (Carlo, 2006). Thinking about dilemma situations where issues of fairness, caring or justice are involved are examples of moral reasoning. Justice oriented, care oriented, and pro-social moral reasoning are the three types of moral reasoning. It has been found that higher levels of pro-social behaviors are associated with higher levels of moral reasoning.

In addition, children who interpret ambiguous events in ways that promote positive social interactions exhibit high levels of pro-social behavior. More pro-social behaviors are found in adolescents who expect their parents to react appropriately to pro-social and antisocial behaviors.

Hoffman (2000) views pro-social moral action as helping someone else who is in some type of distress. He sees that prior to taking action, one experiences what he refers to as empathic distress. Empathic distress is signaled in life situations, precedes the helping behavior, is positively correlated with helping behavior and the distress diminishes in intensity when one helps. Hoffman identifies empathic distress as occurring in five different modes. The first is mimicry, a conditioned response that occurs when one observes someone in distress at the same time they are having their own distress. The second, as a variant of a conditioned response, is direct association, which is a situation that arises when the victim's situation reminds the observer of similar experiences, and third, evokes feelings that fit the victim's situation. Meditated association, the fourth mode, takes place when the victim's emotional state is communicated verbally.

Finally, the fifth mode is role taking. This is analogous to Smith's sympathetic process, in that it requires putting oneself in the other's place and imagining what he feels, which requires an advanced cognitive processing ability. Research indicates that more empathy is aroused when one imagines putting oneself in the other's place rather than focusing on his expressive movements. Furthermore, more empathy is aroused when imagining oneself in the other's place rather than focusing attention directly on the other's feelings. Role taking can be self-focused by imagining how one would feel in the same situation as the other. In other focused role taking, one imagines how the other feels in a given situation resulting in the observer feeling something of the other's feelings. This is analogous to what Smith describes.

Evidence for empathy in pro-social behavior

As has been indicated so far, empathy seems to play an important role in moral development. The capacity to develop moral values occurs through maturing mutual attunement (Morrison and Severina, 1997) and is composed of both affective and cognitive processing (Haidt and Kesebir, 2010).

Morality includes the concepts of fairness, justice, and rights, as well as maxims regarding interpersonal relationships. Haidt and Kesebir (2010) identify morality as a set of interlocking virtues, values, practices, norms and identities that work together to regulate interactions and selfishness to make cooperative life possible. A central focus of morality is the assessment of the wrongness or the rightness of acts or behaviors that knowingly cause harm to people. Experiences of approval and disapproval continue through life in mutually attuned relationships.

The early foundations of morality are present in early childhood, taking the form of the infant's appreciation of standards and responses to the feelings of others. The origins of morality are located in the young child's awareness of self in relation to others. Initially two dimensions of morality are distinguished: inequality and care (Gilligan and Wiggins, 1987). Inequality is reflected in the child's awareness of being less capable and smaller than older people. Focusing on this dimension, morality is defined as justice. This is aligned with the child's progress towards independence and equality. The second dimension is care. How one should act towards another is profoundly shaped by attachment. The ways in which attachment is nurtured in children shape a perspective that views morality as being related to the love and care they received (Gilligan and Wiggins, 1987).

In most of the literature, empathy is seen as a factor that motivates pro-social behavior such as sharing and helping, and it inhibits aggression towards others (see for example, Hoffman, 1982, Miller and Eisenberg, 1988). It often generates feelings of concern for others' need, distress and pain as well as an awareness of the effect of one's behavior on others (see for example, Zahn-Waxler, Radke-Yarrow, and King, 1979). Empathy is also argued to contribute to the development of higher moral reasoning and it is reflected in social behavior (see for example, Eisenberg, 1986, Hoffman, 2000). Empathy is a moral emotion and plays an important part in moral reasoning, values and behavior (Eisenberg,

Spinard and Sadovsky, 2006). While high moral reasoning has been linked to empathy, moral development does not necessarily proceed smoothly. The same children that demonstrated empathic understanding of moral transgressions and efforts to repair within the family may not demonstrate the same capacities with people outside the family (Dunn, 2006). These behaviors depend on the particular relationship within which he is interacting. As a child's capacity for general social competence increases, the likelihood of a child's understanding of other's emotions and responding in a sensitive manner increases as well. There is then a natural link between social competence and empathy.

Conversely, psychopathic tendencies are found in people with low levels of empathy. Children may be at risk for externalizing problems if they are not reactive to mild empathy-inducing stimuli. Socio-emotional problems are found with greater frequency when empathy is lacking in general, and in particular when there is no empathy over arousal when there is personal distress (Eisenberg, Spinard, Sadovsky, 2006). In addition, when there is low empathy, children tend to become highly aroused (with negative emotion) when exposed to other's emotion and become deregulated in their social behavior (Eisenberg, Spinard, Sadovsky, 2006).

Parent's role in development of empathy

We will present a brief review on the normal development of empathy. We will then discuss the family environments that will most likely produce empathic behavior, such as: a) when children are encouraged to express and experience a broad range of emotions, b) when a child's emotional needs are satisfied and excessive self-concern is discouraged, and c) when a child observes and interacts with others who encourage responsiveness and emotional sensitivity (Koestner, Franz and Weinberger, 1990).

Hoffman (2000) describes the development of empathic distress in children. Initially, it is a rudimentary emphatic response that is manifested in global empathy. Infants, even when they are one day old, start crying when they hear someone else cry. A reactive cry is a spontaneous cry of an infant who is actually in discomfort. It is an "innate, isomorphic response to the cry of another being of the same species, which survived natural selection and is adaptive" (Hoffman, 2000, p. 65). Another's distress is felt as distress in the newborn. It is a precursor to empathic distress. Infants make use of others' emotional displays to guide their own behavior; they are not only responsive to other's emotional signals. It could be argued that this reactive cry could be mimicry, or a learned response based on conditioning. However, given its presence at one day, it seems unlikely that there would be conditioning trials and forms of reinforcement that would create a conditioned response.

By about six months, infants start becoming aware of themselves and others as separate beings, and the reactive cry that is confined to early months is gone by this time. The cry is also not instantaneous and agitated.

During the first year, infants understand simple social rules, engage in reciprocal behaviors and begin to accept rules as their own. Inhibition of previously prohibited behavior and compliance to caregiver requests begin to be observed (Oppenheim, Emde, Hasson and Warren, 1997). Towards the end of the first year, infants still respond to a distressed other. But whimpering and silently watching the other accompanies the cry. There is confusion about who is really in distress even though there is an awareness of something unpleasant happening to another. The child seeks comfort in the same way when he is himself distressed. They respond to empathic and actual distress in the same way. Even though during the first year infants are slowly developing an identity separate from others, this is not fully accomplished. They are unclear about the source of their emphatic distress. Hoffman (2000) refers to this phase of development as egocentric empathic distress. In the latter half of the first year, inhibitions of previously uninhibited behavior and compliance to caregiver requests begin to be observed. During situations of uncertainty, an infant's social referencing of others' emotional expressions occurs (Oppenheim, Emde, Hasson and Warren, 1997). In situations of uncertainty, children monitor their mother's emotional expressions and modify their behavior (Dunn, 1987).

A one-and-a-half-year-old may respond emphatically when confronted by another's distress. They exhibit evidence of concern, emotional arousal or share something with the distressed other. Quasi-egocentric distress starts around age two. These children start making helpful advances towards the victim. They are more anchored to external reality. They don't recognize others' inner states even though they have inner states. They use strategies that they themselves feel comforted by in an egocentric way even when they know that the other is in distress. They are confined to preverbal modes. They show a rudimentary form of self-focused role taking. They no longer confuse the victims' or their own actual distress with their empathic distress. The toddler shows an awareness of social standards towards the end of the second year (Zahn–Waxler and Radke–Yarrow, 1990). Early moral development may not require discipline with the emergence of internalized empathy. As the development of empathic capacities emerge, a toddler's aggression may be constrained (Emde, Johnson, Easterbrooks, 1987).

Children start becoming aware of the other's inner states later in the second year. Self-other differentiation and self-recognition develop. They realize that others' inner states at times may differ from their own. They are able to imagine and infer others' perspectives and feelings. They begin to describe others' internal states, their own internal states and begin to talk about emotions (Emde, Johnson, Easterbrooks, 1987). Children at this stage help others more effectively because they empathize more accurately with another's feelings. They become sensitive to family members' distress and anger (Dunn, 1987). All the basic elements of mature empathy are present at this stage and continue to develop and grow throughout life. They now start engaging other focused role taking as well as self-focused role taking. They can empathize with complex feelings. Sharing, helping and cooperation emerge during this period. In sum: even two-year-olds show: a) the states of others can be experienced affectively, b) others' psychological and physical states can be interpreted cognitively, and c) the capacity to alleviate distress of others can be developed (Emde, Johnson, Easterbrooks, 1987).

We see that by the age of two the human capacity for empathy has been well-developed from the foundational beginnings in infancy. As has been indicated, the parental environment plays a significant role in nurturing this development (Dunn, 2006). We will now look more directly at the role that parents play in the development of empathy.

Dunn (2006) has consolidated many of the research understandings on the parent's role in development of empathy. Moral judgments, moral sensibilities and the wider aspects of culture are built through family mediation. The development of social understanding occurs through social interaction in the family, and the development of moral understanding and reasoning is based on the development of social and emotional understanding. Family discipline is seen as important in conscience development. By contrast, others emphasize parent-child relationships rather than parenting. Reciprocity within family relationships is significant. Social understanding more broadly considered is motivated in this relational framework. Children's caring behavior is linked to family experiences. For moral development, positive experiences within the parent-child relationship are essential (Dunn, 2006).

Early conscience development and the pro-social understanding of relationships are related to family discussions of emotions in conflict. Powerful motivations for children to understand moral issues and conventional rules are provided by the affective dynamics of family relationships. Children even in preschool years distinguish between breaches of conventional rules and breaches of moral issues (the welfare of others, positive justice, fairness). The distinction between these two, however, is blurred in family relationships, where a breach of social conventions maybe treated as a breach of personal welfare (Dunn, 2006).

Children discover how to understand other people, the social rules, how to gain other's cooperation, how to provide comfort and how to manage disputes from their family relationships. An important factor in developing the understanding of others comes in their ability to understand their own self-interest. From solving these social problems can come self-efficacy (separate from self-interest). This does not imply opposition to the interest of others. Developing social understanding in which concern for self-interest plays a major role does not come into conflict with empathetic concern for another family member (Dunn, 2006).

The development of the child's internalized guilt feelings is fostered by parental warmth, parental strategies of psychologically oriented discipline and open expression of emotions. However, punitive and harsh discipline seems to interfere with these developments (Dunn, 2006).

Reciprocal relationships are important in the parent-child relationship. Children internalize certain aspects of parents' behavior, and in turn they influence parental behavior. The extent and direction of this influence is affected by the quality of relationship between child and parent (Dunn, 2006).

The significance of the parent-child relationship for moral development and the quality of the parent-child relationship strongly influence a child's individual characteristics (the understanding of emotions and mental states, temperamental characteristics, ability to regulate emotions and verbal ability) and plays an important role in their development (Dunn, 2006).

The children of mothers who use a reasoned argument for a child's behavior in conflictual situations responded differently than children of mothers who did not use a reasoned argument. Specifically, children of mothers who did not use such arguments showed less concern with matters of reparation to the victim of transgressions and moral orientation than children whose mothers did use such arguments (Dunn, 1987).

Children had high scores of reparation when mothers frequently explained to the child the consequences of his behavior for the victim, as well as when multiple forms of affective communications were used. Affective explanations of mothers had children with high altruism scores. Children's altruism was not associated with techniques of physical punishment or physical restraint. Children's altruism was based on mother's moralizing. Children were more likely to make reparations when mothers gave reassurances frequently (Zahn-Waxler and Radke-Yarrow, 1979).

A child's participation in family conversations about emotions play a central role in the development of emotional understanding. The development of empathy and early conscience is also linked to this type of emotional understanding (Dunn, 2006).

There is a positive relation between pro-social development, attachment and parental support. Authoritative parents have children who exhibit high levels of pro-social behavior. Acceptance and understanding are the two main components necessary for value internalization. Judgments of the appropriateness of the parent's reactions, the clarity and consistency of the message, the type of misdeed, the type of discipline, perceived threat to the child's autonomy and the individual characteristic of the child, such as temperament, are central for the child's willingness to accept the moral message. A powerful means to foster desirable moral behaviors and to mitigate antisocial behaviors is the strong desire of children to gain their parent's approval and positive affection. Future pro-social behaviors can be influenced by praise or positive feedback (Carlo, 2006).

Mother's empathy is associated with high empathy scores in daughters (Barnett, King, Howard and Dinno, 1980). The development of empathy is linked with empathic parenting and parents' directiveness. Empathy may be fostered though the encouragement of empathy due to children's increased capacity of role taking, which is also a component of empathy. Moral reasoning in adolescents is associated with parental practices that encourage perspective taking and acknowledge the child's perspective. Cognitive perspective taking and a girl's empathy are associated with emotional communication. Children's perspective taking is positively correlated with maternal rational independence training (Eisenberg and McNally, 1993).

A daughter's empathy at the early to mid-elementary school-age is positively correlated with her mother's empathy (Eisenberg, Spinard and Sadovsky, 2006). A high quality relationship between caregiving and supportive parenting has been linked to empathic development (see for example Eisenberg, Spinard and Sadovsky, 2006). For example, more empathic concern towards the injured other is seen in securely attached children at 22 months. In securely attached children at the age of three to four, empathic and pro-social behaviors are observed. Maternal responsiveness has been found to influence later empathic responding. For example, higher levels of empathy in toddlers at 22 months are predicted by maternal responsiveness at nine months old. Similar results are observed in adolescents. Empathy is associated with warm and supportive parenting. Consistent with this finding, toddlers are found to be low in other oriented concern and high oriented self-concern with parents who display intense and frequent anger. Relatively high empathic children usually are found to be associated with parents who give reason for discipline, set high standards for their children and are not punitive. Empathy is fostered when parental practices increase children's capacity to deal constructively with their own negative emotion (Eisenberg, Spinard and Sadovsky, 2006).

Empathic concern is also linked to parental involvement with children and maternal tolerance for dependent behavior. Altruism in children is linked to adult models of sharing, comforting and helping. An important condition for altruistic behavior is the child's ability to fully understand another person's experiential state. Children have high reparation scores when the mother explains the consequences of the child's behavior, and when the mother uses multiple forms of affective communication. In addition, children have high reparation scores when mothers frequently give assurances. Altruism is also high in children who use affective communication, and whose mothers use moralizing (Zahn-Waxler, Radke-Yarrow and King, 1979).

Empathic anger, guilt and feelings of injustice

The research in this next section points out the development of pro-social moral behavior in ways that aim more towards the type of moral reasoning and behavior that Smith has elaborated upon. This is particularly true when it comes to placing oneself in the position of another and taking moral action based upon that experience.

Hoffman (2000) describes relations between anger, guilt and feelings of injustice. One may empathize with the victim as if they themselves feel attacked. They may also feel angry or may sympathize with the victim and feel angry with the culprit. There are two types of empathic anger. In the first type, the observer picks up the anger of the victim at the abuser. In the second type, the observer feels angry through taking the perspective of the victim. In this case the observer feels both empathic anger and empathic distress for the victim. Guilt may be produced when observers allow the victim's distress to happen or continue due to egotistical motives. Empathy based guilt leads to pro-social acts such as reparation and apologizing. Observers may conclude that the victim's fate was unfair, and their empathic distress, anger or guilt may increase. Observers may view the victim as a victim of injustice in the latter case (Hoffman, 2000).

The key pro-social motive in transgressions involving harm to others is empathy based guilt. Empathic feelings are often expressed when describing guilt over experiences. Parental discipline and empathy based guilt are linked positively. Guilt like behavior when toddlers observe another's distress is similar to empathic distress while observing another's distress. There is considerable evidence that pro-social acts such as reparations and helping others besides the victim are motivated by empathy based transgression guilt. Guilt is considered a positive interpersonal emotion. Based on an empathic desire to make things better when the other is hurt, guilt can be seen as a moral regulating emotion (Hoffman, 2000).

Shame and pride also play a role in moral development and they are based on a dilemma, some sense of struggle or conflict. Indicating that a rule or standard has been successfully applied in a given situation, pride exerts a positive response. Shame, on the other hand, indicates an experience of displeasure when a prohibited act is carried out. For the development of autonomy, modulated shame experiences are necessary. Together with empathy, shame is necessary for the development of moral values (Morrison and Severina, 1997).

As a final note, it has been argued that the capacity for individual regulation is important in empathy related responses (Eisenberg, Spinard and Sadovsky, 2006). Individuals who have good emotional regulation are more likely to be empathetic, while those who are low in regulation are more prone to be occupied with personal distress. This suggests that because many aspects of regulation appear to be temperamentally based, empathy also involves biologically based predispositions in temperament (Eisenberg, Spinard and Sadovsky, 2006).

IV. Conclusions

Smith's foundational concept of sympathy in his TMS bears a strong resemblance to the more contemporary psychoanalytic and developmental concept of empathy. Psychoanalytic theory based on clinical observation and research that has been presented in this paper expands Smith's moral philosophy to include a more applied understanding grounded psychoanalytic theory and the research in child development over the past 50 years.

We reviewed the origins of empathy in psychoanalysis and developmental psychology. We see that empathy (like sympathy) has an important linking effect that allows people to find common connections between themselves and others. In particular, as it relates to Smith's work, there is strong evidence that empathy leads to pro-social behavior/moral behavior across a number of human interactions. In psychotherapy, in addition to being a theoretical concept, we find that it is one of the core elements to any healing therapeutic relationship. In child rearing, empathy is strongly related to emotional regulation and well-adjusted children. In human development beyond childhood, we find that empathy is also related to pro-social behavior. There is also evidence that the lack of empathy leads to anti-social behavior, pointing again to its central role in the facilitation of morality.

At both the level of clinical practice and empirical research, it appears that the foundations for morality/pro-social behavior are based on sympathy/empathy as Smith predicted that they would be.

Notes

1 The term Eifuhlung was originally used by Freud in 1921, and was translated by Strachey as empathy. Freud describes Einfuhlung as a process of putting oneself into another's position unconsciously or consciously. We try to understand the other through this process. He continued to use the word throughout the rest of his life. Kohut (1966) defined empathy as "the mode by which one gathers psychological data about other people and, when they say what they think or feel, imagines their inner experience even though it is not open to direct observation" (p. 261).
2 The Standard Edition of works of Freud translates only three of the 12 other occurrences of einfuhlung as "empathy" and never translates einfuhlen (empathize), which occurs eight times.
3 As is clear in Freud (1928) and his exchange of letters with Ferenczi, Freud indicates that empathy concerns almost everything an analyst should do in a positive direction.

References

Barnett, M.A., King, L.M., Howard, J.A. and Dinno, G.W., 1980. Empathy in young children: Relation to parents' empathy, affection and emphasis on the feelings of others. *Developmental Psychology, 16*(3), pp. 243–244.

Batson, C.D., 1991. *The altruism question: Toward a social psychological answer.* Hillsdale, NJ: Lawrence Erlbaum Associates.

Batons, C.D., Klein, T.R., Highberger, L. and Shaw, L.L., 1995. Immorality from empathy induced altruism: When compassion and justice conflict. *Journal of Personality and Social Psychology, 68,* pp. 1042–1054.

Bion, W. R., 1967. *Second thoughts.* London: Heinemann.

Bolognini, S., 2004. *Psychoanalytic empathy.* London: Free Association Books.

Buchsbaum, H.K. and Emde, R.N., 1990. Play narratives in 36-month old children – Early moral development and family relationship. *Psychoanalytic Study of the Child, 45,* pp. 129–155.

Carlo, G., 2006. Care-based and altruistically based morality. In: Killen, M. and J. Smetana, eds. *Handbook of moral development.* Mahwah, NJ: Hamilton Printing Company. pp. 551–580.

Darwall, S., 1999. Sympathetic liberalism: Recent work on Adam Smith. *Philosophy and Public Affairs, 28*(2), pp. 139–164.

Decety, J. and Cowell, J.M., 2014a. Friends or Foes: Is empathy necessary for moral behavior? *Perspectives on Psychological Science, 9*(5), pp. 525–537.

———, 2014b. The complex relation between morality and empathy. *Trends in Cognitive Sciences, 18*(7), pp. 337–339.

Dunn, J., 1987. The beginnings of moral understanding: Development in the second year. In: Kagan, J. and S. Lamb, eds. *The emergence of morality in young children.* Chicago: University of Chicago Press. pp. 91–111.

———, 2006. Moral development in early childhood and social interaction in the family. In: Killen, M. and J. Smetana, eds. *Handbook of moral development.* Mahwah, NJ: Hamilton Printing Company. pp. 331–350.

Eisenberg, N., 1986. *Altruistic emotion, cognition and behavior.* Hillsdale, NJ: Lawrence Erlbaum Associates.

Eisenberg, N. and McNally, S., 1993. Socialization and mothers' and adolescents' empathy related characteristics. *Journal of Research on Adolescents, 3*(2), pp. 171–191.

Eisenberg, N., Spinard, T. and Sadovsky, A., 2006. Empathy related responding in children. In: Killen, M. and J. Smetana, eds. *Handbook of moral development.* Mahwah, NJ: Hamilton Printing Company. pp. 517–550.

Emde, R., Johnson, W.F. and Easterbrooks, M.A., 1987. The do's and don'ts of early moral development: Psychoanalytic tradition and current research. In: Kagan, J. and S. Lamb, eds. *The emergence of morality in young children.* Chicago: University of Chicago Press. pp. 245–276.

Ferenczi, S., 1928. Die Elastizität der psychoanalytischen Technik. *Internationale Zeitschrift für Psychoanalyse, 14*, pp. 197–209.

Fleischacker, S., 2004. *On Adam Smith's wealth of nations: A philosophical companion.* Princeton, NJ: Princeton University Press.

Fliess, R., 1942. The metapsychology of the analyst. *Psychoanalytic Quarterly, 11*, 211–227.

Freud, S., 1879. Letter from Sigmund Freud to Eduard Silberstein, August 10, 1879. In: Boehlich, W., ed. *The letters of Sigmund Freud to Eduard Silberstein 1871–1881.* Cambridge, MA: Harvard University Press.

———, 1905. Jokes and their relation to the unconscious. In: Strachey, J., ed. *The standard edition of the complete psychological works by Sigmund Freud.* London: Hogarth Press. Vol. VIII, pp. 9–238.

———, 1912. Recommendations to physicians practicing psycho-analysis. In: Strachey, J., ed. *The standard edition of the complete psychological works by Sigmund Freud.* London: Hogarth Press. Vol. XII, pp. 109–120.

———, 1921. Group psychology and the analysis of the ego. In: Strachey, J., ed. *The standard edition of the complete psychological works by Sigmund Freud.* London: Hogarth Press. Vol. XVIII, pp. 69–144.

———, 1930. Civilization and its discontents. In: Strachey, J., ed. *The standard edition of the complete psychological works by Sigmund Freud.* London: Hogarth Press. Vol. XXI, pp. 57–146.

Fricke, C., 2013. Adam Smith: The sympathetic process and the origin and function of conscience. In: Berry, J.C., M.P. Paganelli and C. Smith, eds. *The Oxford handbook of Adam Smith.* pp. 177–200.

Gilligan, C. and Wiggin, G., 1987. The origins of morality in early childhood. In: Kagan, J. and S. Lamb, eds. *The emergence of morality in young children*. Chicago: University of Chicago Press. pp. 277–305.

Gopnik, A., 2009. *The philosophical baby: What children's minds tell us about truth, love and the meaning of life*. New York: Picador.

Greenson, R.R., 1960. Empathy and its vicissitudes. *International Journal of Psycho-Analysis*, *41*, pp. 418–424.

Griswold, C.L., 1999. *Adam Smith and the virtues of enlightenment*. Cambridge: Cambridge University Press.

Grotstein, J. 1994. Projective identification and countertransference. *Contemporary Psychoanalysis*, *10*, 578–592.

Haidt, J. and Kesebir, S., 2010. Morality. In: Fiske, S., D. Gilbert and G. Lindzey, eds. *Handbook of social psychology* (5th ed.). Hoboken: Wiley. pp. 797–832.

Hamlin, J.K., 2014. The origins of human morality: Complex socio-moral evaluations by pre verbal infants. In: Decety, J. and Y. Christen, eds. *New frontiers in social neuroscience*. New York: Springer. pp. 165–188.

Hastings, P.D., Zahn-Waxler, C.N. and McShane, K., 2006. We are by nature moral creatures: Biological basis of concern for others. In: Killen, M. and J. Smetana, eds. *Handbook of moral development*. Mahwah, NJ: Hamilton Printing Company. pp. 483–516.

Hinshelwood, R. D., 1989. *Dictionary of Klenian Thought*. London: Free Association Books.

Hoffman, M.L., 1982. Development of prosocial motivation: Empathy and guilt. In: Eisenberg, N., ed. *The development of prosocial behavior*. New York: Academic Press. pp. 281–213.

———, 2000. *Empathy and moral development: implications for caring and justice*. Cambridge: Cambridge University Press.

Kernberg, O.F., 1987. Projection and projective identification: Developmental and clinical aspects. *Journal of the American Psychoanalytic Association*, *35*, pp. 795–819.

Kohut, H., (1959). Empathy and psychoanalysis: an examination of the relationship between mode of observation and theory. In: Ornstein, Ph. H., ed. *The search for self*. New York: International University Press. Vol. 1, pp. 205–232.

———, 1966. Forms and transformations of narcissism. *Journal of the American Psychoanalytic Association*, *14*(2), pp. 243–272.

———, 1971. *The analysis of the self*. New York: International University Press.

———, 1977. *The restoration of the self*. New York: International University Press.

———, 1984. *How does analysis cure?* Chicago: Chicago University Press.

Miller, P.A. and Eisenberg, N., 1988. The relation of empathy to aggression and externalizing/antisocial behavior. *Psychological Bulletin*, *103*, pp. 324–344.

Money-Kyrle, R., 1956. *Normal countertransference and some of its deviations*. London: Duckwood.

Morrison, N. K. and Severina, S. K., 1997. Moral values: Development and gender influences. *Journal of Academy of Psychoanalysis*, *25*, pp. 255–275.

Olden, C. 1958. Notes on the development of empathy. *Psychoanalytic Studies of the Child*, *13*, pp. 505–518.

Oppenheim, D., Emde, R. N., Hasson, M. and Warren, S., 1997. Preschoolers face moral dilemmas: A longitudinal study of acknowledging and resolving internal conflict. *The International Journal of Psychoanalysis*, *78*, pp. 943–957.

Pao, P. N. 1984. *Therapeutic empathy in the schizophrenic: Empathy II*. Hillsdale, NJ: Analytic Press.

Peart, S.J. and Levy, D.M., 2005. A discipline without sympathy: The happiness of the majority and its demise. *The Canadian Journal of Economics*, *38*(3), pp. 937–954.

Titchener, E. 1909. *Elementary psychology of the thought process.* New York: Palgrave Macmillan.

Truax, C.B. and Carkhuff, R.R., 1967. *Toward effective counseling and psychotherapy.* Chicago: Aldine.

Schafer, R., 1959. Generative empathy in the treatment situation. *The Psychoanalytic Quarterly, 28,* pp. 242–273.

Sullivan, H.S., 1947. *Conceptions of modern psychiatry.* Washington, DC: White Foundation.

Koestner, R., Franz, C. and Weinberger, J., 1990. The family origins of empathic concern: A 26-year longitudinal study. *Journal of Personality and Social Psychology, 58*(4), pp. 709–717.

Zahn-Waxler, C. and Radke-Yarrow, M., 1990. The origins of empathic concern. *Motivation and Emotion, 14*(2), pp. 107–130.

Zahn-Waxler, C., Radke-Yarrow, M. and King, R.A., 1979. Child rearing and children's prosocial initiations toward victims of distress. *Child Development, 50,* pp. 319–330.

Chapter 4

The impartial spectator, conscience and morality

I. Introduction

Sympathy is the building block of morality in the TMS, and the impartial spectator is the moralizing agent. As we have described in Chapter 2, the spectator puts himself in the agent's situation and forms an idea about how the agent is affected in a given situation; he then experiences an emotion analogous to the emotion of the agent. The spectator then compares his feelings with those of the agent. Each participant works hard to reach consensus through the interactions in the sympathetic process. Sympathy, or the sympathetic process, seeks to reach a correspondence or concordance of sentiments. The dynamic interaction between the spectator and the agent generates the development of morality. In Smith's ethical structure, through sympathetic interaction, moral principles are conveyed and taught.[1]

As the following quotes indicate, there is a tension between instincts (passions) and self-command. The passions of the agent might be too low or too high for the spectator to sympathize:

> The propriety of every passion excited by objects peculiarly related to ourselves, the pitch which the spectator can go along with, must lie, it is evident, in a certain mediocrity. If the passion is too high, or if it is too low, he cannot enter into it.
>
> (TMS, p. 32)

It is under the critical and watchful eyes of the spectator that the agent softens his temper in some cases and elevates it in others. In cases where emotions are "violent and disagreeable", the agent must "lower his passions that pitch, in which the spectators are capable of going along with him" (TMs, p. 27). "[T]urbulent passions" have to be brought to "that tone and temper" so that the impartial spectator can go along with them. The chaos of unbridled passion threatens self-command. The person who exerts self-command feels that he has acted with propriety.

As such, the spectator has a disciplining effect. We learn self-command from the spectator:

it is always from that spectator, from whom we can expect the least sympathy and indulgence, that we are likely to learn the most complete lesson of self-command.

(TMS, p. 178)

The higher value that is placed on self-command is evident in the following statement: "Self-command is not only itself a great virtue, but from it all the other virtues seem to derive their principal lustre" (TMS, p. 284). Self-command is the mother of all virtues, as well as the foundational principle upon which morality is based on. Since a man might be "seduced" to violate all principles due to his passions, self-command is necessary, indicating a clear conflict between passions and self-command. Our pleasure from self-command increases with the degree of self-command we exert. Smith, of course, was well aware that self-command cannot always be perfect. However, even in these cases we may still be approximating perfection.

Next we turn to a discussion of the impartial spectator. In Section III we describe conscience. Section IV contains a discussion of morality. Finally, our discussion is presented in Section V.

II. The impartial spectator

Who are spectators? Smith uses many different phrases for spectatorship, such as "we", "everybody", "every impartial spectator", "every indifferent by-stander", "every human heart", the "spectator" (occasionally "spectators"). The spectator owes his existence to real spectators who are fellow members of society. The agent internalizes the external spectator and hence the spectator is created in the imagination of the agent. Smith's ideal spectator is a disinterested party that uses understanding and deliberation. The spectator challenges his self-interest by imagining that he too is being observed at a distance by a spectator. We are all spectators of each other. We are spectated on and we spectate simultaneously.[2]

Not only self-command is given a very high value by Smith, it is clear that it is a trait the impartial spectator needs to have mastered in order to be able to teach self-command to the agent. The first spectators are parents. A child learns self-command from his parents. When a child goes to school, whatever aspects of self-command that have not been covered by the parents, he learns at school. In addition, since we are all spectators and agents of each other, we continuously learn to have self-command.

Only due to the presence of spectators we come to know who we are within the morals of the community and are able to evaluate our own actions. Smith describes this process:

Were it possible that a human creature could grow up to manhood in some solitary place, with any communication with his own species, he could no

more think of his own character, of the propriety or demerit of his own
sentiments and conduct, than of the beauty or deformity of his own mind,
than of the beauty or deformity of his own face. All these are objects that
he cannot easily see, which naturally he does not look at, and with regard
to which he is provided with no mirror that can present them to his view.
Bring him into society, and he is immediately provided with the mirror
which he wanted before.

(TMS, p. 129)

Smith's moral philosophy is characterized as "social theory of self" (Haakonssen, 1996). In Smith's view, self is formed in our interactions with other people.
Our self-conception is established through a sympathetic process.

In addition to not knowing who he is, if a man were a stranger to society
from birth, he would not have a moral sense:

> Bring him into society, and all his own passions will immediately become
> the causes of new passions. He will observe that mankind approve of some
> of them, and are disgusted by others.

(TMS, p. 129)

In sum, to be a human creature, we have to be connected to others, which
comes from recognition of one another as spectators.

It is when Smith discusses amiable and respectable virtues and self-command
that he introduces the term "impartial spectator". The impartial spectator is
a judge ("impartial judge") and a critic who decides whether an approbation is due through the sympathetic process.[3] Haakonssen (1996) argues that
the impartial spectator provides "the imagined external consummation of our
moral ideals that cannot be achieved in this world" (p. 151). There might be as
many impartial spectators as there are agents because each agent imagines his
own impartial spectator.

Since the agent is imagining how he would be judged by an impartial spectator, the judgments the actor is imagining are his own, which Smith describes in
the section on how we judge our sentiments and conduct:

> We examine our persons limb by limb, and by placing ourselves before a
> looking-glass, or by some such expedient, endeavour, as much as possible,
> to view ourselves at the distance and with the eyes of other people. . . .
> When I endeavour to examine my own conduct, when I endeavour to
> pass sentence upon it, and either to approve or condemn it, it is evident
> that, in all such cases, I divide myself, as it were, into two persons; and that
> I, the examiner and judge, represent a different character from that other I,
> the person whose conduct is examined into and judged of. The first is the
> spectator, whose sentiments with regard to my own conduct I endeavour
> to enter into, by placing myself in his situation, and by considering how
> it would appear to me, when seen from that particular point of view. The

second is the agent, the person whom I properly call myself, and of whose conduct, under the character of a spectator, I was endeavouring to form some opinion. The first is the judge; the second the person judged of. But that the judge should, in every respect, be the same with the person judged of, is as impossible, as that the cause should, in every respect, be the same with the effect.

(p. 131)

Smith also states that since we cannot survey our motives and sentiments and pass judgments on them, our judgments

must always bear some secret reference, either to what are, or to what, upon a certain condition, would be, or to what, we imagine, ought to be the judgment of others.

(TMS, pp 128–129)

The impartial spectator is the agent in the character of the imagined impartial spectator. "The great demigod within the breast" is better situated than external spectators to make judgments about the agent's behavior. Smith uses expressions such as "man within the breast", "the great judge and arbiter", "higher tribunal" in referring to this imagined impartial spectator. As such the impartial spectator is an introject, he is "the man within the breast", which is similar to the Freudian notion of "super-ego" (Freud, 1930), as has been pointed out by Raphael (2007) and as we elaborate on in Chapter 7.

The spectator's impartiality is crucial. He has to overcome self-love or self-interest. This is done by imagining a spectator who observes him at a distance.

We must view [opposing interests between us and of another], neither from our own place nor yet from his, neither with our own eyes nor yet with his, but from the place and with the eyes of a third person, who has no particular connexion with either, and who judges with impartiality between us.

(TMS, p. 157)

Preceding this paragraph, Smith has an interesting comparison to this process:

I can form a just comparison between those great objects and the little objects around me, in no other way, than by transporting myself, at least in fancy, to a different station, from whence I can survey both at nearly equal distances, and thereby form some judgment of their real proportions. Habit and experience have taught me to do this so easily and so readily.

(TMS, p. 156)

Ideally, the impartial spectator is detached from the demands of his own and others' emotions, though sympathetically engaged. The impartial spectator judges the degree of approbation due from a critical perspective. He is not unemotional. As Campbell (1971) argues, the impartial spectator is subject to cultural influences and feelings. It is not a perfectly informed rational being. He is "indifferent" in the sense that he is disinterested. He judges without prejudice stemming from his own emotions or by a desire to improve his condition by manipulating the situation.[4]

The only information available to the impartial spectator is the information the agent has. If the spectator does not have the information the agent has, the "great demigod within the breast" is in a better place to make judgments. The agent seeks to answer what would be the judgment of the external spectator if the spectator knew what the agent knows. The agent benefits from the information he has about his situation and tries to see his own situation in a disinterested way.

Another issue with regards to the impartial spectator is that the man within sometimes may be "astonished and confounded by the vehemence and clamour of the man without" (TMS, p. 150).

> In such cases, the only effectual consolation of humbled and afflicted tribunal, to that of the all-seeing Judge of the world, whose eye can never be deceived, and whose judgments can never be perverted.
>
> (TMS, p. 153)

Thus, God is the impartial spectator of the universe.

III. Our judgments regarding ourselves and conscience

Smith emphasizes that we judge ourselves in the same way we judge others. We have to remove ourselves from "our natural station" and view them "at a certain distance from us".

> This is the only looking glass by which we can, in some measure, with the eyes of other people, scrutinize the propriety of our own conduct.
>
> (TMS, p. 131)

We become capable of self-judgment through the sympathetic process. "We endeavour to examine our own conduct as we imagine any other fair and impartial spectator would examine it" (TMS, p. 129). We might be partial to our own interests; however, Smith does not see this without remedy. We imagine that we are in the presence of the impartial spectator.

In judging our character and conduct we can use two standards: exact perfection and propriety, and an approximation to propriety, which is more common. The first of these standards is what the wise and virtuous man directs his attention to. When there is not exact perfection, however, we can improve it by:

the slow, gradual, and progressive work of the great demigod within the
breast, the great judge and arbiter of conduct. . . . Every day some feature is
improved; every day some blemish is corrected.

(TMS, p. 291)

According to Smith, it is natural to have preference for oneself but it is morally
unacceptable. As interpreted by Fleischacker (1991), Smith solves this problem
through the impartial spectator because it provides a means for escaping from
self-delusion. The impartial spectator has a crucial role in correcting self-love:

> It is from him only that we learn the real littleness of ourselves, and of
> whatever relates to ourselves, and the natural misrepresentations of self-love
> can be corrected only by the eye of this impartial spectator.

(TMS, p. 158)

In addition, men's views about themselves are partial and men have a tendency
to deceive themselves, and are tempted to act out of self-love, which is the
"source of half the disorders in human life" (TMS, p. 184). But this impulse is
not without remedy:

> It is not the soft power of humanity, it is not that feeble spark of benevo-
> lence which Nature has lighted up in the human heart, that is thus capable
> of counteracting the strongest impulses the strongest impulses of self-love.
> It is a stronger power, a more forcible motive, which exerts itself upon such
> occasions. It is reason, principle, conscience, the inhabitant of the breast, the
> man within, the great judge and arbiter of our conduct.

(TMS, p. 158)

Smith once again turns to Nature and says that Nature has not left this without remedy. By observing others, we form general rules, and from these general rules we learn what is approved or disapproved of. By using the general
rules, we correct "the misrepresentations of self-love concerning what is fit and
proper to be done in our particular situation" (TMS, p. 186). It is the regard
to the general rules or its disregard that distinguishes "a man of principle and
honour and a worthless fellow". Thus, morality is founded upon general rules.
Smith likens the general rules to the laws of the Deity, "promulgated by those
vicegerents which he has thus set up within us" (TMS, p. 192). The vicegerents
punish the violations of the general laws by self-condemnation and shame.

General rules are founded upon sense and feeling, not reason:

> But though reason is undoubtedly the source of the general rules of moral-
> ity, and of all the moral judgments which we form by means of them; it
> is altogether absurd and unintelligible to suppose that the first perceptions
> of right and wrong can be derived from reason, even in those particular

cases upon the experience of which the general rules are formed. These first perceptions, as well as all other experiments upon which any general rules are founded, cannot be the object of reason, but of immediate sense and feeling.

(TMS, p. 377)

The cumulative results of the interaction between the spectator and the agent create an internalized aggregate that can be referred to as conscience. Conscience is the way we approve or disapprove of ourselves based on the judgments of the impartial spectator. For Smith, conscience is the consequence of the sympathetic process and results from an internal conversation between the agent and the impartial spectator.[5] "[H]abit and experience have taught us to [appeal to conscience] so easily and so readily, that we are scarce sensible that we do it" (TMS, p. 157). It is learned from others who take the role of indifferent spectators, and it is an acquired faculty. Berry (2003) refers to it as a "learnt resource". Once conscience is acquired, the propriety of one's feelings, actions and intentions can be judged in a similar way other people are judged. Conscience for Smith is a mirror of social feelings, and as such it is a social product. In a quote we gave earlier from Smith, he states that man cannot think of his character without society; men need a mirror. The mirror is society: "It [his judgment of himself] is placed in the countenance and behaviour of those he lives with" (TMS, p. 129).

As can be seen in the following quote, even though Smith viewed that "the all-wise Author of Nature" appointed man to judge others, it is ultimately man's own conscience who is the judge.

The all-wise Author of Nature has, in this manner, taught man to respect the sentiments and judgments of his brethren; . . . He has made man, if I may say so, the immediate judge of mankind; and has, in this respect, as in many others, created him after his own image, and appointed him his vicegerent upon earth, to superintend the behaviour of his brethren. . . . But though man has, in this manner, been rendered the immediate judge of mankind, he has been rendered so only in the first instance; and an appeal lies from his sentence to a much higher tribunal, to the tribunal of their own consciences, to that of the supposed impartial and well-informed spectator, to that of the man within the breast, the great judge and arbiter of their conduct. The jurisdiction of the man without, is founded altogether in the desire of actual praise, and in the aversion to actual blame. The jurisdiction of the man within, is founded altogether in the desire of praise-worthiness, and in the aversion to blame-worthiness.

(TMS, pp. 149–150)

Thus, the real spectators, "the man without", and the impartial spectator, "the man within", may have different judgments. On conscience, Raphael (2007) states that

The judgment of conscience is superior to that of actual spectators simply because the agent can know better than bystanders what he has done or not done, and what was his motive for action as he did.

(p. 45)

According to Smith, an agent's conscience is a "higher tribunal". The function of external spectators is psychological and educational. One can make his moral self-judgment, independent of others, once conscience is acquired.[6] Conscience for Smith is not purely a reflection of social attitudes. It sometimes goes against popular opinion. In a letter written to Sir Gilbert Elliot on October 10, 1759, Smith states,

You will observe that it is intended both to confirm my Doctrine that our judgments concerning our own conduct have always reference to the sentiments of some other being, and to shew that, notwithstanding this, real magnanimity and conscious virtue can support itself under the disapprobation of all mankind.

(Mossner and Ross, 1977, p. 37)

If the judgments of the impartial spectator were merely always reflection of the prevailing opinion, there would be no change of moral values, but we would be in a morally static society.[7]

For Smith, conscience, once internalized, begins to have something of a life of its own, even if it is somewhat limited. Conscience then does slowly evolve through the gradual absorption of individual perspectives and the critique of social norms that would take place in the face of at least initial disapprobation. This accounts for the evolution of social change and values within Smith's system, even though it otherwise appears to be quite monolithic.

There is again a premium on self-command over feelings in the section entitled "of the influence and authority of conscience". Self-command must be acquired from

that great discipline which Nature has established for the acquisition of this and every other virtue; a regard to the sentiments of the real or supposed spectator of our conduct.

(TMS, p. 167)

Wise and just men are "bred in the great school of self-command" (TMS, p. 169). They control their feelings. Self-approbation depends on the degree of self-command we have. "Where little self-command is necessary, little self-approbation is due" (TMS, p. 170). Manhood is founded upon self-command. The virtuous man has the "most perfect command of his original and selfish feelings", which has the sympathetic feelings of others (TMS, p. 176). Self-command prospers most under difficult and challenging conditions.

IV. Morality

Smith's construction of morality is strongly based in psychology. The process of sympathy itself is a psychological process. The psychology of the agent and the spectator dynamically interact. There is the psychology of both the spectator and the agent and they work hard to change their sentiments which are psychologically based, to reach a concordance of sentiments. According to Fleischacker (1996), the moral world in the TMS is constructed from innate, amoral tendencies of human nature. Raphael (2007) views that Smith was seeking a genetic explanation based on psychological as well as sociological elements. According to Carrasco (2011), "our innate desire for pleasure" (psychology) is like the "infrastructure" that supports the "superstructure" of morality that emerges through a sympathetic process. Many authors argue that morality is justified in psychology. (For example, Campbell (1971), Otteson (2002), Forman-Brazilai (2010), von Villiez (2006).) According to Carrasco, on the other hand, Smith starts from an innate psychological constitution to an account of how moral judgments are made. Smith's introduction of the impartial spectator means that he moves from psychological to moral sympathy according to Carrasco.

Smith states that his inquiry is about fact, not about what is right. Moral life for Smith is created through interactions between people that condition a consensual set of behaviors and norms. Morality is achieved through social coordination and self-command in the sympathetic process. The capacity for sympathy and the human desire for sympathy make it possible for these corrective actions to take place. As we have elaborated upon in the previous section, spectators have a corrective effect on agents; they can bring about a change in the agent by revealing whether they sympathize or not, and the agent's desire to have sympathy and concordance leads him to change. One can modify behaviors and character through viewing himself from the position of the impartial spectator. The spectator also works on modifying his sentiments to reach concordance of sentiments.

In this dynamic process, the spectator relies on "the soft, the gentle, the amiable virtues, the virtues of candid condescension and indulgent humanity" (TMS, p. 29). The agent works hard to bring down his emotions relying on "great, the awful, and respectable, the virtues of self-denial, of self-government" (TMS, p. 29). In a more modern language of psychoanalysis, what Smith is advocating for is for the instincts to be tamed by self-command. He advocates for conscious self-command to rule over the unbridled instincts. There is an analogy to Freud, who asserted that the internalized superego restrains instinctual drives.

According to Smith, it is Nature that teaches spectators and actors to reach harmony. In Smith's words:

> Nature, when she formed man for society, endowed him with an original desire to please, and an original aversion to offend his brethren. She taught him to feel pleasure in their favourable, and pain in their unfavourable

regard. She rendered their approbation most flattering and most agreeable to him for its own sake; and their disapprobation most mortifying and most offensive.

(TMS, p. 135)

The moral world strives to be a harmonious world, where concordance of sentiments leads to consensus. We have a moral self only in a human society. A social bond is created through sympathy. Approval pleases everyone and disapproval creates displeasure. Moral judgments are reached by imagining ourselves as an ideal impartial spectator. Morality is a social practice. Through repetition of sympathy, moral life is passed from generation to generation. Berry (2003) refers to this as "stickiness" of "social institutions".

Since morality is created through a dynamic interaction between the spectator and the actor, it replaces the power of the individual by the power of the community due to the spectator and the actor seeking harmony with each other's emotions. Freud (1930) makes an analogous statement. "The replacement of the power of the individual by the power of a community constitutes the decisive step of civilization" (p. 95). The invisible hand of the spectator is at work in making judgments and revising their own judgments.

The sentiments of the actor and the spectator, even though they will not be in perfect correspondence, though they will never reach a perfect unison, their concord is what is required and wanted for the harmony of the society: "Though they will never be unisons, they may be concords, and this is all that is wanted or required" (TMS, p. 27).

As we have described in Chapter 2, sympathy is a process through which the agent adjusts his passions based on the judgments of the impartial spectator. The agent, who works hard to have the concordance of sentiments in this process, obviously has motive for action. Moral judgments are a consequence of the impartial spectator having or not having sympathy with the agent. However, were it not for the sympathetic process itself, moral judgments would not be possible. Thus, sympathy is both a motive for action and a basis for moral judgment.[8]

There are two kinds of moral judgments based on sympathy. The first refers to propriety or impropriety of actions. If the agent's actions are suitable to the agent's situation, there is propriety. It is based on whether the spectator would act the same way in the same situation. Smith argues that there is a difference between virtue and propriety.

[T]o act with the most perfect propriety, requires no more than that common and ordinary degree of sensibility or self-command which the most worthless mankind are possest of, and sometimes even the degree is not necessary.

(TMS, p. 31)

On the other hand, even though actions may fall short of propriety, there could be virtue. In particular, the cases that require "greatest exertion of self-command" are of greatest virtue every impartial spectator can enter into. Even this may fall short of perfection, but it may be a much "nearer approximation to perfection" (TMS, p. 31).

The second moral judgment refers to merit or demerit. If the action of the agent creates beneficial results which are to be praised, we judge that action as having merit, and if on the other hand it leads to harmful ends, deserving punishment, we judge the action as having demerit. Merit is compounded. It constitutes direct sympathy for the agent and indirect sympathy with those who face the consequences of the agent's actions.

Propriety depends on motive and merit depends on the intended effects:

> The sentiment or affection of the heart from which any action proceeds, and upon which its whole virtue or vice must ultimately depend, may be considered under two different aspects, or in two different relations; first, in relation to the cause which excites it, or the motive which gives occasion to it; and secondly, in relation to the end which it proposes, or the effect which it tends to produce.
>
> In the suitableness or unsuitableness, in the proportion or disproportion which the affection seems to bear to the cause or object which excites it, consists the propriety or impropriety, the decency or ungracefulness of the consequent action.
>
> In the beneficial or hurtful nature of the effects which the affection aims at, or tends to produce, consists the merit or demerit of the action, the qualities by which it is entitled to reward, or is deserving of punishment.
>
> (TMS, p. 22)

Our moral faculties were given to us for the direction of our conduct. The only way humans are capable of directing their actions is by following the general rules, which Smith calls duty. The very existence of human society is based on "the tolerable observance" of these duties. If mankind were not to follow these rules, human society would "crumble", and the Deity plays an important role in following these rules:

> This reverence is still further enhanced by an opinion which is first impressed by nature, and afterwards confirmed by reasoning and philoso-phy, that those important rules of morality are the commands and laws of the Deity, who will finally reward the obedient, and punish the transgres-sors of their duty.
>
> (TMS, p. 190)

Heath (1995) criticizes Smith's system as not being able to explain the emer-gence of morals from a system where no morals exist. However, as argued by

Otteson (2002), that is not the project Smith undertakes in the TMS. Smith's project was to explain how a moral sense develops through interactions with others in society where there are already moral standards in place. It can also be extrapolated from the above referenced quotes by Smith that were it possible for someone to live in isolation, there would be no necessity for morality. He sees morality as evolving directly from the genesis of social interaction, that is motivated by the "horror or solitude", and further developed through social interaction that is facilitated by the impartial spectator and the agent.

Morality in Smith's system is described in several ways. Rothschild (2001) refers to it as "conversational morality", Otteson (2002) as "market", Haakonssen (1981) as a mechanism for social institutions which creates common social standards, Clark (1992) as "conversation". Peters (1995) highlights its "publicity". Myers (1975) states that Smith's moral philosophy is "firmly based on ... the common interpersonal pressures arising out of everyday life as these pressures act on people through the principle of sympathy". Forman-Brazilai (2010) puts it as "activity of the mind", as in Radner (1980). In addition, she emphasizes that "this activity of the mind takes place in a social context among other minds, mixing together in shared spaces"[9] (p. 63). We agree with what Rothschild (2001) states on morality: "The principle of moral judgment, that is to say, is that there is no fundamental principle of moral judgment. There is no foundation; all there is the correction and convergence of sentiments" (p. 231).

V. Discussion

In this chapter, we have outlined and interwoven Smith's construct of the impartial spectator; the internalization of the impartial spectator creating a capacity for self-command, self-judgment and conscience, and then leading to a larger moral structure. This interactive learning process is facilitated by sympathy. Analogously, from a psychoanalytic perspective, what is taking place is an interaction between the superego and the instincts. This interaction civilizes the instincts so that individuals can have relative harmony in a community.

As each individual interacts with the impartial spectator and begins to internalize the consensual morality, there is a growing capacity for what Smith sees as the primary virtue: self-command. Self-command is integral in the ongoing development of conscience, and collectively it facilitates the development of larger moral structures that encompass a community.

Another important process that emerges out of this aspect of Smith's work is the dynamic interaction that is necessary for the individual and collective development of morality. This first takes place between the impartial spectator and the agent. It creates an internal dialogue that finally develops into the construction of a more comprehensive morality. Each phase of this development is predicated upon this interactive dynamic, which ultimately leads to collective development of morality.

Notes

1 Griswold (2010) argues that Smith's theory is a spectator theory, which we agree with, since it is the spectator who enters into the other's situation and makes moral judgments. Darwall (1999), on the other hand, argues that Smith's theory is not spectatorial and states: "And Smith holds that to judge whether a motive or feeling is warranted or proper, we must take up, not some external perspective, but that of the person who has the motive or feeling – the agent's standpoint, in the case of motivation; the patient's standpoint, in the case of feeling" (p. 141).

2 Young (1997) argues that the spectator mechanism plays a role in the market both in the early and rude state and in commercial societies, connecting Smith's moral theory with his economics. For example, in the early and rude stage, the impartial spectator's processes "inform the origin of the division of labor, exchange and price" (p. 69). In the commercial stage, Young argues that the spectator plays a role in establishing "non-labour forms of income as component parts of natural price and establishing some forms of pay and profit differentials" (pp. 72, 73) and wage differentials.

3 Griswold (2006) argues that we imagine the impartial spectator through illusive sympathy. By illusive sympathy, we imagine a non-existent spectator. We then imagine how we are seen from that imagined position. "Our sympathizing with ourselves is not itself an act of 'illusive' sympathy, but it is exercised from a standpoint created by 'illusive' sympathy" (p. 91).

4 "[T]o be impartial is to treat competing preferences and interests on their own merits without being biased by one's own", which requires that we know "what these interests are and for what they are competing" (Piper, 1991, pp. 746–747).

5 Raphael and Macfie (1976) point out that there is an important difference between conscience reflecting the feelings of real external spectators in Smith's view. On the one hand, the man within may be inferior if he is overcome by partiality. On the other hand, the man without may not have relevant information that the agent has, and in that sense the judgment of conscience can be more reliable than the judgment of external spectators.

6 There are, however, controversial accounts of how conscience is acquired. According to Brown (1994) and Rothschild (2001), external spectators cannot be moral judges at all. Firth (2007) and Hanley (2009) view that a consciences person does not have to take into account other people's views; conscience arises from a transcendent source. Yet, Fleischacker (1991) states that "viewing moral laws as if they issued from God, . . . was highly unusual in the eighteenth century". Griswold (1999) also views morality not arising from the divine. Forman-Brazaili (2010) has the opinion that the agent's society or cultural community limits the agent's moral judgment.

7 Yet, as summarized in Forman-Brazilai (2010, pp. 91–92), there is an ongoing debate in the literature on whether conscience is a reflection of social attitudes. Berry (2003) refers to it as "mere reflex of prevalent social norms". Campbell (1971) writes, "to talk of the impartial spectator is simply a shorthand way of referring to the normal reaction of a member of a particular social group, or of a whole society when he is in the position of observing the conduct of his fellows" (p. 145). Fleischaker (2004) states that the impartial spectator is "an extension or idealization of our society's mode of moral judgment" (p. 8). Hope (1984) views the impartial spectator in light of conventionalism. According to Andrew (1998), it is an "internalized radar of social expectations" (p. 82). Others disagree. Bolstanki (1999) argues that the impartial spectator is "aperspectival". Haakonssen (1981), Griswold (1999) and Pitts (2005) recognize the socially embedded nature of conscience, yet that conscience can be independent. Sen (1987) argues that the impartial spectator can remove himself from accepted norms. Brodie (2006) notes that the impartial spectator is not simply a repository of social opinions.

8 There are different views in the literature regarding whether sympathy is a basis for moral judgment or a motive for action. Raphael and Macfie (1976) claim that sympathy is used

as the basis for moral judgment. Raphael's view is that "[Smith] uses his notion of sympathy to explain . . . moral judgment or approval" (1985, p. 29). Fleischacker (1991), on the other hand, states, "Rather, sympathy functions as the mechanism by which the impartial spectator can operate, but it is only the sympathy of the *impartial spectator* that provides a standard for moral judgment" (p. 258). On the issue of whether sympathy is a motive for moral action or not, Peart and Levy (1999) argue that when sympathy turns to affection, there is motivation for action. Montes (2003) emphasizes that sympathy is not only a basis for moral judgment but also it is a motive for action. However, Brodie (2006) states that sympathy is not a motive for moral action.

9   The author discusses at length three dimensions of space: the physical, the affective and the historical/cultural. On the first, the impartial spectator is better able to enter into the agent's situation as the distance diminishes. On the second, men can feel more for those with whom they have a particular connection. Finally, even though the spectator is able to transcend these two biases, the author argues that the impartial spectator in Smith's account does not entirely surmount cultural bias.

Reference

Andrew, G.E., 1998. Anarchic conscience and enlightenment reason. In: Yamamoto, T., ed. *Philosophical designs for a social-cultural transformation (Ecole des Hautes Etudes en Sciences Culturelles and Rowman and Littlefield).* Lanham, MD: Rowman & Littlefield.pp. 77–85.

Berry, C., 2003. Sociality and socialization. In: Brodie, A., ed. *Cambridge companion to the Scottish Enlightenment.* Cambridge: Cambridge University Press. pp. 243–257.

Bolstanki, L., 1999. *Distant suffering: Morality, media and politics.* Cambridge: Cambridge University Press.

Brodie, A., 2006. Sympathy and the impartial spectator. In: Haakonssen, K., ed. *The Cambridge companion to Adam Smith.* Cambridge: Cambridge University Place. pp. 158–188.

Brown, V., 1994. *Adam Smith's discourse: Canonicity, commerce and conscience.* New York: London.

Clark, H.C., 1992. Conversation and moderate virtue in Adam Smith's 'Theory of Moral Sentiments'. *Review of Politics, 54*(2), pp. 185–210.

Campbell, T.D., 1971. *Adam Smith's science and morals.* London: George Allen and Unwin.

Carrasco, M.A., 2011. From psychology to moral activity. *Adam Smith Review, 6*, pp. 9–29.

Darwall, S., 1998. Empathy, sympathy, care. *Philosophical Studies, 89*, pp. 261–282.

———, 1999. Sympathetic liberalism: Recent work on Adam Smith. *Philosophy and Public Affairs, 28*(2), pp. 139–164.

Firth, A., 2007. Adam Smith's moral philosophy as ethical self-formation. In: Firth, A., G. Cockfield and J. Laurent, eds. *New perspectives on Adam Smith's theory of moral sentiments.* Cheltenham: Edward Elgar. pp. 106–123.

Fleischacker, S., 1991. Philosophy in moral practice: Kant and Adam Smith. *Kant-Studien, 82*, pp. 249–269.

———, 1996. Values behind the market: Kant's response to *The Wealth of Nations. History of Political Thought, XVII*(3), pp. 379–407.

———, 2004. *On Adam Smith's Wealth of Nations: A philosophical companion.* Princeton, NJ: Princeton University Press.

Forman-Brazilai, F., 2010. *Adam Smith and the circles of sympathy: Cosmopolitanism and moral theory.* Cambridge: Cambridge University Press.

Freud, S., 1930. Civilization and its discontents. In: Strachey, J., ed. *The standard edition of the complete psychological works.* London: Hogarth Press. Vol. XXI, pp. 57–146.

Griswold, C.L., 1999. *Adam Smith and the virtues of enlightenment*. Cambridge: Cambridge University Press.

———, 2006. Imagination: Morals, science, and arts. In: Haakonssen, K., ed. *The Cambridge companion to Adam Smith*. Cambridge: Cambridge University Press. pp. 22–56.

———, 2010. Smith and Rousseau in dialogue: Sympathy, pitie, spectatorship and narrative. In: Brown,V. and S. Fleischacker, eds. *Adam Smith Review*, *5*, pp. 59–84.

Haakonssen, K., 1981. *The science of a legislator: The natural jurisprudence of David Hume and Adam Smith*. Cambridge: Cambridge University Press.

———, 1996. *Natural law and moral philosophy: From Grotius to the Scottish enlightenment*. Cambridge: Cambridge University Press.

Hanley, R.P., 2009. *Adam Smith and the character of virtue*. Cambridge: Cambridge University Press.

Heath, E., 1995. The commerce of sympathy: Adam Smith on the emergence of the morals. *Journal of History of Philosophy*, *33*, pp. 447–466.

Hope,V., 1984. Smith's demigod. In: Hope,V., ed. *Philosophers of the Scottish Enlightenment*. Edinburgh: Edinburgh University Press. pp. 157–167.

Montes, L., 2003. Das Adam Smith problem: Its origins, the stages of current debate, and one implication for our understanding of sympathy. *Journal of History of Economic Thought*, *25*(1), pp. 63–90.

Mossner, E.C. and Ross, I.S., 1977. *The correspondences of Adam Smith*. Oxford: Clarendon Press.

Myers, M.L., 1975. Adam Smith as a critic of ideas. *Journal of History of Ideas*, *32*(2), pp. 281–296.

Otteson, J.R., 2002. *Adam Smith's market place of life*. Cambridge: Cambridge University Press.

Peart, S.J. and Levy, D.M., 1999. Sympathy and approbation in Hume and Smith: As solution to the other rational species problem. *Economics and Philosophy*, *20*(2), pp. 331–349.

Peters, J.D., 1995. Publicity and pain: Self abstraction in Adam Smith's Theory of Moral Sentiments. *Public Culture*, 7, pp. 657–684.

Piper, A. M. S., 1991. Impartiality, compassion, and modal imagination. *Ethics*, *101*, pp. 726–757.

Pitts, J.A., 2005. *A turn of empire: The rise of imperial liberalism in Britain and France*. Princeton, NJ: Princeton University Press.

Radner, J.B., 1980. The art of sympathy in eighteen-century British moral thought. *Studies in Eighteenth-Century Culture*, *9*, pp. 189–210.

Raphael, D. D., 1985. *Adam Smith*. Oxford: Oxford University Press.

———, 2007. *The impartial spectator: Adam Smith's moral philosophy*. Oxford: Clarendon Press.

Raphael, D.D. and Macfie, A.L. eds., 1976. *Adam Smith: The theory of moral sentiments*. Oxford: Clarendon Press.

Rothschild, E., 2001. *Economic sentiments: Adam Smith, Condorcet, and the Enlightenment*. Cambridge, MA: Harvard University Press.

Sen, A., 1987. *On ethics and economics*. Oxford: Basic Blackwell.

Villiez, C.V., 2006. Double standard-naturally! Smith and Rawls: A comparison of methods. In: Montes, L. and E. Schleisser, eds. *New voices on Adam Smith*. London: Routledge. pp. 115–139.

Young, T.J., 1997. *Economics as a moral science*. Lyme: Edward Elgar Publishing Limited.

Chapter 5

The role of the Deity in Smith's moral system

I. Introduction

This brief chapter is purely a descriptive background to Chapters 6 and 7 in order to provide a more complete view of Smith's moral system. Smith describes the Deity as a beneficent and comprehensive force in human life. The Deity is the designer of the universe and the invisible hand that guides the universe. By extension, Smith sees morality as a manifestation of the Deity's design, in which sympathy is the mechanism for the implementation of this design. He sees the resulting structure or principals of morality as directions of an omniscient Deity, and they are disseminated through human vicegerents in the person of the impartial spectator. To be concise, Smith defines morality as being in concert with the Deity and directives that are given to us by the Deity. He sees the Deity as intending disorders, because they have utility, and Smith encourages wise people to accept this destiny. Ultimately the promotion of human happiness, the protection of the vulnerable and the order of society are all the results of the Deity's influence on moral structure.

II. The Deity in Smith's system

In our reading of the TMS, the foundation of Smith's moral philosophy is the existence of a Deity. "Smith develops his system of ethics on the basis of a doctrine of a harmonious order in nature guided by God ..." (Viner, 1927, pp. 200–201).[1] Others argue that Smith's moral philosophy could exist without a Deity.[2] (For a review of the literature on conflicting arguments regarding the role of the Deity, see Hill, 2001.) Independent of whether a system of morality such as Smith's could be formulated without a Deity, Smith relies on the Deity for the formulation and perpetuation of morality, as we show in this chapter.

Smith refers to a divine being using many different phrases. Among them are: "The Author of Nature", "the great Director of Nature", "the great judge of hearts", "the final cause", "an invisible hand", "the divine being", "God", "Deity", "Superintendent" and "Providence".

Smith conceptualizes a benevolent Deity as the designer and administrator of the universe. It is the "great, benevolent, and all-wise Being who directs all the movements of nature" (TMS, p. 277). He sees nature as having implanted in human beings' sentiments that which would result in the happiness and welfare of mankind. Human beings have independence, but at the same time they carry out the Deity's plans for order in human affairs. Smith conceptualizes benign Nature as a guiding providence, with its beneficent purposes operating to produce the "happiness and perfection" of mankind. He sees society as moving towards the Deity's design. Mankind's thriving, prosperity, material comfort and perpetuation are also the business of God.

Smith's moral system is based on the presence of the Deity. "Important rules of morality are the commands and laws of the Deity, who will finally reward the obedient, and punish the transgressors of their duty" (TMS, p. 190). The impartial spectator represents the Deity. We are terrified when the Deity disapproves our behavior and overjoyed when we have his approval. In Smith's words:

> [God] created [the impartial spectator] after his own image, and appointed him his vicegerent upon earth, to superintend the behavior of his brethren. They are taught by nature, to acknowledge that power and jurisdiction which has thus been conferred upon him, to be more or less humbled and mortified when they have incurred his censure, and to be more or less elated when they have obtained his applause.
>
> (TMS, p. 149)

Fundamentally for Smith morality is the harmony of human behavior, through the sympathetic process, with the Deity's design. The spectator correctly determines moral acts based on the balance of sentiments that are in harmony with this design. One's sentiments are properly balanced and consistent with the design by following the guidance of "great judge and arbiter of our conduct". Sympathy is the mechanism through which the Deity's design is implemented.

Nature is our superintendent. Our moral faculties can be based on a modification of reason, an "original instinct, called a moral sense", or "upon some principle of nature" (TMS, p. 191). Our conduct is based on these, and we were given these by Nature. It is our moral sense that guides us. Our moral sense tells us the degree to which our passions and appetites should be restrained or indulged. Smith states the following:

> They [our moral faculties] carry along with them the most evident badges of this authority [authority of Nature], which denote that they were set up within us to be the supreme arbiters of all our actions, to superintend all

our senses, passions, and appetites, and to judge how far each of them was either to be indulged or restrained.

(TMS, p. 191)

It is also Nature that gives man original desires: "an original desire to please" and "original aversion to offend his brethren". Approbation of the society flatters us, and we find disapprobation "mortifying". However, this is not sufficient for us to be fit for society. The desire to be approved of is at the root of being fit for society:

> Nature, accordingly, has endowed him, not only with a desire of being approved of, but with a desire of being what ought to be approved of; or of being what he himself approves of in other men. The first desire could only have made him wish to appear to be fit for society. The second was necessary in order to render him anxious to be really fit.

(TMS, p. 136)

For Smith the Universe appears to be guided by an invisible hand.[3] Smith's view is that social order is founded upon a superordinate rationality that is greater than that of human beings, based on the invisible hand of God, who has "from all eternity contrived and conducted the immense machine of the universe" (TMS, p. 278). Smith views the rationality of the Deity and its use of the invisible hand as being a greater intelligence than that of humans. The interests of society and the individual are reconciled by an invisible hand of the Deity. The invisible hand leads the rich to make distributions to meet others' needs:

> They [rich] are led by an invisible hand to make nearly the same distribution of the necessaries of life, which would have been made, had the earth been divided into equal portions among all its inhabitants, and thus without intending it, without knowing it, advance the interest of the society, and afford means to the multiplication of the species.

(TMS, p. 215)

Smith further asserts that the wise and virtuous men at all times sacrifice their private interest for the good of the whole. Even when the "benevolent and all-wise Being" allows "partial evil" that is good for "the universal good", the wise and virtuous man considers all the misfortunes

> which may befall himself, his friends, his society, or his country, as necessary for the prosperity of the universe, and therefore as what he ought, not only to submit to with resignation, but as what he himself, if he had known all the connexions and dependencies of things, ought sincerely and devoutly to have wished for.

(TMS, p. 277)

Smith continues this theme by making an analogy to soldiers marching to the defense of an indefensible situation that is a "forlorn station". For these soldiers, "the prosperity of a greater system" is more important than their own systems. "No conductor of an army can deserve more unlimited trust, more ardent and zealous affection, than the great Conductor of the universe" (TMS, p. 278). A wise man views that the order to a "forlorn station of the universe" was given to him for the "good of the whole". For Smith, a wise man, like a good soldier, has the duty to consider the good of the whole, embracing it with joy.

Further, Smith continues by laying out an omniscient perspective that even views misfortunes as being for the good of the whole. Even in the face of most tragic events, we have the "consolation" of Nature. We find consolation from the "man within the breast" and if possible from "that benevolent wisdom which directs all the events of human life" (TMS, p. 345). Even the misfortunes are there due to the necessity for the "prosperity and perfection of the whole". Even when we have "most unfortunate and disastrous" events, Nature consoles us:

> That consolation may be drawn, not only from the complete approbation of the man within the breast, but, if possible, from a still nobler and more generous principle, from a firm reliance upon, and a reverential submission to, that benevolent wisdom which directs all the events of human life, and which, we may be assured, would never have suffered those misfortunes to happen, had they not been indispensably necessary for the good of the whole.
>
> (TMS, pp. 344–345)

Smith counsels the wise person to accept the "destiny of Providence" with joy and without complaint. Even when there is misfortune, we accept the destiny of Providence. We believe that if we had known "all the connections and dependencies of the different part of the universe", that would be the destiny we would "wish for" (TMS, p. 325).

All the "vices and follies of mankind" were intended by the Deity. Even when a man is weak we admire the "wisdom of God". Thus, God has implanted our weaknesses and our strengths in us. The "great disorder" in our morals is admired because it has its utility. Our admiration of wealth and success is "necessary for establishing ranks and order of society" (TMS, p. 297). "The peace and order" in a society is more important than relieving mankind from his misery. Due to this admiration, we more easily submit to those superiors "whom the course of human affairs may assign to us" (TMS, p. 298). Yet, this admiration of wealth is a deception. Due to this deception, we sacrifice tranquility; only at old age a man realizes that he had given up "security and contentment" and finds that "wealth and greatness are mere trinkets of frivolous utility" (TMS, p. 218). This deception imposed by Nature, however, has a purpose in that it "keeps in continual motion the industry of mankind" (TMS, p. 214).

Smith further offers that the Deity has endowed human beings with self-love, which sets the spring that leads to the motion of human industry. He sees human beings pursuing their own interests out of self-love, which leads to socially beneficial outcomes. The Deity has endowed man with self-love, yet, "reason, principle, conscience, the inhabitant of the breast, the man within, the great judge and arbiter of our conduct" is larger than our own self-love. In addition, we have other drives, and all of them have a purpose (TMS, pp. 158). Humans are endowed with progressive drives; Nature "formed man for society" and endowed him with instincts that make social life possible.

We learn the "littleness of ourselves" from the impartial spectator. Our self-love is balanced out by the complementarity of the impartial spectator. The impartial spectator counsels us to sacrifice our interest for the wellbeing of others. However, we are interested in the wellbeing of others due to the love of being noble and honorable, not because of our love for others. Smith states:

> It is he who shows us the propriety of generosity and the deformity of injustice; the propriety of resigning the greatest interests of our own, for the yet greater interests of others, and the deformity of doing the smallest injury to another, in order to obtain the greatest benefit to ourselves. It is not the love of our neighbour, it is not the love of mankind, which upon many occasions prompts us to the practice of those divine virtues. It is a stronger love, a more powerful affection, which generally takes place upon such occasions; the love of what is honourable and noble, of the grandeur, and dignity, and superiority of our own characters.
>
> (TMS, p. 158)

Benefice, though, is the "consciousness of deserved reward", it is like "the ornament which embellishes" a building. Justice, on the other hand, is "the main pillar" that holds the society together, like upholding "the whole edifice". When there is no justice, the world "crumble[s] into atoms]". Justice is observed because Nature had given us terror of punishment when punishment is merited:

> In order to enforce the observation of justice, therefore, Nature has implanted in the human breast that consciousness of ill-desert, those terrors of merited punishment which attend upon its violation, as the great safe-guards of the association of mankind, to protect the weak, to curb the violent, and to chastise the guilty.
>
> (TMS, p. 101)

The desire for justice has been placed in us by Nature to preserve society. Smith says that if a murderer is not punished, the impartial spectator "would call upon God to avenge, in another world, that crime which the injustice of mankind had neglected to chastise upon earth" (TMS, p. 107). He goes on to say that Nature gives us hope that injustice will be punished "in a life to come".

Nature is a sophisticated, enormous, subtle machine. Two great purposes of Nature are the propagation of the species and the support of the individual. An omnipotent, beneficent and omniscient Deity supervises this machine as the designer of the universe.

> In every part of the universe we observe means adjusted with the nicest artifice to the ends which they are intended to produce; and in the mechanism of a plant, or animal body, admire how everything is contrived for advancing the two great purposes of nature, the support of the individual, and the propagation of the species. But in these, and in all such objects, we still distinguish the efficient from the final cause of their several motions and organizations. . . . The wheels of the watch are all admirably adjusted to the end for which it was made, the pointing of the hour. All their various motions conspire in the nicest manner to produce this effect. If they were endowed with a desire and intention to produce it, they could not do it better. Yet we never ascribe any such desire or intention to them, but to the watch-maker, and we know that they are put into motion by a spring, which intends the effect it produces as little as they do. But though, in accounting for the operations of bodies, we never fail to distinguish in this manner the efficient from the final cause, in accounting for those of the mind we are very apt another. When by natural principles we are led to advance those ends, which a refined and enlightened reason would recommend to us, we are very apt to impute to that reason, as to their efficient cause, the sentiments and actions by which we advance those ends, and to imagine that to be the wisdom of man, which in reality is the wisdom of God. Upon a superficial view, this cause seems sufficient to produce the effects which are ascribed to it; and the system of human nature seems to be more simple and agreeable when all its different operations are in this manner deduced from a single principle.
>
> (TMS, p. 102)

In the above quote, God is in the role of the watch-maker, the first cause, and designer of the watch's final cause, while humans are the spring. As the watch-maker to a watch, the Deity is to the universe. The hand of the designer arranges the springs and the system is set in motion. Only the product is observed, however. Human beings, as active agents, realize the Deity's design.

The resultant social rules are the commands of the Deity, and are "promulgated by those vicegerents which [God] has thus set up within" (TMS, p. 192). The "general rules" are to be regarded as "the laws of an All-powerful being". "Supreme rule of conduct" is having a regard for the "will of Deity". Commands were given "by the Infinite Wisdom and Infinite Power", and they are promulgated by the impartial spectator. The "Great Superior" rewards people according to their deeds. Those who violate the general rules are punished by "those vice-gerents of God within us", which results in "inward shame" and "self-condemnation", while those who obey them have "tranquility of mind", "contentment" and "self-satisfaction". For Smith, it is absurd and vain not to obey commands of the Infinite Wisdom. Nature has endowed human beings, regarding vices, with a "desire to heap upon them every sort of disgrace and disaster" (TMS, p. 195). In terms of virtues, man has been endowed by Nature, with a "desire to see them crowned with wealth, and power, and honours of every kind" (TMS, p. 195). The level of punishments and rewards are only to the degree which "perfection and happiness of human nature" require. Obeying the will of God is virtuous. Human beings have independence; however, they are involved in fulfilling the Creator's plans.

According to Smith, our duties are given to us by God. The first rule of duty is to obey the Deity. "The sole principle and motive of our conduct in the performance of all those different duties, ought to be a sense that God has commanded us to perform them" (TMS, p. 199). Our love for the Deity gives us a desire to make ourselves agreeable to him. There is virtue in acting obediently to the Deity. There can be two reasons for this: because the Deity is a "Being of infinite power", or because "there is a congruity and fitness" in obeying the Creator. In the first case, virtue consists in prudence, since we have to obey the will of the Deity. In the latter case, it consists in propriety because "the ground of our obligation to obedience is the suitableness or congruity of the sentiments of humility and submission to the superiority of the object which excites them" (TMS, p. 361).

We are the objects of esteem and love when we act with love and charity. The actions that are motivated in this manner are praise-worthy and deserve merit. By acting these ways, we become "more proper objects of his love and esteem". If we act in other ways, we violate the scheme that is established by the Deity for happiness and perfection of the world. We cooperate with the Deity by acting morally.

> By acting according to the dictates of our moral faculties, we necessarily pursue the most effectual means for promoting the happiness of mankind, and may therefore be said, in some sense, to co-operate with the Deity, and to advance as far as in our power the plan of Providence. By acting other ways, on the contrary, we seem to obstruct, in some measure, the scheme which the Author of nature has established for the happiness and perfection of the world, and to declare ourselves, if I may say so, in some measure the enemies of God.
>
> (TMS, p. 193)

For Smith, the Creator has infinite goodness. We admire God's wisdom and goodness. "In the divine nature" the sole principle of action is love or benevolence. The main principle of action of the Deity is benevolence because the

Deity needs nothing external and he is happy in himself. Everyone, the "meanest" and the "greatest", are under the "care and protection" of the benevolent "All-Wise-Being". It is the business of God to care for the "universal happiness of all rational and sensible beings" (TMS, p. 279). The primary aim of the Deity is the happiness of human kind and to facilitate human flourishing and "guard against misery".

> To man is allotted a much humbler department, but one much more suitable to the weakness of his powers, and to the narrowness of his comprehension; the care of his own happiness, of that of his family, his friends, his country.
>
> (TMS, p. 279)

> No other end seems worthy of that supreme wisdom and divine benignity which we necessarily ascribe to him; and this opinion, which we are led to by the abstract consideration of his infinite perfections, is still more confirmed by the examination of the works of nature, which seem all intended to promote happiness, and to guard against misery.
>
> (TMS, p. 193)

We promote the happiness of mankind and other "rational creatures", which is the "original purpose intended by the Author of nature" (TMS, p. 193), by acting morally. We declare ourselves as the enemies of God by acting in other ways.

The Deity has designed the universe for the happiness of mankind. The man who believes that benevolent God wants happiness for everyone has our greatest admiration:

> The idea of that divine Being, whose benevolence and wisdom have, from all eternity, contrived and conducted the immense machine of the universe, so as at all times to produce the greatest possible quantity of happiness, is certainly of all the objects of human contemplation by far the most sublime. . . . The man whom we believe to be principally occupied in this sublime contemplation, seldom fails to be the object of our highest veneration; and though his life should be altogether contemplative, we often regard him with the idea of that divine Being, whose benevolence and wisdom have, from all eternity, contrived and conducted the immense machine of the universe, so as at all times to produce the greatest possible quantity of happiness, is certainly of all the objects of human.
>
> (TMS, p. 278)

Human nature and psychological make-up are adjusted for specific tasks: "[God's] wisdom . . . contrived the system of human affections, as well as that of every other part of nature" (TMS, p. 270). Benevolence and enforcing the "sacred laws of justice" are consequences of "this constitution of Nature". Smith states that man "who can subsist only in society, was fitted by nature to that situation for which he was made" (TMS, p. 100).

Conclusion

As can be seen from the above-cited material, Smith sees morality as a worldly extension of the influence of a Divine force or being, in which the sympathetic process serves as the mechanism for the implementation of this design. In particular, he sees this influence as all-encompassing in human life and of a decidedly beneficent nature. While he does not mention or promote any specific religious preference, the readers will undoubtedly notice a distinctly Judeo-Christian flavor to this facet of his theorizing. Indeed, Smith was acting as a vicegerent within the moral system that he conceptualized by explicating and promoting the moral theory he has proposed and expounded in his works. He makes a clear distinction between Divine and human will, and that humans operate within the realm of a much larger design than their own.

Notes

1 Others also hold the view that the Deity plays a role in Smith's system. See, for example, Hill, 2001, Bitterman, 1940, Veblen, 1919, Taylor, 1929, Fleishacker, 2005.
2 See, for example, Kleer, 1995, Haakonssen, 1981, Campbell, 1971, Morrow, 1923, Raphael, 1975, Evensky, 2005, Morrow, 1923, Lingren, 1973, Raphael, 1975, Kristol, 1980, Martin, 1990, Spiegel, 1976, Davis, 1990, Rothschild, 1994.
3 The first usage of the "invisible hand" metaphor is in Smith's *History of Astronomy*. Here the invisible hand is that of Jupiter, or any major classical God. Second is in the TMS as we see in the above. The third is in the WN, where he describes that even though individuals have appropriate capital to promote their individual interests, led by Providence, social interests are advanced.

References

Bitterman, H.J., 1940. Adam Smith's empiricism and the law of nature. *Journal of Political Economy*, *48*(4), pp. 487–620.

Campbell, T.D., 1971. *Adam Smith's science of morals*. London: George Allen and Unwin.

Davis, G.R., 1990. Adam Smith on the providential reconciliation of individual and social interests: Is man led by invisible hand or by sleight of hand? *History of Political Economy*, *22*(2), pp. 341–352.

Evensky, J., 2005. *Adam Smith's moral philosophy*. Cambridge: Cambridge University Press.

Fleishacker, S., 2005. *On Adam Smith's Wealth of Nations: A philosophical companion*. Princeton, NJ: Princeton University Press.

Haakonssen, K., 1981. *The science of a legislator: The natural jurisprudence of David Hume and Adam Smith*. Cambridge: Cambridge University Press.

Hill, L., 2001. The hidden theology of Adam Smith. *European Journal of History of Economic Thought*, *8*(1), pp. 1–29.

Kleer, R.A., 1995. Final causes in Adam Smith's theory of moral sentiments. *Journal of the History of Philosophy*, *33*(2), pp. 275–330.

Kristol, I., 1980. Rationalism in economics. *The Public Interest*, *61*(Special Issue), pp. 201–218.

Lingren, J.R., 1973. *The social philosophy of Adam Smith*. The Hague: Martinus Nijhoff.

Martin, D.A., 1990. Economics as ideology: On making the "invisible hand" "visible". *Review of Social Economy*, *48*(1), pp. 272–287.

Morrow, G.R., 1923. The significance of the doctrine of sympathy in Hume and Adam Smith. *Philosophical Review*, *32*(1), pp. 60–78.

Raphael, D.D., 1975. *Adam Smith*. Oxford: Oxford University Press.

Rothschild, E., 1994. Adam Smith and the invisible hand. *American Economic Review*, *84*(2), pp. 319–322.

Spiegel, H.W., 1976. Adam Smith's heavenly city. *History of Political Economy*, *8*(4), pp. 478–493.

Taylor, O.H., 1929. Economics and the idea of Jus Naturale. *Quarterly Journal of Economics*, *44*, pp. 205–241.

Veblen, T. 1919. *The preconceptions of economic society: The place of science in modern civilization and other essays*. Reprint 1899. New York: Russell & Russell.

Viner, J., 1927. Adam Smith and laissez faire. *Journal of Political Economy*, *35*(3), pp. 198–232.

Chapter 6

A known world

An analysis of defenses in Adam Smith's *The Theory of Moral Sentiments*

I. Introduction

As we have described in Chapter 2, the development of Adam Smith's system of ethics and moral structure is based on what he calls sympathy. We argue that for a person to go from an unconscious unreflective state that seeks sympathetic interactions and approval from others to a more deliberate consensual morality, it is necessary to employ psychological defenses. Carrasco (2011) states, quoting Griswold (1999), "[the] desire for mutual sympathy is the first motivation for moral conduct or as Griswold says the mid-wife of virtues". (p. 16). Analogously we argue that to go from what Carrasco refers to as "psychological sympathy" to "moral sympathy" necessitates a defensive structure. One of the essential elements for any social and moral structure is an integral psychological defense system that supports it. While it is often taken for granted, it is a necessary part of human interactions.

It is important to be clear about what we mean by a "defense system", which we use in this chapter, and in Chapters 7 and 8, which we undertake in the next section. We are referring to the capacity within individuals to contain their more chaotic human passions, which becomes even more necessary as interactions grow to be more complex: particularly the capacity to delay the gratification of instinctual needs and impulses (Freud, 1920). It is therefore necessary to employ defenses that allow us to protect ourselves against the intrusion of inner impulses that would disrupt the social order and defenses that would protect us from the overwhelming influence of others that would also disrupt internal and social order. It is in this light that we use the term "defenses" as a necessary and important structural component in forming an attitude towards life. So, when we speak of Smith's use of defenses in his moral philosophy, we are attempting to analyze the strengths and limitations that are the natural extension of any defensive system. We view defenses as adaptive to a social and moral world. On that basis, we analyze the psychological defensive system that Smith employs in the TMS. By a known world we mean a world in which consensual rules are implemented and followed by all people creating a stable system. Thus, the known world is a system that allows the implementation of a moral structure.

We analyze the need for a known world in his system, what this known world includes, what it excludes and what are its consequences.

Smith's primary defensive structure is made up using rationalizations for his positions, the moralization of the rightness of his positions and the rational intellectualization of his positions. These are all methods that allow for the separation (or splitting) of thought from affect (Freud, 1936; McWilliams, 1994). In addition, he carefully and exactingly displaces anger according to his moral structure on to the proper objects of resentment. This type of displacement also requires both the repression and suppression of one's affective impulses to accomplish its purpose. All of these strategic defensive arrangements make possible the structure of his known world.

In this chapter, we argue that a system of defenses is necessary for the creation of Smith's moral structure. The system of defenses used in the TMS, like any other defensive system, has both strengths and limitations. Its strengths facilitate the structure of the moral system that Smith promotes, and within that structure it places limits on unique individual creativity, change, dynamism and spontaneity. In the next section, we describe what we mean by defenses employing psychoanalytic literature. In Section III we provide a brief overview of the sections in the TMS that we analyze. Section IV provides our analysis of defenses and Section V is the discussion section.

II. Defense

We need to refer back to the development of this concept in psychoanalysis and take it forward to our current use of the term. Within the original context of psychoanalysis, defenses were used interchangeably with the term resistances and seen as a negative force. In this context, "defenses" were employed by one's conscious attitude, or ego, to use the psychoanalytic term, to resist psychoanalytic interpretations and were seen as a negative force to resist treatment (Freud, 1921). By the mid to later part of the 1930s, the work of Anna Freud (1936) and Hartman (1939) looked to free the ego from an impossibly subordinate role relative to the instincts. Anna Freud's (1936) work was truly groundbreaking in that she was the first to articulate the necessity for defenses and saw them as integral to human development and character. Her work served to take defenses out of the previously exclusive realm of resistances. Earlier resistances were viewed as something negative that needed to be overcome in analysis because they held back development. Anna Freud reconceptualized them as being important to development.

As stated in Pumpian-Midlin (1967), Takatoff stated that Anna Freud as early as in 1936 observed that "preliminary stages of defense" were phase specific adaptive reactions. Takatoff also observed that defensive mechanisms that are socially sanctioned and reinforced by reality tend to persist. She concluded that whether behavior patterns become adaptive or remain primarily defensive is determined by the social reinforcement of certain behavioral patterns.

Others began to look at defenses from the perspective of their necessity for adaptation. Barret and Yankelovich (1970) described this evolution starting with Anna Freud by saying that she

> showed the ego and its workings in a new light. Where previously the ego's defenses had been regarded as obstacles to successful therapy (the defenses were technically regarded as "resistances") she showed that these resistances were, in fact, highly adaptive at least in their origins. She further demonstrated that . . . each individual's defenses (intellectualization, reaction formation, ego restriction, etc.) were characteristic to his total adaptation to life, forming a distinctive part of his personality.
>
> (Barret and Yankelovich, 1970, p. 96)

This began an evolution within psychoanalysis that included Kris (1951) and Erikson (1950) among others that viewed the "defenses" as an important structural component that facilitated human adaptation for human development. These defensive adaptations cover the spectrum from managing the daily life struggles of anxiety and ambiguity on the one hand, to managing deep emotional affect on the other. As a result of this defensive structure, life becomes more manageable and less unpredictable. Depending on the nature of our defensive structure, which becomes a component part of our character structure, we have the advantage of a more manageable life and the limitation that any protective structure brings because it excludes certain experiences. Therefore, it can be said that one's defensive structure is a "compromise" (Freud, 1923).

Brenner (1982) offered a further revision of the classical Freudian approach towards defenses. He pointed out that anything could be regarded as defensive when it functions to reduce anxiety or to drive tensions away. Hartmann, Kris and Loewenstein (1964) viewed defenses as ego functions to cope with external reality and drive demands. Schafer (1968) focused on delineating the dynamic properties of the ego. He emphasized that defenses can express undesirable impulses that allow gratification and at the same time underscored that defenses attempt to block the expression of undesirable content. An example of this might be channeling the anger and frustration caused by an unsatisfactory interaction, and focusing it on furthering efforts to overcome the frustrating or anger-inducing situation.

An important shift in the analysis of defenses has been in viewing defenses as a set of relational and cognitive processes that emphasize the "interpersonal" context in the use of defenses. (See Cooper, 1989, for a review of "two-person" analysis of defenses, and Eagle, 2011, on the shift to contemporary psychoanalysis.) Winnicott (1965), by stating that a baby does not exist without the care giver, viewed defenses as adaptations to traumatic environmental failure, differentiating this from defense organized against the expression of impulses. This perspective no longer viewed the individual as a closed system.

Modell (1975) suggested that defenses were organized from situations where there was early empathetic failure, which lead to the need to fall back into the self and the avoidance of expressions of need towards others. Thus, he emphasized a "two-person" theory of defense. Kohut (1984) highlighted that defensive structures were attempts to protect an enfeebled self. He pointed out that defenses were often organized against failures of self-objects (those people in one's early environment in particular, who were not able to adequately preform necessary care functions). His formulations were in line with those of Fairbairn (1952), Winnicott (1965), Guntrip (1969) and Modell (1975), emphasizing that the self might need to be protected in its state of vulnerability. He minimized the importance of instinctual drives and process. Sandler (1976) also asserted that defenses are manifested interpersonally. Kernberg (1975) viewed defensive organization as operating both in object relations contexts and in intrapsychic contexts. Greenberg and Mitchell (1983) and Mitchell (1998) described a reciprocal process in which the patient and the therapist affect one another, using the notion of intersubjectivity. In this view defenses are organized as a part of mutual regulation and influence. Novick and Novick (2001) emphasized that a "two-person" focus on the therapeutic relationship and the forms of interaction between patients and the therapist could be combined with a classical "one-person" focus on the patient's defenses.

Psychological defense mechanisms represent an important component of our capacity to maintain emotional homeostasis (Valliant, 2002). Defense systems evolve and operate much like the immune system without our conscious awareness. Defenses were originally viewed as the unconscious mechanisms that contained and redirected disturbing impulses and drives; however, as psychoanalytic theory evolved, defense mechanisms came to be viewed as having an adaptive value (Bowins, 2004). Bibring et al. (1961) stated that defenses have a dual function. One is that they are in the service of constructive, maturational, progressive growth and mastery of the drives and they have an autonomous, adaptive function. The other is that they ward off anxieties in relation to unconscious conflict. It is these same mechanisms that serve both defensive and adaptive purposes, ether singly or together, sequentially or simultaneously. Any behavioral expression (conscious and observable or unconscious and inferable) can serve as adaptive, defensive or impulsive, again simultaneously and/or sequentially.

As human capacities have evolved and have integrated more civil behavior, the mechanisms for accommodating the immediate tension and discomfort of such pro-social behavior needed to evolve too. These adaptive defenses play a key role in the assimilation of more complex sets of behavior that go into moral structure.

Defense mechanisms have evolved to reduce the intensity, frequency and duration of adverse feeling states. The adoption of moral behavior requires the individual to contain immediate emotional impulses and desires for gratification, and reduce the intensity of their frustration that arises from not immediately gratifying those needs. The use of defensive processes is an integral component in mediating immediate desire and delaying its gratification. This delay of gratification is then reinforced by the positive consequences such an ability has on fulfilling interactive agreements, and building trust in the public square and the market place, as we will elaborate on in Chapter 8.

Hartman (1939) indicates that environmental situations often play a part in determining the need for adaptation. Underlying the concept of adaptation is that living organisms come to fit their environment. Adaptation is a reciprocal relationship between the environment and the organism. Adaptation may result from the changes which the individual effects on his environment, thus humans adapt the environment to human functions and then the human being adapts to the environment he created.

Hartman (1939) also states that man acquires a crucial part of his adaptation through a learning process. Both constitutional factors and the external environment influence the process of adaptation. Heredity factors, tradition and survival all impact how a man adapts to his environment. From the beginning of life, the task of man to adapt is present. He stresses that the primary importance of social factors in human development and their biological significance are important for adaptation. There could also be progressive and regressive adaptation. An individual gains increasing independence through evolution. Thus, the reactions that originally occurred in relation to the external world are increasingly displaced into the interior of the organism (Hartman, 1939).

Contemporary psychoanalysis has expanded the conceptualization of defense to accommodate the growth and development of theory and practice. As the work has come to make the interpersonal process and the self the focus of practice, the understanding of the defensive process has been modified. "Defense" has therefore come to include not only the use of defenses to come to terms with needs that arise from primary drives, but also includes the defenses from the affects that arise from interpersonal interactions and primary self-organizations.

It is in this light that we use the term "defenses" as a necessary and important structural component to forming an attitude towards life. So, when we speak of Smith's use of defenses in his moral philosophy, we are attempting to analyze the strengths and limitations that are the natural extension of any defensive system. We view defenses as adaptive to a social and moral world. We are applying basic psychoanalytic understanding of defenses to Smith's elaborate 18th century theory in order to bring to light the defensive structure that is needed to go from a natural unreflective state to a more ego-ideal based moral structure that Smith advocates.

III. Analysis of defenses in the TMS

Prior to presenting our analysis, we refer the reader to Chapter 2 on sympathy, and we provide an overview of three other fundamental parts in the TMS: merit and de-merit, duty and virtues. We choose these parts because of their fundamental role in creating a known world.

In his discussion in the part entitled "of merit and demerit: or, of the objects of reward and punishment", Smith tells us that an action deserves reward, "which appears to be the proper and approved of object of that sentiment" (TMS, p. 79). Similarly, an action deserves punishment if it is the proper and approved of object of that sentiment. It is gratitude that prompts us to reward and resentment that prompts us to punish, and that we would like to be instrumental in rewarding and punishing. The passions of gratitude and resentment are seen as proper if they are approved of. These passions are approved of ". . . when the heart of every impartial spectator entirely sympathizes with them" (TMS, p. 81). To sympathize with the gratitude of the person who receives the benefit from the actions of the agent there must be propriety in the motives of the agent. A similar argument holds for resentment.

Duty is our application of judgments of propriety and merit to ourselves, rather than to others. We approve or disapprove of our conduct in the same manner we do of others' conduct. We wish to examine our own conduct through the eyes of the impartial spectator. In order to attain the satisfaction of gaining the admiration of others, we must again be the impartial spectators of our character and conduct. Approbation of others confirms our self-approbation, and their praise increases our sense of praise-worthiness. For Smith, the sole principle of our conduct should be our sense of duty.

Smith addresses what is virtuous. He says that virtue consists in "the tone of temper, and tenour of conduct, which constitutes the excellent and praise-worthy character, the character which is the natural object of esteem, honour, and approbation" (TMS, p. 313). The fundamental virtues are prudence, benevolence and self-command.

> The care of health, of the fortune, of the rank and reputation of the individual, the objects upon which his comfort and happiness in this life are supposed principally to depend, is considered as the proper business of virtue which is commonly called Prudence.
>
> (TMS, p. 249)

Of benevolence, Smith tells us that

> . . . our good-will is circumscribed by no boundary, but may embrace the immensity of the universe. Even the 'meanest' as well as the 'greatest' man are cared and protected by 'that great, benevolent, and all-wise Being, who directs all the movements of nature; and who is determined . . . to maintain . . . the greatest possible quantity of happiness.'
>
> (TMS, p. 277)

Self-command is "not only itself a great virtue, but from it all the other virtues seem to derive their principle luster" (TMS, p. 284). Self-command is bringing down our emotions to what others (especially the impartial spectator) can enter. Self-command is a part of every virtue. However, it is not a sufficient condition for the entirety of virtue. One could have great command over the fear of death. When they are combined with justice and benevolence, they are great virtues and increase the glory of other virtues. However, they may sometimes be "dangerous". "The most intrepid valour may be employed in the cause of the greatest injustice" (TMS, p. 284).

These structural components, sympathy, merit, duty and virtue are the corner stones of creating Smith's known world. Sympathy is the structural mechanism by which we connect to the other. Because we have mutual sympathy we have the basis for morality. This is the basis for reflection about how we want to be treated and how we want to treat others. The remainder of the sections, duty, merit and virtue, are the rules and character traits that systematically carry out this morality based on sympathy.

Part I: of the propriety of action

Throughout this section we will discuss the necessary defensive attitudes that are essential to develop the moral structures that are integral to Smith's "known world". Adam Smith's system of ethics and moral structure is based on what he calls sympathy. Smith tells us that "Though our brother is on the rack, as long as we ourselves are at our ease, our senses will never inform us of what he suffers" (TMS, p. 11). By imagination we put ourselves in his situation and form an idea of his sensations. This quote is an example of how Smith employs splitting as a defense maneuver. Smith splits the extreme effect of torture from the intellectual analysis of the process of sympathy. In so doing he establishes how important splitting is to this human experience. His objectified attitude allows Smith to speculate about morality because he is split off from the dominating affect that torture evokes. Smith gives credence to the emotional experience and at the same time he exclusively evaluates it intellectually. He creates a linear and logical structure that we are terming a known world by splitting the emotional experience from the cognitive structure of morality that he is creating.

In his interaction with the spectator, the agent often brings his emotions down a pitch to reach a concordance of passions. As Smith puts it, "we . . . endeavor to bring down our passions to that pitch, which the particular company we are in may be expected to go along with them" (TMS, p. 28). As such there is a premium put on the containment of one's emotional pitch for the sake of social order. Thought and affect are splitting off. This allows the intellectual rationale of bringing down "our passions . . . to go along with them" (TMS, p. 28).

The actor and the spectator seek harmony with each other's emotions, thus replacing the power of the individual by the power of the community. This is due to mutual sympathy. The harmonious world that is created through mutual sympathy is the moral world, the known world. Smith's perspective on the passions goes from the personal level, the interplay of the agent and spectator, and moves on to the development of a larger social structure. When this social structure reaches a critical mass, it then becomes the basis for his social order, and the structure of what in this chapter we have deemed the known world.

Smith outlines his elaborate understanding of the human passions that are in need of self-command. Indeed, self-command becomes the basis for self-government, and the usefulness of those virtues that support the social order. It can be seen once again how necessary it is for a clear defensive system to enable the action of self-command. The chaos of unbridled passion threatens the self-command that is essential to the personal and collective moral system. Smith clearly discriminates among the expression of certain feeling states. On the one hand, he is very open to the acknowledgement of most all aspects of human emotion and feeling states. However, on the other hand, particularly to the modern reader, he is quite unrestrained with his level of discrimination between what is acceptable and what is not acceptable, and is very exacting in his preferences. For example, Smith tells us that

> We are disgusted with that clamorous grief, which without and deli-cacy, calls upon our compassion with sighs and tears and importunate lamentations.
>
> (TMS, p. 29)

Similarly, he tells us

> The insolence and brutality of anger, in the same manner, when we indulge its fury without check or restraint, is, of all objects, the most detestable.
>
> (TMS, p. 30)

On the other hand, according to Smith, "to feel much for others and little for ourselves . . . constitutes the perfection of human nature" (TMS, p. 30).

Smith goes on to demonstrate his differentiation relative to the passions. He defines: passions which take their origin from the body; passions that take their origin from the imagination, such as love; unsocial passions, such as hatred and resentment; social passions, such as generosity, humanity, kindness, compassion, mutual friendship and esteem, all the social and benevolent affections; and the selfish passions, such as grief and joy.

These passions are discriminated on the basis of his sense of propriety and virtue as they relate to the social structure. Smith argues against expression of what he refers to as the bodily passions, such as sex and hunger. Bodily passions are beneath dignity in their expression, and he advocates for a strong level of repression and the exercise of suppression where there is conscious acknowledgement. In his discussion of bodily passions, he employs both moralization and compartmentalization to rationalize his known world. Smith goes as far as to say that while on the one hand we have sympathy with bodily pain, on the other hand if a violent outcry is made from pain, he states that the spectator would never fail to despise him. This is typical of Smith's attitude towards all passions that take their origin from the body. He acknowledges it but is against its expression. In this case, he distinguishes what is not acceptable, then he advocates for suppression.

He moves on and talks about the passions that derive their origin from the imagination and speaks of love between the two sexes. Even though he acknowledges that love is an important human emotion on the one hand, he takes a strong stand against its expression on the other. Smith further declares that although love's expression might be "ridiculous" and though it might have dreadful consequences, its intentions are not mischievous.

The unsocial passions of hatred and resentment are also derived from the imagination, and as with love, he advocates strongly against their expression, seeing them as not being graceful or becoming. He next turns to the social passions of generosity, humanity, kindness, compassion, mutual friendship and esteem, "all the social passions of benevolent affections" (TMS, p. 47). These passions please the impartial spectator in almost every occasion. Smith goes on to talk about what he calls the selfish passions of grief and joy. He sees them as neither amenable nor terrible.

Smith acknowledges that we have a desire to be respected and respectable. On the one hand, he acknowledges that one way to achieve that is to become rich and powerful; however, he also says that

> This disposition to admire the rich and powerful and to despise to neglect persons of poor and mean condition though necessary to establish and maintain the distinction of ranks and the order of society is the great and most universal cause of the corruption of our moral sentiments.
>
> (TMS, p. 72)

Here Smith is both rationalizing and moralizing the need for distinction of rank and wealth. On the other hand, the other way to become respected and respectable is through the practice of virtue. Smith states that only a select group of people admires others for their virtue, while the mob generally admires people for their wealth and power.

This final section of sympathy continues to shape the creation of the "known world" through its rationalization for a stable social order. He creates this "known world" through the splitting of thought from affect, moralization of the rightness of his positions, the rationalization of his position and then intellectualizing his overall structure. Starting here with sympathy, Smith shows the development of a meticulously constructed, rational structure. Implicit in his system is a desire for social order, stability, propriety and consistency. These are the hallmarks of what we are postulating as a known world. Psychological defenses are necessary to make this structure possible in the face of the fundamental human condition, which includes emotion and irrationality.

From a defensive perspective, it is first necessary to separate affect from cognition. This separation is accomplished through rationalization, moralization and intellectualization. Briefly, he rationalizes the need for the separation of affect from cognition. He then uses extensive moralization to bolster the need to exalt certain passions as virtuous while others are not. He accomplishes his discriminations through a rigorous application of purely intellectual reason. His structure requires (as he in fact indicates) the selective repression of certain emotions such as pain. Smith also uses the displacement of emotion (particularly anger) from one source to a legitimate target. The legitimate target of anger is based on the spectator's evaluation. Finally, as was indicated earlier, Smith consigns certain feeling states to a devalued position and associates them with weakness.

Psychological defenses enable the building of his structure. Smith's defensive system necessarily includes and excludes certain life experience. This exclusion of experience both facilitates his structure and limits its flexibility and application because it eliminates certain aspects of human experience. This also includes the development of a systematic method for a collective morality and structure. In so doing it excludes uniqueness and individual development that fall outside of his known parameters.

Part II: Merit and demerit: objects of reward and punishment

In this section Smith is rationalizing the use of merit and demerit as a means of shaping social behavior. This is the implementation of his rationalized hierarchical values from which reward and punishment are deemed appropriate. He is concerned with

> the beneficial or hurtful nature of the effects which aims at, or tends to produce, consists of the merit and demerit of the action, the qualities by which it is entitled to reward or is deserving of punishment.
>
> (TMS, p. 22)

Merit and demerit are the active mechanisms that govern behavior. In this section Smith provides us the rules of his "known world" by stating what deserves reward and what deserves punishment. It is gratitude that prompts us to reward and resentment that prompts us to punish, and that we like to be instrumental in rewarding and punishing. The net effect of the ongoing practice of these rewards and punishments is to create a consensual morality practiced by the collective culture and reinforced by the active use of merit and demerit or rewards and punishments.

The objects of gratitude and resentment are seen as proper if they are approved of. As with sympathy, these passions are approved of "... when the heart of every impartial spectator entirely sympathizes with them, when every impartial spectator entirely enters into, and goes along with them" (p. 81). The impartial spectator represents the moral structure that constitutes the proper objects of gratitude or resentment. In Smith's reassertion of the importance of the impartial spectator, we are again seeing the uniformity of his thought across every aspect of his theorizing. He rationalizes the use of punishment and reward to implement this position.

He then compares the virtues of benefice and justice. On benefice he tells us the following: "Actions of beneficent tendency, which proceed from proper motives, seem alone to require reward; because such alone are the approved objects of gratitude ..." (TMS, p. 91). Along this same line the man who does not reward his benefactor when he has the power to do so is also "is guilty of the blackest ingratitude" (TMS, pp. 91–92). Also, hurtful actions that proceed from improper motives deserve punishment. The motivation for such resentment and punishment is given to us by nature for defense only. Resentment is seen as a safeguard of justice and the security of innocence. Smith is speaking about resentment as a philosophical and societal defense against hurtful actions and injustice on the part of the agent.

The text goes on to address another important virtue in this section, which is justice. Justice is unique from the other virtues. Griswold (1999) tells us that justice for Smith is first a social and political virtue, and that it may be extracted by force. The rules of justice are precise; Smith compares them to the rules of grammar. Justice is a "negative virtue" and "only hinders us from hurting our neighbor". He asserts that retaliation is an important instrument to bring about justice:

> Every man doth, so shall it be done to him, and retaliation seems to be the great law which is dictated to us by nature. . . . The violator of laws of justice ought to be made himself that evil which he has done to another; and since no regard to the sufferings of his brethren is capable of restraining him, he ought to be over-awed by the fear of his own.
>
> (TMS, p. 96)

Here Smith rationalizes the use of retaliation as a basis for social control. Using retaliation, Smith endeavors to create guilt and remorse. He points out that remorse plays an important role in adhering to justice:

> it is made up of shame from which the sense of impropriety of past conduct; of grief of the effects of it; of pity for those who suffer by it; and of the

dread and terror of punishment from the conscious of the justly provoked resentment of rational creatures.

(TMS, p. 99)

The violator of justice feels "all the agonies of shame, and horror, and consternation" (TMS, p. 98). It should be noted that shame is the signal that lets the agent know that he has deviated from a particular moral structure, or the known world that compels the agent to follow the rules of the structure. When looked at this way, Smith is building on what from a psychoanalytic perspective are the component parts of the superego structure.

Smith assumes as one of the bases for his moral/superego structures that one finds indefinite solitude horrifying. This is what keeps someone who has violated some aspect of this structure from fleeing justice by flying away from the social group. "But solitude is still more dreadful than society . . . the horror of solitude drives him back to society" (p. 99). In order not to be left in this situation, the agent is compelled to adhere to the rules of the known world.

In contrast to shame and punishment, feelings of being the natural object of love and gratitude, esteem and approbation arise in a man who has performed generous actions. He finds himself applauding himself as the impartial judge would, which is a very agreeable state. There is harmony and friendship that such a person experiences with mankind. All of these sentiments constitute the conscious incorporation of merit. This is also illustrative of how the reinforcement and rationalization of proper behavior is facilitated within the moral structure. Human consciousness and awareness of both the merits and demerits of our actions speak to the internalization of Smith's known world. From a psychoanalytic perspective, this constitutes the internalization of a consensual superego structure.

Smith says,

> All members of human society stand in need of each other's assistance. . . . Where the necessary assistance is reciprocally afforded from love, from gratitude, from friendship, and esteem, the society flourishes and is happy.
>
> (TMS, p. 100)

There is great value in such harmonious assistance with one another. According to Smith, society cannot subsist when members hurt and injure one another. Here he makes a strong case for the self-perpetuating nature of his known world based on the conscious awareness of idealized potential for happiness and social harmony.

He reasserts the necessity and importance of justice to reinforce this harmony and the warning that injustice threatens it:

> in order to enforce the observation of justice, therefore, Nature has implanted in the human breast that consciousness of ill-desert, those terrors of merited punishment which attend upon its violation, as the great

safe-guards of the association of mankind, to protect the weak, to curb the violent, and chastise the guilty.

(TMS, p. 101)

In so saying he indeed personifies what Freud (1923) came to refer to as the superego.

In this section, Smith is solidifying his moral structure by adding the governing components of merit and demerit. As we indicated in this section, the accomplishment of merit and demerit requires the exercise of both moralization and rationalization to justify the use of punishment and reward to reinforce his views on social justice.

Part III: Of the foundation of our judgments concerning our own sentiments and conduct, and of the sense of duty

In this section Smith goes into what he refers to as duty, which he sees as the applications of judgments of propriety and merit to ourselves. We approve or disapprove of our own conduct in the same way that we do the conduct of others. We examine our conduct through the eyes of the impartial spectator. This observation of others is accomplished by removing ourselves from the immediate situation by imagination and viewing our sentiments and motives, and then making judgments about them.

Modern psychoanalytic thinking (Kohut, 1968, 1971, Winnicott 1967) supports Smith's assertion that interpersonal object relations that bring about "mirroring" are integral to human development. The mirroring of significant others, particularly the mother in early development, is fundamental to how we come to know our genuine or "true" selves. These experiences of ourselves through the eyes of those who are significant to us also help in development of our sense of morality, cultural identity and consensual norms. This mirroring from significant others also conveys a defensive structure that is integral to the personal and cultural norms that are conveyed in these interactions.

Smith talks about the human need for communication with other members of our own species and how such societal interactions shape our perceptions about ourselves. Smith tells us that if "human creatures" were to grow up in a solitary place, they would not have any conception of themselves. Smith sees each human being as inextricably intertwined with others; indeed, we are social beings and are only at home in relation to others. We have moral criticism of others and others have it of us. "This is the only looking-glass by which we can, in some measure, with the eyes of other people, scrutinize the propriety of our own conduct" (TMS, p. 131). Smith focuses on what would be termed the development of the "superego" functions of morality. Thus, the known world is created through these interactions, which includes the development of propriety, merit and demerit. This superego development evolves through the observation and mirroring of significant others.

Smith goes on to further assert that not only do we want praise, but also we want to be praise worthy. The approbation of others confirms our self-approbation and their praise increases our sense of praise-worthiness. Smith makes a very strong argument that one of the great motivators is what Freud (1920) later saw in a similar light and termed the "pleasure principal".

Smith goes on to express strong views about Nature.

> The all-wise Author of Nature has . . . taught man to respect the sentiments and judgments of his brethren; to be more or less pleased when they approve of his conduct, and to be more or less hurt when they disapprove of it. He has made man, if I may say so, the immediate judge of mankind; and has in this respect . . . created him after his own image, and appointed him his vicegerent up on earth, to superintend the behavior of his brethren.
>
> (TMS, p. 149)

He clearly advocates that Nature gives the impartial spectator the authority to determine where we ought to go.

A strong emphasis is placed on self-command. Self-command is acquired from the great discipline of Nature and gains the regard of the spectator of our conduct. Smith equates the level of self-approbation that one has with the level of self-command. Nature rewards proportionally to the level of self-command and good behavior that one has mastered. He further rationalizes that those who are best able to acquire complete control of their joys or sorrows are those who feel the most for the joys and sorrows of others. Those who have the most exquisite humanity are those who are most capable of acquiring the highest degree of self-command. Smith's statements about Nature indicate a defensive grandiosity, as he seems to be arbitrating for God, which is the basis for his moral/superego development. His rationalization of moral/superego development as being based on Nature/God anchors his defensive structure in the deity.

For Smith, half of the human disorders are the result of self-deceit. He then describes general rules as a remedy for this. This leads to the point that Smith is making in this section, these general rules are referred to as a sense of duty, "a principle of the greatest consequence in human life, and the only principle by which the bulk of mankind are capable of . . . directing their actions" (TMS, p. 188). He views these rules as sacred and necessary.

Smith becomes obsessively redundant on this matter when he restates that our moral facilities were intended to be governing principles of human nature. These rules are to be regarded as the "commands and laws of the Deity, promulgated by those vicegerents which he has thus set up within us" (TMS, p. 193). He sees this as the gesture of a beneficent God that set all of these rules up for the happiness of mankind:

> When the general rules which determine the merit and demerit of actions, come to be regarded as the laws of an All-powerful being, who watches

over our conduct, and who, in a life to come, will reward the observance, and punish the breach of them; they necessarily acquire a new sacredness from this consideration.

(TMS, pp. 197–198)

Smith finally declares directly that the sole principle of our conduct should be our sense of duty. When our actions arise from a sense of duty and with regard to general rules, then all questions are answered.

The general rules appear to be circular. God created these rules and the right-minded approve of what is virtuous, then they become general rules. It is our duty to follow the general rules. Greater good comes from virtue. If we agree to be virtuous, then we are in a much better social cultural environment. If we do this, it will create the greatest freedom for the greatest number of people. The ordering is as follows: virtues, accomplishment, social system with greater commerce and greater freedom.

Smith accomplishes this large linear system of thought by employing a great deal of rationalization. This system is supported by his deference to the higher wishes of the Deity. He seems to have made a grandiose identification with the Deity to accomplish this large task. In short, he attempts to subdue the instincts and put them in the control of his rational morality under the authority of God.

Part VI: of the character of virtue

Virtue is a cornerstone that is present throughout TMS. In this section Smith describes and defines the traits that are necessary for his moral structure and moral world. For Smith, virtue shapes the "tone and temper, and tenor of conduct, which constitutes the excellent and praise-worthy character, the character which is the natural object of esteem, honor, and approbation" (TMS, p. 313). In short, virtue for Smith is the ideal attitude by which we approach our life and that of others, and virtue shapes the attitude that we exercise when carrying out our lives, and manifest in relation to our "own happiness and secondly, as it may affect that of other people" (TMS, p. 248). As can be seen, virtue then interacts with all the other principles that he so meticulously articulates. He presents an intellectually articulate and linearly rational argument for the integral use of virtue in his moral structure. In his idealization of virtue, there is a defensive perfectionism that postulates an ideal attitude. This aspect of his defensive structure sets out a perfectionistic ideal that does not include the human reality which often falls short.

Virtue is discussed throughout the TMS. For example, when Smith discusses sympathy early in TMS, he describes the efforts of the spectator to enter into the emotions of the agent. And for the agent to bring down his emotions to what the spectator can go along with. This is founded on two different sets of virtues: self-command and propriety. It also allows the agent to find the appropriate pitch for a given emotion. Another example comes in his section on merit and demerit, where he talks about the virtue of justice. Justice is a social virtue that is required for the existence of society. Justice bears the distinction of being the one virtue that may be enforced by force and have a greater precision than other virtues.

Smith's fundamental virtues from which others are derived are: prudence, benevolence and self-command.

> The care of health, of the fortune, of the rank and reputation of the individual, the objects upon which his comfort and happiness in this life are supposed principally to depend, is considered as the proper business of virtue which is commonly called Prudence.
>
> (TMS, p. 249)

Security is identified as the first object of prudence; and a prudent man is serious in his studies, is sincere, is always capable of friendship and is not offensive in his conversations. In addition, a prudent man is industrious, frugal and sacrifices the present for future enjoyments. Following from this attitude a prudent man lives within his income, is contented with his situation and does not subject himself to any responsibility that is not imposed by duty. The prudent man is also just. He does not harm others, cheat or steal. He does not have ambition to dominate others. Smith sums up the acts of a prudent man by declaring that he has the entire approbation of the impartial spectator. Prudence is a very important virtue for Smith; he demonstrates this by writing a long paragraph about each of the attributes of a prudent man, and he exactingly describes each attribute.

In this discussion Smith describes in hierarchical detail the idealization of virtue in all of its manifestations. In order to accomplish the idealization of the virtues of prudence, benevolence and self-command, he uses intellectualization, rationalization, moralization and compartmentalization of virtues into specific categories of behavior and motives. As a result of such a perfectionist attitude, and such rational defenses, human feelings (particularly those that do not fit into preformed rational forms) are put in a devalued realm.

It follows that Smith also places a great deal of importance on exercising self-command in relation to others and sees no good reason to hurt the happiness of our neighbors unless there is a proper resentment for an injustice that has been attempted or actually committed.

On how the character of the individual affects the happiness of other people, Smith tells us that every man is first recommended to his own care. Then there is an expanding circle of individuals that we are to care for: our immediate family; our extended family. There is a partiality towards members of our own circle.

> The general rule is established, that persons related to one another in a certain degree, ought always be affected towards one another in a certain

manner, and that there is always the highest impropriety, and sometimes even a sort of impiety, in their being affected in a different manner.

(TMS, p. 258)

He considers what he calls natural affection the "effect of the moral than of the supposed physical connection ..." (TMS, p. 262).

He then turns to friendships. The necessity and convenience of mutual accommodation among well-disposed people generates a friendship similar to what takes place in those who are born in the same family. He considers attachments that are founded upon "esteem and approbation of his conduct and behavior ... the most respectable" (TMS, p. 264). The attachment based on "the love of virtue" is the most virtuous. After those people come those who are rich and powerful, the poor and the wretched. The former, however determine the peace and order in society, which is more important than the relief of the miserable. Once again, we see a rationalization of rank, distinction and class difference. This rigidly defined hierarchy idealizes certain attachments and social rankings and necessarily devalues others. This defensive idealization serves to include those attitudes and behavior that perpetuate his moral structure and exclude those that do not.

As an extension of the love of virtue, Smith declares that Nature has formed men for mutual kindness, and that "kindness is the parent of kindness" (TMS, p. 265). He makes it clear that the evolution of virtue comes from a universal benevolence that knows no bounds, and is interwoven with a Divine Creator.

The idea of that divine Being whose benevolence and wisdom have from all eternity contrived and conducted the immense machine of the universe so as at all times to produce the greatest possible quality of happiness is certainly of all the objects of human contemplation by far the most sublime.

(TMS, p. 278)

Here Smith gives the impartial spectator the authority of God. Once again, this grandiose identification with the Deity supports the perfectionistic idealization of his hierarchy, and is the fundamental defensive position to his moral structure. Without his appeal to an absolute authority as the rational for his system, the defensive justification of his structure would not work.

Of self-command, Smith says:

The man who, in danger, in torture, upon the approach of death, preserves his tranquility unaltered, and suffers no word, no gesture to escape him which does not perfectly accord with the feelings of the most indifferent spectator, necessarily commands a very high degree of admiration.

(TMS, p. 280)

Similarly, he sees the command of anger as a great and noble power. According to Smith, the disposition to anger, hatred, envy, revenge and malice, the passions that drive men from one another, would offend the impartial spectator. Here Smith idealizes an extreme view of self-command even in the face of self-destruction, and then moralizes the virtuousness of such a defensive position.

Acting according to the rules of perfect prudence, justice and benevolence may be considered perfectly virtuous. However, he says, a man's own passions are likely to mislead him. These other virtues then must be supported by self-command. Self-command is emphasized throughout the TMS as "not only itself a great virtue, but from it all the other virtues seem to derive their principle luster" (TMS, p. 284). One of the principle acts of self-command is bringing down our emotional expressions to what others (i.e. the impartial spectator) can enter into.

Throughout this section Smith makes the argument for self-command in relation to one's life. In particular, he focuses on the emotions of fear and anger, which require the greatest exercise of virtue. Indeed, he sees the spontaneous indulgence of these and of other such emotions as vanity. Consistent with his meticulous observations and exacting prescriptions, he also orders the passions in terms of their difficulty to contain. On the one hand, there is anger and fear that require the highest degree of virtuous self-command to the restraint of affection that requires less. On the other hand, the exercise of virtue is intended to provide harmony within the individual and harmony within the greater society. Smith puts it clearly:

> The virtues of prudence, justice and beneficence have no tendency to produce any but the most agreeable effects. Regard to those effects as in originally recommends them to the actor so does it afterwards to the impartial spectator. In our approbation of all those virtues our sense of the agreeable effects of their utility either to the person who exercises them or to some other persons joins with our sense of their propriety and constitutes always a considerable frequently the greater part of that approbation.
>
> (TMS, p. 309)

This section points out Smith's diligent exercise of a defensive structure to create and maintain a known world. He has skillfully intellectualized the exercise of virtue and has moralized the hierarchy of virtuous acts. This structure is rationalized through the appeal to, and grandiose identification with, a deity to support his structure. Self-command is an important structural component of virtue and dictates the most obsessive compartmentalizing of human impulse and interactions. As such, spontaneous and intuitive human actions are put in a devalued position. In addition, individual feeling states are devalued in favor of collectively approved attitudes and actions.

III. Discussion

This chapter looks at the TMS and the essential psychological defensive arrangements that Smith employs to implement his theory of moral structure. In particular, we are arguing that the transition from the initial condition of sympathy that Smith postulates, to the implementation of his moral structure, requires a psychological defense system to facilitate that transition. As such, in this chapter we attempt an analysis of Smith's defensive viewpoint.

We have presented the fundamentals of his elaborate and elegantly structured theory that results in what has been referred to in this chapter as a known world. Smith's work is dependent upon the use of psychological defenses to (1) implement his moral theory in the face of the natural unreflective and instinctual human condition, and (2) to facilitate its necessary internal consistency. As stated earlier in this chapter, defenses are necessary operational components to any system that is applied to human behavior, and as such have both strengths and deficits. We often take for granted the need for defenses because they are so much a part of our particular social structure. Indeed, the human need for defenses allows us to come to terms with and make sense of the otherwise chaotic nature of internal need and external reality, and cannot be overstated. A further example of this will be discussed in Chapter 7. Smith's theory creates a social and moral structure that prescribes a set of priorities and behaviors. In order to implement these priorities and behaviors, there is a need to manage the instinctual affective life within an individual that interacts with these priorities. Indeed, this is where a defensive structure becomes necessary.

Our capacity for sympathy also reveals the need to limit the influence of others' experience upon us and creates the need for defenses to limit the overwhelming affects that sympathy creates in our interactions with others.

In the broadest perspective Smith's theory is defending against the fundamental instincts of aggression and sexuality. In particular, it defends against the affects that are the result of the dynamic conflict of these instincts both within an individual and in relation to others. Further, his system evolves into the prescription of an elaborate arrangement of social interactions where he defends against the potential of losing his relationship to others. He adopts an exclusively rational perspective that makes his system vulnerable (as any individual would be) to the eruption of irrational affect, unforeseen circumstances or the spontaneous expressions of feeling that do not fall into the prescribed category of feeling values that his structure dictates. In particular, he defends against the *expression* of affective states such as rage, anger, hate, frustration, sexual desire and affection, in a spontaneous way that falls outside his structure.

In Smith's view, we are saddled with opposing forces of an inner human condition, which includes instinctual impulses on the one hand, and on the other hand are also endowed by God with "all-seeing . . . powers of judgment" (Rotshchild, 2010, p. 27). In order to resolve these discrepancies within the human being, we argue that a defensive system is necessary to bring about this "all seeing" ego ideal.

One of the most dominant defenses employed by Smith is that of splitting: the turning of emotional states into good and bad, black and white or right and wrong. In particular, his system has little room for the subtleties of context or uniqueness. His theory defends against the expression of affect by evaluating such expression with the "disapprobation of the spectator." He further reinforces this split by rationalizing and moralizing about the "virtue" of the suppression of affective states.

All of Smith's structures (virtue, propriety, merit, duty) are applications of his foundational defense system that we have outlined. In his thoughtful and meticulous way, he has masterfully woven together these structures to create a logically tight system of morality and behavior. The strength of Smith's purely rational approach is that it can be internally consistent, linear, follow logical rules and can conceptually account for a large portion of behavior and details. It further supports a majority collective view of human action based on the external need for relationship with others, which is mediated by the "approbation" of others. On the other hand, this rational approach leaves little room for individual differences, creativity, change, dynamism and spontaneity within its system. Because of its exclusive focus on the dependency of the individual on the approbation of others, it also leaves out people who "march to their own drummer" such as: Martin Luther, Martin Luther King, Gandhi and Einstein, all of whom were able to go in their own direction, sometimes at great peril and at the risk of great disapprobation by the dominant culture. The attributes and personal styles that are left out of Smith's "known world" would easily be the subject of yet another study.

This chapter was published by Ozler and Gabrinetti: "A known world: An analysis of defenses in Adam Smith's *The Theory of Moral Sentiments*", *Adam Smith Review, 8*, pp. 256–276, March 2013.

References

Barret, W. and Yankelovich, D., 1970. *Ego and instinct: The psychoanalytic view of human nature-revised*. New York: Random House.

Bibring, G.L., Dweyer, T.F., Huntington, D.S. and Valentine, A.F., 1961. A study of the psychological process in pregnancy of the earliest mother-child relationship. *Psychoanalytic Study of the Child, 16*, pp. 9–72.

Bowins, B., 2004. Psychological defense mechanisms: A new perspective. *American Journal of Psychoanalysis, 64*, pp. 1–26.

Brenner, C., 1982. *The mind in conflict*. New York: International Universities Press.

Brodie, A., 2006. Sympathy and the impartial spectator. In: Haakonssen, K., ed. *The Cambridge companion to Adam Smith*. Cambridge: Cambridge University Press. pp. 22–56.

Bromberg, P.M., 2007. Reply to review of awakening of the dreamer: Clinical journeys by Philip M. Bromberg. *Psychoanalytic Dialogues, 17*, pp. 769–787.

Brown, V., 1994. *Adam Smith's discourse: Canonicity, commerce and conscience*. London: Routledge.

Campbell, J., 1972. *The hero with a thousand faces*. Princeton, NJ: Princeton University Press.

Carrasco, M.A., 2011. From psychology to moral normativity. *The Adam Smith Review, 6*, pp. 9–29.

Cooper, S.H., 1989. Recent contributions to the theory of defense mechanisms: A comparative view. *Journal of the American Psychoanalytic Association, 37*, pp. 865–891.

Eagle, M.N., 2011. *From classical to contemporary psychoanalysis: A critique and integration*. New York: Routledge.

Erikson, E.H., 1950. *Childhood and society*. New York: Norton.

Faribairn, W.R.D., 1952. *Psychoanalytic Studies of the personality*. New York: Tavistock Publishing Limited.

———, 1931. Features in the analysis of a patient with a physical genital abnormality. *Psychoanalytic Studies of Personality*, pp. 197–222.

Fricke, C., 2011. Introduction: Adam Smith and the conditions of a moral society. *The Adam Smith Review, 6*, pp. 3–8.

Freud, A., 1936. *The writings of Anna Freud, vol. II*. New York: International University Press.

Freud, S., 1920. Beyond the pleasure principle. In: *The standard edition of the complete psychological works by Sigmund Freud* (J. Strachey [in collaboration with A. Freud & assisted by A. Tyson], Trans.) London: Hogarth Press. Vol. XIII, pp. 7–66.

———, 1921. Group psychology and the analysis of the ego. In: *The standard edition of the complete psychological works by Sigmund Freud* (J. Strachey [in collaboration with A. Freud & assisted by A. Tyson], Trans.) London: Hogarth Press. Vol. XVI, pp. 69–144.

———, 1923. The ego and the id. In: *The standard edition of the complete psychological works by Sigmund Freud* (J. Strachey [in collaboration with A. Freud & assisted by A. Tyson], Trans.) London: Hogarth Press. Vol. XIII, pp. 12–68.

Griswold, C.L., 1999. *Adam Smith and the virtues of Enlightenment*. Cambridge: Cambridge University Press.

———, 2006. Imagination: Morals, science, and arts. In: Haakonssen, K., ed. *The Cambridge companion to Adam Smith*. Cambridge: Cambridge University Press.

Greenberg, J. and Mitchell, S., 1983. *Object relations in psychoanalytic theory*. Cambridge, MA: Harvard University Press.

Guntrip, H., 1969. *Schizoid phenomena: Object relations and the self*. New York: International Universities Press.

Hartman, H., 1939. *Ego psychology and the problem of adaptation*. New York: International University Press.

Hartmann, H., Kris, E. and Loewenstein, R.M., 1964. *Papers on psychoanalytic psychology: Psychological issues*. New York: International Universities Press.

Kernberg, O.F., 1975. *Borderline conditions and pathological narcissism*. New York: Aronson.

Kohut, H., 1968. The psychoanalytic treatment of narcissistic personality disorders. *Psychoanalytic Study of the Child, 23*, pp. 86–113.

———, 1971. *The analysis of the self: A systematic approach to the psychoanalytic treatment of narcissistic personality disorders*. New York: International Universities Press.

———, 1984. *How does psychoanalysis cure?* Chicago: University of Chicago Press.

Kris, E., 1951. The development of ego psychology. *Samiksa the Indian Journal of Psychoanalysis, 5*, 153–168.

McWilliams, N., 1994. *Psychoanalytic diagnosis: Understanding personality structure in the clinical process*. New York: The Guildford Press.

Mitchell, S.A., 1998. The analyst's knowledge and authority. *The Psychoanalytic Quarterly, 67*, pp. 1–31.

Modell, A.H., 1975. A narcissistic defense against affects and the illusion of self-sufficiency. *The International Journal of Psychoanalysis, 56*, pp. 275–283.

Novick, J. and Novick, K.K., 2001. Two systems of self-regulation. *Psychoanalytic Social Work, 8*, pp. 95–122.

Özler, S., 2012. Adam Smith and dependency. *Psychoanalytic Review, 99*(3), pp. 333–358.

Pumpian-Midlin, E., 1967. Defense organization of the ego and psychoanalytic technique. *Journal of the American Psychoanalytic Association, 15*, pp. 150–165.

Rotshchild, E., 2010. The theory of moral sentiment and the inner life. *The Adam Smith Review, 5*, pp. 25–36.

Sandler, J., 1976. Countertransference and role-responsiveness. *International Review of Psychoanalysis, 3*, pp. 43–47.

Schafer, R., 1968. The mechanisms of defense. *The International Journal of Psychoanalysis, 49*, pp. 49–62.

Schore, A.N., 2007. Review of the dreamer: Clinical journeys by Philip M. Bromberg. *Psychoanalytic Dialogues, 17*, pp. 753–767.

Smith, A., 2007. *The theory of moral sentiments.* In: Haakonssen, K., ed. Cambridge: Cambridge University Press.

Sugden, R.D., 2002. Beyond sympathy and empathy: Adam Smith's concept of fellow-feelings. *Economics and Philosophy, 18*, pp. 63–87.

Sullivan, H.S., 1953. *The interpersonal theory of psychiatry.* New York: W.W. Norton.

Vaillant, G.E., 1982. The historical origins and future of Sigmund Freud's concept of the mechanisms of defense. *International Review of Psycho-Analysis, 19*, pp. 35–50.

———, 2002. *Aging well.* Boston: Little, Brown and Co.

Winnicott, D.W., 1965. *The maturation process and the facilitating environment: Studies in the theory of emotional development.* London: Hogarth.

———, 1967. Mirror-role of the mother and family in child development. In: *Playing and reality.* New York: Basic Books. pp. 111–118.

Chapter 7

Defenses and morality

Adam Smith, Sigmund Freud and contemporary psychoanalysis

I. Introduction

In this chapter, we analyze the development of a through line from the work of Adam Smith (1759) in his TMS on the impartial spectator and morality, through Sigmund Freud's work on the internalization of morality through the superego. This research revealed that defenses are an integral part of the acquisition and implementation of a moral system. We then continue this analysis by following the development of morality in contemporary psychoanalysis and the implications of this progression.

This examination brought to light the significant differences between open and closed systems of defenses (Novick and Novick, 2013). In particular, we argue that Smith's system of morality and defenses was a closed system. By a closed system we mean a system that "avoids reality and is characterized by power dynamics, sadomasochism, omnipotent defenses, and stasis" (Novick and Novick, 2013, p. 191). The opposite of the closed system is an open one, "attuned to reality and characterized by joy, love, competence and creativity. Adaptive self-regulation and self-protection stem from these factors" (Novick and Novick, 2013, p. 191). We continue this argument by showing that Freud makes significant progress towards an open system relative to Smith, and it is fully accounted for in the two-person system of contemporary psychoanalysis.

A premise that is essential to any discussion of the imposition of morality is that defenses are an integral part in the internalization of a moral structure, and one's conscious relationship to those defenses ultimately plays a very important role in one's continuing moral and individual development, as we argued in Chapter 6. Indeed, that relationship seems to determine whether or not moral development can occur at all.

We argue that that Smith's work in the mid-18th century was a predecessor to Freud's work in the early 20th century. Their work in remarkably different ways shows that both Smith and Freud relied on defenses to develop their moral structures. We discuss the similarities and differences between Smith's and

Freud's approaches. We then take account of how the move from a one-person perspective to a two-person perspective on defenses and moral development has been articulated in the more contemporary psychoanalytic literature. We include a discussion of the evolving attitudes towards defenses in psychoanalytic theory, the strides that have been made in humanizing the more sadistic qualities of the defenses (Freud, 1923) and of the superego's role in the implementation of morality (Barnett, 2007). In particular these issues are highlighted by the differences between more "open" and "closed" (Novick and Novick, 2013) defense systems.

The remainder of this chapter is organized as follows. In the second section we discuss Freud's concept of superego. In the third section a comparison of the impartial spectator and the superego is provided. In the fourth section, we provide an overview of defenses in Smith's TMS and in Freud's works. Section V contains a discussion of superego, morality and defenses in contemporary psychoanalysis. The final section is a discussion.

II. Freud's superego concept and morality

Morality and the impartial spectator in the TMS were discussed in Chapter 4. Before we turn to a comparison between the concepts of the impartial spectator and the superego, we will present the most salient aspects of Freud's superego and its development that are relevant for our undertaking. We remind the reader that Freud was familiar with Adam Smith's work, as he indicated in a letter he wrote to Silberstein in August of 1879; he states, "I have some marvelous books to read . . . a great philosopher . . . Adam Smith's fundamental book on the wealth of nations . . ." (p. 174).

Freud's (1923) term superego was first used in "The Ego and the Id", and came out of his sometimes-confusing conceptualizations on the topic in his earlier writings. The superego, according to the structural theory, has three interrelated functions: self-observation, the ego ideal and conscience. Let us, however, first start with the development of his ideas on these themes, briefly summarizing the articles in a chronological order.

In *Totem and Taboo*, Freud (1913) discusses morality that is imposed by society. For example, he described the horror of incest. He also states that religion and morality find their genesis with the Oedipus complex. In this early description, morality is ascribed to social forces that can be learned, and not from internal developmental processes.

In "On Narcissism: An Introduction", Freud (1914) introduces the concept of "ego ideal" and the self-observing agency related to it. In this depiction he describes a mental agency that critically observes the mind by standing separate from it. He further endows this agency with the ability to both stand separately and hold the ideals and standards set by the parents. This is his earliest mention of an internal observing moral agency that forms the basis of what was ultimately described as the superego.

In "Mourning and Melancholia", Freud (1917) goes on to expand his conceptualization of this critical agency, stating that:

> one part of the ego sets itself over against the other, judges it critically, and as it were, takes it as its object. . . . What we are here becoming acquainted with is the agency commonly called 'conscience'; we shall count it, along with the censorship of consciousness and reality-testing, among the major institutions of the ego.
>
> (p. 247)

Freud (1921, pp. 109–110) further expands and elaborates this line of thought in *Group Psychology and the Analysis of the Ego*, where he speaks of ego being divided into two parts. He states that one part comprises the "ego-ideal" or the "self-observation" of the "moral conscience", which takes up a critical attitude towards the second part, which is the ego.

These writings lead up to what is ultimately the use of the term "superego" in his work "The Ego and the Id" (Freud, 1923). There he refers to the superego by stating that it "may be called the 'ego ideal' or 'super-ego'" (p. 28). This articulates that the Oedipus complex has a special significance in the formation of the superego. It was in this work that his well-known expression was first used: "The ego ideal is therefore the heir of the Oedipus complex" (p. 36). In this article he sees that behind the ego ideal lies an individual's idealized first identification with the father, "his identification with the father in his own personal prehistory" (p. 31).

In reviewing this sequence of development, Freud (1923) indicates that he considers the origin of the superego to be based on biological as well as historical factors. Specifically, he cites the "lengthy duration in man of his childhood helplessness and dependence . . . and the diphasic onset of man's sexual life" (p. 35) as being major contributing factors in the strong establishment of the superego within the personality. He views conflicts between the ego and the ideal ultimately as being due to the contrast between the internal and external world. He then elaborates:

> The tension between the demands of conscience and the actual performances of the ego is experienced as a sense of guilt. Social feelings rest on identifications with other people, on the basis of having the same ego ideal.
>
> (Freud, 1923, p. 37)

In "Inhibitions, Symptoms and Anxiety", Freud (1926) defines inhibition as a restriction, or a loss of an ego function. The inhibiting agency is either the superego or the ego. He states that the loss of the superego's love threatens the ego, which may result in a sense of guilt and consequent self-punishment. He says ego can be distinguished from superego when there is a tension between them.

Some reflections on the nature of culture are introduced in "The Future of an Illusion" (Freud, 1927). He gives an account of what he later refers to as "the cultural superego". According to him, development of civilization and human survival depend upon the abandonment of primitive instinctual wishes such as incest and cannibalism. In his description, the cultural superego helps enforce the rules of civilized behavior as well as being a coercive agency.

Freud (1930) discusses the superego at some length in *Civilization and its Discontents*. The main theme here is "the irremediable antagonism" between the restrictions imposed upon "civilized" man and instinctual demands. He attributes a positive role to guilt in the growth of civilization. He also suggests that when the external authority is internalized, we can speak of conscience and a conscious sense of guilt.

He sees that the sense of guilt is produced by civilization. It is the most important problem of development. Humanity pays a price for the increased sense of guilt upon which the advance of civilization and increased consciousness depend. He clarifies the concepts of conscience and guilt by stating that the superego is a critical agency and the conscience is a function of that agency. Freud also considers the role of superego on the cultural development of a community. The cultural superego makes strict demands on the individual. If these demands are disobeyed it sets off a fear of conscience. An important demand here is ethics, which concerns the relationships among people.

Here Freud (1930) elaborates by arguing that a person's instinctual aggressiveness is interjected, internalized and directed towards his or her own ego.

> There it is taken over by a portion of the ego, which sets itself over against the rest of the ego as superego, and which now, in the form of 'conscience', is ready to put into action against the ego the same harsh aggressiveness that the ego would have liked to satisfy upon other, extraneous individuals.
>
> (p. 123)

Indeed, in the *New Introductory Lectures*, Freud (1933) distinguishes a special agency in the ego he calls "conscience", and he suggests that this agency should be kept independent. He continues:

> to suppose that conscience is one its functions and that self-observation, which is an essential preliminary to the judging activity of conscience, is another of them. And since when we recognize that something has a separate existence we give it a name of its own, from this time forward I will describe this agency in the ego as 'super-ego'.
>
> (p. 60)

He also distinguishes the superego from ego ideal. The former is the "vehicle" of the ideal that the ego measures itself against to strive towards perfection. Superego therefore is the enforcement agency.

Freud (1933) turns to "the higher side of human life" (p. 67). He notes that the superego is the source of all moral restrictions, striving for perfection. Parents and other authorities are crucial in its formation. He also notes that the superego helps in understanding social behavior, in that past values and traditions live on as the superego's moral contents or "ideologies".

In "An Outline of Psycho-analysis", Freud (1938) further emphasizes that the long period of childhood and dependence on parents leads to prolonged parental influence on both the moral content and its enforcement. He once again calls the special agency that results from such a prolonged period of parental influence the superego. He continues to emphasize that those who substitute for parents, such as teachers and models in public life of admired social figures, become important in both moral content and the development of the superego as the enforcing agent.

III. A comparison of the impartial spectator and the superego

Adam Smith did not develop a psychological theory of the depth of Freud's work on the unconscious, nor explicate the sexual drive. He also did not have the advantage of years of clinical observation to understand the many implications that come from the internalization of parental, cultural and larger collective influences, or the implications of transference and projection that can be intertwined with superego processes. That being said, several authors have pointed out certain foundational similarities between their two positions. We will review a few of these comparisons made by others and then draw some specific comparisons and contrasts of our own between these two seminal thinkers.

Raphael (2007) states that Smith's theory, particularly as it relates to the impartial spectator, bears a resemblance to Freud's account of the superego. He comments:

> This is similar to Smith's view in taking conscience to be a second self built up in the mind as a reflection of the attitudes of outside persons.
>
> (p. 48)

The similarity of the two views is also highlighted in Brissenden (1969), who points out that even though Adam Smith did not have a concept of the unconscious or the primacy of the sexual drive, the sense of self in Smith evolves out of the

> dynamic relationship between the instinctual drives of the individual and the moral attitudes of the society in which he finds himself, even though he sees this as a consciously directed process, as a process of learning the habit of 'self-command'.
>
> (p. 949)

As such, Brissenden indicates, Adam Smith anticipates Freud. Brissenden also sees the dynamic account of the impartial spectator that becomes incorporated in the agent's developing personality as the basis for "the man within the breast", as Smith refers to it.

> This dynamic account of the origins of social conscience has a great deal in common with Freud's notion of the development of super-ego.
>
> (p. 950)

Another similarity between Smith and Freud is that Smith had an awareness of guilt, "and this awareness of guilt is related, to use the Freudian terminology, to 'the tension between the demands of conscience and the actual performances of the ego'" (Brissenden, 1969, p. 951). Brissenden (1969) also notes:

> Freud sees in the formation of the super-ego and an explanation of why moral attitudes customarily carry a religious sanction: of why man finds it necessary to invent a God to believe in. Adam Smith sees both an explanation of the origins of religious belief and a justification of its validity. In fact he argues that it is because the general rules of morality have a demonstrable influence and authority 'that they are justly regarded as the Laws of the Deity'.
>
> (p. 950)

For Smith, moral laws are derived inductively from experience, and represent the will of the Deity and we are obliged to obey them. We provide a description of the role of the Deity in Smith's system in the appendix of this chapter.

Smith and Freud each evolved their own perspectives about the nature of human interactions. There were some fundamental similarities that would allow us to consider that Smith's work on the impartial spectator was a precursor to Freud's development of the superego. It can be argued that while they held different perspectives, they are in basic agreement about the phenomenological contents that went into their respective conceptualizations.

For instance, in the TMS Smith saw the impartial spectator as the arbitrator of cultural norms, which are taught within the family, and recognized that these values ultimately become internalized in the individual. Freud (1923) cited similar contents of culture that are translated through the family as the basis of the superego. Further, they both emphasized the civilizing role of the culture that comes through others in the broader culture, which has the potential to transform the otherwise adverse individual into one of its proponents. However, they would not agree on the origin of these cultural norms. As noted by Brissenden (1969), Smith sees the origin of these values as coming from God; we are his "vice-regents" and it as our moral duty to convey his will. Freud, on the other hand, took a much more pragmatic view of this matter, in that he saw cultural values and norms as a practical agreement that evolved through the development of civilization to keep us from doing great harm to one another. That being said, Smith and Freud had some common agreement about the sometimes overwhelming power of these internalized cultural and familial forces within people's lives. Freud recognized the tremendous influence that the internalization of superego values had on an individual, and how this force exerted an overpowering power within one's life, but did not see this as the command of a God.

Smith proposed in the TMS a well-articulated understanding of human instinctual forces and their influence on human behavior. Smith's understanding of the instincts is nowhere near the scope and elegance that Freud elaborately articulated over his many volumes, based on his understanding of the unconscious dynamics of instinctual forces within the personality; however, at its base, both men agreed on their foundational importance. Further, both Smith and Freud recognized that the instincts were the basis of human action. Finally, they would have generally agreed that having any kind of a moral structure was a significant accomplishment in the face of instinctual drives, and because of the potential destructive quality of raw instinctual drives, such a moral structure was very important.

A major difference between Freud and Smith is that Smith did not have the benefit of Freud's more secular and pragmatic view of the human condition. This led Freud to voice a more accepting and compassionate attitude towards the human struggle. He recognized that civilization had evolved consensual moral structures that were pragmatically necessary for social order, and that these structures, which he came to conceptualize as the contents of the superego, were in conflict with the fundamental instinctual drives. He therefore had compassion for the struggle between moral demands and instincts because he recognized that no one was going to be in complete harmony with them. Freud's more compassionate attitude makes room for an open understanding and acceptance of the need for defenses to deal with the guilt that people experience in falling short of superego demands. For instance, the need to rationalize one's inability to live up to an ideal under difficult life circumstances is essential in the face of difficult if not impossible human struggles. On the other hand, Smith, because he believed that the dictates of the impartial spectator were ultimately the will of God, was left with what can be termed a more traditional religious struggle, in that if one were not to follow the moral prescriptions of the impartial spectator, this was analogous to disobeying God. Aside from his writings about mutual sympathy, compassion for moral shortcomings in the face of the Deity is conspicuously absent from Smith's work. This can be extremely onerous for the subject of such guilt. Various religious structures have different ways of dealing with such shortcomings; however, these are not a part of Smith's conceptualization.

A second related and significant difference between Smith and Freud is that Smith did not have the benefit of Freud's elaborate understanding of the unconscious. This difference makes itself clear in the application of moral structure to a person's life. Smith saw the application of moral behavior as an act of "self-command" – you are either doing it properly or you are not. Moreover, as mentioned earlier, the failure of self-command at a moral level was tantamount to disobeying a moral structure with the authority of a God. Freud, on the other hand, because of his understanding that moral structure was being imposed through the agency of the superego on one's instinctual nature, recognized that defenses would be necessary to justify the need for morality to our consciousness or ego, as well as defenses that would allow us to rationalize and justify our inability to live up to those moral/superego demands. Indeed, Freud's conscious inclusion of defenses makes for a different attitude towards one's limitations in coming to terms with superego demands. Rather than seeing our limitations as failures in the face of some absolute authority, Freud saw the need for compassion, due to the fact that we struggle to come to terms with the ideals that are included in the superego. No doubt Freud's practical work with patients led to his deep respect for the power of the superego within the individual, and the need to "soften" its more "sadistic" impact (Freud, 1923).

IV. Defenses in Smith's the TMS and in Freud

Smith

In this section we give some examples and discuss the defensive attitudes that are essential to develop the moral structure integral to Smith's system, which we described in detail in Chapter 6.

Smith clearly acknowledged human emotions and their power to influence behavior. He went on to judge the "bodily passions", such as sex and hunger, as being beneath one's dignity when it came to expression. He saw "self-command" as the skill that a person needed to develop to come to terms with these "passions". Although he does not name it as such, Smith, through the use of "self-command", advocates for the repression of instinctual desire. He makes the point in several areas that "self-command" is threatened by unbridled passion, and often backs this up by pointing out that the non-expression of these passions is pleasing to the impartial spectator "in almost every occasion". Smith uses moralization and compartmentalization to rationalize the morality that he advocates.

Smith uses splitting as a defense maneuver when he talks about our senses not being informed when "our brother is on the rack". Sympathy is presented as an intellectual analysis of the situation, since the emotional experience is split off. Smith rationalizes the repression of emotions as being very important to preserve social order. He explains that in order to gain the sympathy of the impartial spectator, the actor has to bring his or her emotions down to a level that the impartial spectator can go along with. There is a bias of reason over emotion, which is accomplished by the splitting of thought or reason from affect, and the repression of affect.

Smith's moral system has a hierarchy of values for which reward and punishment are deemed appropriate and rationalized. Smith affirms that we are prompted to punish when we feel resentment and prompted to reward when we feel gratitude. We are instrumental in rewarding and punishing. Consensual morality then gets practiced in the dominant culture and is reinforced by the active use of merit and demerit or rewards and punishments.

His system has a linear and rational standpoint and is achieved by the use of a complex series of rationalizations. These rationalizations are supported by deference to the wishes of the Deity. In places it appears that Smith has made a grandiose identification with the Deity in order to complete this task. Ultimately, the instincts are subdued, and they are put in the control of his rational morality under the authority of God.

An important part of this moral system is kindness. Smith (1759) declares that "kindness is the parent of kindness" (p. 265) and asserts that Nature has formed men for mutual kindness. This virtue comes from a universal benevolence that knows no bounds and is interwoven with a Divine Creator.

> The idea of that divine Being whose benevolence and wisdom have from all eternity contrived and conducted the immense machine of the universe so as at all times to produce the greatest possible quality of happiness is certainly of all the objects of human contemplation by far the most sublime.
>
> (p. 278)

This perfectionistic ideal in Smith's hierarchy is supported by his reference to the Deity. It is a fundamental defensive position in his moral structure.

Virtue is skillfully and intellectually incorporated into his system. Smith moralizes the hierarchy of virtuous acts and then rationalizes the hierarchy by his appeal to the Deity. For example, kindness is a valued expression of feeling and emotion, while anger and pain are not. Also, "self-command" is an important structural component of virtue. As used by Smith, it dictates the most obsessive compartmentalizing of human interactions and impulse. As a result of this view, spontaneous and intuitive human actions are also put in a devalued position. In addition, individual feeling states are devalued in favor of consensually approved attitudes and actions.

In viewing Smith's theory from the viewpoint of the work of Kohlberg (1976) on moral development, we note that Smith's conceptual organization of moral development does not include levels of understanding that incorporate a larger conceptual frame of the social order, and does not include moving on to a more autonomous or principled moral behavior involving a "social-contract and universal-ethical principles" (Kohlberg and Hersh, 1977, p. 55). These levels of moral development involve a greater awareness of larger and more relative levels of social interaction. Smith's conceptualization of moral development seems to fall within Kohlberg's conventional level of moral development, at stage three, where "good behavior is that which pleases or helps others and is approved by them" (Kohlberg and Hersh, 1977, p. 55). Smith's moral structure would not include the kind of self-reflection that would allow for the acknowledgment of personal shortcomings and the recognition of the defensive attitudes that would allow for self-acceptance.

Given that Smith's moral development does not include reflection upon defensive adaptive behavior (which is described in Chapter 6), this leads us to consider what level of defensiveness is generally operating in his system. While we have included numerous defensive positions used by Smith in the TMS, it is clear that his general system of morality is governed by the "approbation" of the impartial spectator. This general attitude falls into what Cramer (2006) refers to as the primary defense of denial. This particular way of using denial involves the construction of a personal fantasy, or in this case an idealized structure that is put in place of reality: "The individual's involvement in this fantasy rivals the perception of reality and replaces it in significant portions of her experience. These fantasies may also be imposed on reality with an insistence that other people agree with the fantasy and ignore reality" (Cramer, 2006, p. 45).

The examples of defenses provided here are necessary to show how Smith built his moral structure. This defensive system necessarily excludes certain life experience and eliminates certain aspects of human involvement. Individual uniqueness and its development seem to fall outside of his moral structure. Smith's defense system is a "closed" defense system, instead of an "open" defense system (using Novick and Novick's [2013] terminology). This is a significant distinction. Smith constructs an elaborate moral structure that relies on the consent of the "impartial spectator"; however, it is closed to examining the defenses that would allow for individual and unique experience. It necessarily eliminates realities that fall outside of its structure and confines the individual to a limited scope within that structure. Novick and Novick state the contrast well:

> One system, the open system, is attuned to reality and characterized by joy, love, competence and creativity. Adaptive self-regulation and self-protection stem from these factors. The other, the closed system, avoids reality and is characterized by power dynamics, sadomasochism, omnipotent defenses and stasis.
>
> (p. 191)

Smith's intended goal might not have been a closed system as described by Novick and Novick (2013), but lacking a mechanism to examine its defensive structure, this is the unintended consequence.

Freud's use of defenses in superego development

In contrast to Smith, Freud talks openly about defenses and their integral role in superego development. In that respect, his awareness of the need for defensiveness puts him at a distinct advantage in relation to Smith. In particular, Freud is able to discuss the implications and the dynamics of defensive processes and how bringing these contents to consciousness mediates their negative effect and at least liberates the individual from carrying the defensive conflict unconsciously.

In his landmark article, "The Ego and the Id", Freud (1923) lays out the foundation of his understanding of the three-part system of personality, which now includes the superego. With the introduction of the superego, which in this chapter is also referred to as the ego ideal, Freud talks about the mechanisms that are necessary for its development to take place. He starts out by discussing early object-cathexes (investments of energy) and their resolution. As the significant objects within a child are let go of as objects for direct cathexis, an internalization of their representations occurs within the child and leaves a trace upon the child's character. In particular, Freud (1923) refers to at least three specific defenses that are necessary for the development of the superego. First, for the child to let go of his primary object cathexis requires an "abandonment of sexual aims, a desexualization – a kind of sublimation therefore" (p. 30). Second, as the nascent superego develops and encounters the oedipal conflict, the boy gives up his primary focus upon the mother in favor of identification with the father and identification with the masculine. Third, from this point Freud describes the necessity to repress the oedipal struggle in order to move on with his development. This repression is further consolidated with a reaction formation towards both of his previous oedipal desires: first, renouncing the desire for the mother, and then renouncing the murderous fantasies towards the father.

The foundational understanding for Freud in relation to the superego is that the "ego-ideal [superego] is the heir to the Oedipus complex" (Freud, 1923, p. 48). All of Freud's writing about the superego presumes the oedipal struggle has been achieved. This allows for individuals to make a strong attachment to the primary parents, and to experience the ambivalence of love and hate that manifests in relation to them as primary objects.

Freud (1923) often points to the fundamental struggle between primary drives and the need for repression. The primary drives are for sexual and sexually derived pleasures on the one hand, and the need for repression in the face of the parental prohibitions against sexual and aggressive acting out on the other. One of the by-products of this struggle is guilt. Guilt is the conscious experience of the struggle between primary needs and repression, that is, the love for the father and the desire to kill him. Guilt is the result of that ambivalence and resultant conflict. Freud also spoke of the ongoing need for sublimation to redirect instinctual desires into work, art or other creative compromise.

Both Freud (1923) and, later, Strachey (1934) discuss the need to "soften" or mediate the superego's overwhelming effect on the ego, which unchecked brings about the formation of unconscious defensive positions. The basic understanding that both brought to light is that these superego contents are usually primitive, and are often poorly adapted to reality due to the fact that they were initially adopted in an unreflective way. The psychoanalytic process works to slowly bring these contents and their resistances/defenses to consciousness, mediated by the analyst, "softening" the superego's capacity to further catalyze unconscious conflicts.

There have been substantial advances in our knowledge in relation to both superego processes and the interconnecting defenses that are a part of superego processes since the time of Freud. We briefly outline the through line that has continued from the early work of Smith to Freud and through more contemporary writers, while keeping an eye on the fundamental forms that were pioneered by these two important theorists. In addition, we also look at the understanding that was endemic in Freud's work: that psychoanalysis provides the potential for greater consciousness of one's superego and defensive structure and takes one's defensive attitude from a more "closed" system to a more "open" system (Novick and Novick, 2013). In other words, as an individual moves from a more "closed" system, or personal attitude, the more compassionate and flexible he or she becomes in relation to life's functioning. In this way psychoanalysis, starting with Freud and moving through more contemporary views, has sponsored the potential evolution of moral/superego development beyond more "conventional" levels of moral development (Kohlberg and Hersh, 1977). The more open attitude towards defenses sponsored by psychoanalysis and its development have allowed the potential for what Kohlberg (Kohlberg and Hersh, 1977) referred to as "Postconventional, Autonomous, or Principled" (p. 55) levels of moral development. These levels allow for conscience to be based on both social/contractual wellbeing as well as on the ability to reflect upon universal human values and their application of "justice, of the reciprocity and equality of human rights, and the respect for the dignity of human beings as individual persons" (Kohlberg and Hersh, 1977, p. 55). This more open defensive attitude allows an individual to incorporate new experiences and structures throughout the lifespan.

V. Superego, morality and defenses in contemporary psychoanalysis

Superego and morality

The ongoing development of theory within psychoanalysis has also continued the expansion of more comprehensive understandings of the superego as a vehicle for morality. We review some of the historic trends that have advanced the understanding of superego development and its role in transmitting morality.

Anna Freud (1936) commented on superego development by following up on her father's work, and like him postulates that superego formation is only possible after the resolution of the Oedipus complex. She also brought new light to the repression/resistance work of her father relative to superego conflicts. Her ground-breaking work (Freud, 1936) was pivotal in shaping the modern view towards defenses as integral and important to personality, and not just resistances, as we elaborated on in Chapter 6. This chapter elaborates on that position, pointing out that defenses are necessary for a person to come to terms with the superego's implementation of a moral structure.

Psychoanalytic thought from the time of Anna Freud moved towards object relations, which emphasized the "human relationship", the psychological importance of the "self" and the desire for the "self" to make contact with the "other" (Barnett, 2007). This perspective sees the development of the self as coming about through interaction with another, in contrast to the classical view that the object (other) is simply the aim of a biological drive. The emphasis here is on the relationship between the ego and its internalized objects, though classical concepts such as conflict and anxiety were still retained. Melanie Klein (1930; 1933) focuses on an internal world of objects and unconscious phantasy. She concludes that a primitive form of superego was present in the first year of life, which consisted of part objects, suggesting that the Oedipus complex had early roots.

In the post-Kleinian tradition, Wilfred Bion (2000) was particularly interested in the "moral impulse". Bion took the initial discussions by Freud and, later, Klein and extended them, suggesting that the moral impulse is extremely primitive. He aims to show that this early morality could become perverted and employed against the self. He links the extremely primitive nature of the early superego with severe pathology. He thought it is important to distinguish this primitive superego from more sophisticated, more developed and rational systems of morality. Bion's work offers that these primitive object relations, which are part of an equally primitive superego function, can only be mediated as a result of a long and careful analysis of these contents, slowly rendering them to consciousness and to the potential for a more rational and humane morality.

Ronald Fairbairn developed a comprehensive object relations theory independent of drives, in which he argued that the infant is object seeking rather than pleasure seeking. He was critical of the classical theory with regard to superego and the Oedipus complex, yet he developed the terms internal saboteur and, later, moral defense. In his theory of endo-psychic structure, he focuses on what he refers to as "the internal saboteur". Even though it largely corresponds to the superego, in function it is an ego structure, not an internal object, it is also a compound of the superego and its associated "object". However, Fairbairn retains the superego concept to account for the internal saboteur and a sense of guilt. In Fairbairn's approach, the ego ideal establishes the basis of moral values in the inner world. He wrote, "The superego is built in layers corresponding to stages in Oedipal development. It also revealed that the nucleus of superego is pregenital in origin, [and] belongs to an oral level" (Fairbairn, 1931, p. 221). Fairbairn's understanding lends support to the contention that the less conscious and integrated the moral system, the more it acts as a defense system in and of itself. Conversely, the more conscious the moral system, the less it resembles a defense system and the more it represents a moral structure that is a function of the ego.

Winnicott's concept of superego drew from Freud, Anna Freud, and Melanie Klein, and it was also strikingly different. In his seminal writing "The Innate Morality of the Baby" (Winnicott, 1964, pp. 106–107), he articulates an internalization of superego development that appears more comprehensive and attuned to subtleties. He goes beyond the simple notion that we learn our moral structure from our family, and articulates the integration of moral capacity from pre-oedipal development on through the oedipal struggle. Similar to Bion, Winnicott sees morality as innate. He expresses that this understanding is crucial for those whose role it is to facilitate the emergence of a human being. As the child experiences guilt, there is a growing capacity to feel a sense of responsibility.

Winnicott (1965, pp. 73–82) later uses the concept of "concern" in place of "guilt". In the child's mind there are two aspects of the mother: the mother as the person who wards off the unpredictable and the mother as object that satisfies the infant's urgent needs. When the object mother and the environment mother come together in the infant's mind, concern develops. Winnicott describes the development of a mature healthy superego as a gradual process, along with the development of capacity for concern. In a healthy development process, the infant introjects a pre-oedipal, maternal superego that is connected to the capacity for concern. The infant's ego employs certain controlling forces in the development of guilt. Winnicott calls this superego. He puts an emphasis on the social context in regard to the development of true morality.

Barnett (2007) fundamentally argues that the superego remains a valuable concept. It provides insight and understanding in the promotion of civilized values and morality. The superego, according to Barnett, is closely related to the morality of the society in which an individual lives. He bases these conclusions on a paper by Rickman (1951), who asserts that moral function is a combination of social and biological functions. The infant has a great need for a stabilizer, and an important component of this is the protective and moral function. Moral function can be understood as an external source and an individual's adaptation of his or her biological endowment to the cultural environment. Rickman contends:

> The growth of moral function [is] the change from dogmatism to exploration and choice; from sudden, all or none explosive responses in situations involving moral choice in graduated controlled responses; from reflex or reactive actions to consideration; from automatism to love.
>
> (2007 cited in Barnett, p. 152)

In "Why It Is Good to Be Good", Riker (2011) describes the grounds for moral life based on Kohutian concepts. According to Riker, an individual is good when he or she is characterized by moral virtues, concern for the welfare of others and a willingness to be just and fair towards other human beings. The self-psychological explanation of morality is based on integrity, the need to engage in empathetic reciprocity, the need to develop moral virtues and a need to expand ideals into ethical universals. It is by acknowledging its dependence and vulnerability that the self becomes ethical, not because it identifies itself with universal values. It is crucial for the development of self that we surround ourselves with people who can perform self-object functions throughout life. Self-object reciprocity requires that someone is willing to empathically care for others as he or she expects them to do so towards him or her. Furthermore, Riker argues, more "aliveness" of the soul is dependent upon one's character and empathetic disposition in all situations. The person then is not dependent upon circumstances to determine who he or she is.

LaFollette (1995) argues that morality and personal relationships are supportive in two ways: (1) Close personal relationships give us the knowledge and the motivation to develop impartial moral habits, and (2) intimacy flourishes in an environment that impartially recognizes the needs and interests of all. Close personal relationships are grist for the moral mill, and they empower us to act morally. We learn to identify with the interests of others through interacting with them. If we develop empathy towards our friends, we will be likely to generalize it to others. We learn to respond to the interests of acquaintances and even strangers since empathy is nonspecific.

Honneth (1995) also argues that morality develops through interacting with others. More specifically, mutual recognition is necessary for the reproduction of social life. Emotional concern that comes from familiar relationships of love and friendship, approval that is associated with solidarity and legal recognition are three distinct forms of recognition. In this way, morality grows out of these interactions in which we have recognition and mutual regard.

As can be seen, these practitioners and theorists allow their subjects a greater sense of agency than Smith might have ever imagined. Indeed, as we move from Smith to Freud, there is a greater openness that comes as a result of the conscious inclusion of defensive processes in the internalization of moral structure. As the work has continued to develop in psychoanalytic thought, it has greatly expanded the conceptual framework of both Smith and Freud, who saw the need for morality based on the necessity to mediate the instincts. The more contemporary views on development have expanded to include a greater degree of ego autonomy, a greater influence of object relations and the expansion of a self that allows for a greater degree of human capacity and flexibility than Smith or perhaps even Freud might have imagined.

Defenses in contemporary psychoanalysis

Early theorizing about defenses emphasized the "intrapsychic" mechanisms of the individual on managing conflict, and were initially conceptualized as resistances. The understanding of the importance and necessity of defenses have evolved significantly from this original position.

As mentioned in the previous section, Anna Freud's (1936) work was truly ground-breaking in that she was the first to articulate the necessity for defenses and saw them as integral to human development and character. Her work served to take defenses out of the previously exclusive realm of resistances. As we described in Chapter 6, resistances were viewed as something negative that needed to be overcome in analysis because they held back development. Anna Freud reconceptualized them as being important to development.

Even though the following three paragraphs are contained in Chapter 6, we reiterate them here as a reminder to the reader. Brenner (1982) pointed out that anything could be regarded as defensive when it functions to reduce anxiety or to drive tensions away. Hartmann, Kris and Loewenstein (1964) viewed defenses as ego functions to cope with external reality and drive demands. Schafer (1968) emphasized that defenses can express undesirable impulses that allow gratification and at the same time underscored that defenses attempt to block the expression of undesirable content.

An important shift in the analysis of defenses has been in viewing defenses as a set of relational and cognitive processes that emphasize the "interpersonal" context in the use of defenses. (See Cooper, 1989, for a review of "two-person" analysis of defenses, and Eagle, 2011, on the shift to contemporary psychoanalysis.) Winnicott (1965), by stating that a baby does not exist without others, viewed defenses as adaptations to traumatic environmental failure, differentiating this from defense organized against expression of impulses. This perspective no longer viewed the individual as a closed system.

Modell (1975) suggested that defenses were organized in situations of empathic failure, leading to falling back on the self and avoidance of expression of needs towards others. Thus he emphasized a "two-person" theory of defense. Kohut (1984) highlighted that defensive structures were attempts to protect an enfeebled self. He pointed out that defenses were often organized against failures of self-objects. His formulations were in line with those of Fairbairn (1952), Winnicott (1965), Guntrip (1969) and Modell (1975), emphasizing that self might need to be protected in its state of vulnerability. He minimized the importance of instinctual drives and process, deviating from Modell. Sandler (1976) asserted that defenses are manifested interpersonally. Kernberg (1975) viewed defensive organization as operating both in object relations contexts and in intrapsychic contexts. Greenberg and Mitchell (1983) and Mitchell (1998) described a reciprocal process in which the patient and the therapist affect one another, using the notion of intersubjectivity. In this view defenses are organized as a part of mutual regulation and influence. Novick and Novick (2001) emphasized that a "two-person" focus on the therapeutic relationship and the forms of interaction between patients and the therapist could be combined with a classical "one-person" focus on the patient's defenses.

Contemporary psychoanalysis has expanded the conceptualization of defense to accommodate the growth and development of theory and practice. As the work has come to make the interpersonal process and the self more the focus of practice, the understanding of the defensive process has been modified. "Defense" has therefore come to include not only the use of defenses to come to terms with needs that arise from primary drives, but also includes the defenses from the affects that arise from interpersonal interactions and primary self-organizations.

VI. Discussion

Smith saw the development and transmission of morality as coming through the family and being a reflection of the community and the culture. Foundationally, he saw that humans were endowed by nature with a desire to do what would be approved of. Smith's structures (virtue, propriety, merit, duty) are applications of his fundamental moral structure and, though not stated on his part, his defense system. In his thoughtful and meticulous way, he masterfully wove together these structures to create a logic-tight system of morality and behavior. A strength of Smith's rational approach is that it is internally consistent, linear, follows logical rules and conceptually accounts for a great deal of behavior and details. He accomplished this by deferring to a majority collective view of human action based on the external need for interaction with others, which is mediated by the "approbation" of others.

Smith recognized that moral structure was being imposed upon human instinctual nature. He did not, however, account for how difficulties in this implementation might be mediated. His rational approach did not have the benefit of understanding the unconscious defenses that are necessarily a part of the imposition of a moral structure upon instinctual life, relying rather on the "approbation" of others that leads to guilt to keep oneself in line. Further, his reliance on "self-command" to carry out the prevailing cultural morality does not make room for individual differences, creativity, change, dynamism and spontaneity because there is no consciousness brought to bear on the defensive structure that an individual needs to employ in order to comply with this structure. One's instinctual and human differences do not seamlessly adapt to such external structures. Without the compassion born out of the acceptance of diversity of human differences, there is no flexibility and acceptance of human circumstance or difference. "It would be hard for Smith to fully account for individuals who 'march to their own drummer' such as: Martin Luther, Martin Luther King, Gandhi, Einstein, and Freud, all of whom were able to go in their own direction, sometimes at great peril and at the risk of great disapprobation by the dominate culture, without seeing them as deviant rather than creative and generative" (Özler and Gabrinetti, 2014, p. 27).

Freud began in the same vein as Smith in that he observed that moral structure was passed on through the family. Similar to Smith, he also saw cultural values and morals coming through the family. Freud also recognized that moral structure was being imposed on instinctual nature; however, because of his clinical experience he had a much more compassionate relationship to human limitations and guilt, and saw the need to "soften" the harsh and sometimes sadistic superego's application of moral demands.

An important by-product of the psychoanalytic process that comes to light in this discussion are the differences between conscious and unconscious defenses. Psychoanalytic theory and technique across all schools of psychoanalysis in each their own way make conscious those defenses that are used to protect us. As Novick and Novick (2013) point out, the difference between "open" and "closed" systems of defense is the difference between being "attuned to reality" and "avoiding reality". In this process of making conscious, we are able to create a certain degree of freedom and flexibility. When an individual has a conscious awareness of a defensive process that may be limiting, he or she is in the position to make a choice, particularly if the defense is no longer necessary to the person's wellbeing. On the other hand, if the defense is still important to an individual's current psychic integrity, psychoanalysis allows for both an understanding of and compassion for its current use. This stands in marked contrast to a more closed system, such as that represented by Smith or any other system that seeks to implement a moral code without consciously considering the human struggle that it engenders.

The attitude towards the superego went through significant evolution with the work of Anna Freud (1936). Her contributions to the understanding of the defenses specifically allowed for a more sympathetic view. Her work broadened and operationalized Freud's original formulations and attitudes with regard to defenses. This effort emphasized the positive use of defenses and took defense out of the exclusive realm of resistances. This attitude has been integrated into the general fabric of psychoanalytic theory and has made a significant contribution to a more empathetic and greatly expanded view of defenses and the acceptance of human limitation. More recently, the work of Cooper (1989) looked at more contemporary views of defense and pointed out their utility within a variety of psychoanalytic theorists. Germaine to the current discussion, he illustrated the adaptive use of defenses across theories, regardless of what is being defended against within the various theoretical perspectives.

This larger view of the human process and condition has evolved from a more fixed attitude towards human limitation and morality, as represented in Smith's ground-breaking work. The work has evolved through Freud's recognitions and the explication of the superego to incorporate a greater empathy towards human limitation. This attitude has continued to develop in current psychoanalytic theory and allows for a level of creativity, spontaneity and imagination that more accurately reflects the infinite adaptability of the human condition.

An earlier version of this chapter was published by Gabrinetti and Ozler: "Defenses and morality: Adam Smith, Sigmund Freud and Contemporary Psychoanalysis", *The Psychoanalytic Review*, *101*(5), pp. 735–765, October 2014.

References

Barnett, B., 2007. *"You ought to!": A psychoanalytic study of the superego and conscience.* London: Karnac.

Bion, W.R., 2000. *Clinical seminars and other works.* London: Karnac.

Brenner, C., 1982. *The mind in conflict.* New York: International Universities Press.

Brissenden, R.F., 1969. Authority, guilt and anxiety in the *Theory of Moral Sentiments. Texas Studies in Literature and Language, 11*, pp. 945–962.

Broadie, A., 2006. Sympathy and the impartial spectator. In: Haakonssen, K., ed. *The Cambridge companion to Adam Smith.* Cambridge: Cambridge University Press. pp. 158–188.

Cooper, S.H., 1989. Recent contributions to the theory of defense mechanisms: A comparative view. *Journal of American Psychoanalytical Association, 37*, pp. 865–891.

Cramer, P., 2006. *Protecting the self: Defense mechanisms in action.* New York: Guilford.

Eagle, M.N., 2011. *From classical to contemporary psychoanalysis: A critique and integration.* New York: Routledge.

Evensky, J., 2005. *Adam Smith's moral philosophy: A historical and contemporary perspective on markets, law, ethics, and culture.* Cambridge: Cambridge University Press.

Fairbairn, W.R., 1931. Features in the analysis of a patient with a physical genital abnormality. *Psychoanalytic Studies of Personality,* pp. 197–222.

———, 1952. *An object relations theory of the personality.* New York: Basic Books.

Freud, A., 1936. The ego and the mechanisms of defence. Translated by C. Barnes. London: Hogarth.

Freud, S., 1913. Totem and taboo. In: Strachey, J., ed. *The standard edition of the complete psychological works of Sigmund Freud.* London: Hogarth Press. Vol. 24, pp. 131–162.

———, 1914. On narcissism: An introduction. In: Strachey, J., ed. *The standard edition of the complete psychological works of Sigmund Freud.* London: Hogarth Press. Vol. 14, pp. 67–102.

———, 1917. Mourning and melancholia. In: Strachey, J., ed. *The standard edition of the complete psychological works of Sigmund Freud.* London: Hogarth Press. Vol. 14, pp. 237–258.

———, 1920. Beyond the pleasure principle. In: Strachey, J., ed. *The standard edition of the complete psychological works of Sigmund Freud, Volume 18.* London: Hogarth Press. pp. 1–64.

———, 1921. Group psychology and the analysis of the ego. In: Strachey, J., ed. *The standard edition of the complete psychological works of Sigmund Freud.* London: Hogarth Press. Vol. 18, pp. 65–144.

———, 1923. The ego and the id. In: Strachey, J., ed. *The standard edition of the complete psychological works of Sigmund Freud.* London: Hogarth Press. Vol. 19, pp. 1–66.

———, 1926. Inhibitions, symptoms and anxiety. In: Strachey, J., ed. *The standard edition of the complete psychological works of Sigmund Freud.* London: Hogarth Press. Vol. 20, pp. 75–176.

———, 1927. The future of an illusion. In: Strachey, J., ed. *The standard edition of the complete psychological works of Sigmund Freud.* London: Hogarth Press. Vol. 21, pp. 1–56.

———, 1930. Civilization and its discontents. In: Strachey, J., ed. *The standard edition of the complete psychological works of Sigmund Freud.* London: Hogarth Press. Vol. 21, pp. 57–146.

———, 1933. New introductory lectures on psycho-analysis. In: Strachey, J., ed. *The standard edition of the complete psychological works of Sigmund Freud.* London: Hogarth Press. Vol. 22, pp. 1–182.

———, 1938. An outline of psycho-analysis. In: Strachey, J., ed. *The standard edition of the complete psychological works of Sigmund Freud.* London: Hogarth Press. Vol. 23, pp. 139–208.

———, 1992. Letter from Sigmund Freud to Eduard Silberstein, August 10, 1879. In: Boehlich, W., ed. *The letter of Sigmund Freud to Eduard Silberstein 1871–1881.* Cambridge, MA: Harvard University Press.

Greenberg, J. and Mitchell, S.A., 1983. *Object relations in psychoanalytic theory*. Cambridge, MA: Harvard University Press.

Griswold, Jr., C.L., 1999. *Adam Smith and the virtues of Enlightenment*. New York: Cambridge University Press.

———, 2006. Imagination: Morals, science, and arts. In: Haakonssen, K., ed. *The Cambridge companion to Adam Smith*. New York: Cambridge University Press. pp. 22–56.

Guntrip, H., 1969. *Schizoid phenomena: Object relations and the self*. New York: International Universities Press.

Hartmann, H., Kris, E. and Loewenstein, R., 1964. *Papers on psychoanalytic psychology: Psychological issues*. New York: International Universities Press.

Honneth, A., 1995. *The struggle for recognition: The moral grammar of social conflicts*. London: Polity Press.

Kernberg, O.F., 1975. *Borderline conditions and pathological narcissism*. New York: Aronson.

Klein, M., 1930. The importance of symbol-formation in the development of the ego. *International Journal of Psychoanalysis, 11*, pp. 24–39.

———, 1933. *The early development of conscience in the child*. In: *Love, guilt, and reparation, and other works, 1921–1945*. London: Hogarth, pp. 344–369.

Kohlberg, L., 1976. Moral stages and moralization: The cognitive developmental approach. In: Lickona, T., ed. *Moral development and behavior: Theory, research and social issues*. New York: Holt, Rinehart & Winston. pp. 170–205.

Kohlberg, L. and Hersh, H.R., 1977. Moral development: A review of the theory. *Theory Into Practice, 16*(2), pp. 53–59.

Kohut, H., 1984. *How does psychoanalysis cure?* Chicago: University of Chicago Press.

Lafollette, H., 1995. Morality and personal relationships. In: Lafoletter, H., ed. *Personal relationships: Love, identity, morality*. Oxford: Blackwell. pp. 194–211.

Mitchell, S.A., 1998. The analyst's knowledge and authority. *The Psychoanalytical Quarterly, 67*, pp. 1–31.

Modell, A.H., 1975. A narcissistic defense against affects and the illusion of self-sufficiency. *International Journal of Psychoanalysis, 56*, pp. 275–283.

Novick, J. and Novick, K.K., 2001. Two systems of self-regulation. *Psychoanalytical Social Work, 8*, pp. 95–122.

———, 2013. Two systems of defenses. *Psychoanalytical Social Work, 100*, pp. 185–200.

Özler, S. and Gabrinetti, P.A., 2014. A known world: An analysis of defenses in Adam Smith's *the theory of moral sentiments*. In: Forman-Barzilai, F., ed. *Adam Smith Review*. pp. 256–276.

Raphael, D.D., 2007. *The impartial spectator*. New York: Oxford University Press.

Rickman, J., 1951. The development of moral function. In: King, P., ed. *No ordinary psychoanalyst: The exceptional contributions of John Rickman*. London: Karnac. pp. 314–336.

Riker, J.H., 2011. *Why it is good to be good: Ethics, Kohut's self psychology and modern society*. Lanham, MD: Jason Aronson.

Sagan, E., 1988. *Freud, women, and morality: The psychology of good and evil*. New York: Basic Books.

Sandler, J., 1976. Counter-transference and role-responsiveness. *International Review of Psychoanalysis, 3*, pp. 43–47.

Schafer, R., 1968. The mechanisms of defense. *The International Journal of Psychoanalysis, 49*, pp. 49–62.

Sheppard, A., 2009. Winnicott's concept of innate morality and the development of capacity for concern. *Canadian Journal of Psychoanalysis, 17*, pp. 290–297.

Smith, A., 1759. In: Haakonssen, K., ed. *The theory of moral sentiments*. Cambridge: Cambridge University Press.

Strachey, J., 1934. The nature of the therapeutic action of psychoanalysis. *International Journal Psychoanalysis*, *15*, pp. 127–159.

Sugden, R.D., 2002. Beyond sympathy and empathy: Adam Smith's concept of fellow-feelings. *Economics and Philosophy*, *18*, pp. 63–87.

Summer, F., 2013. *The psychoanalytic vision: The experiencing subject, transcendence and the therapeutic process*. New York: Routledge.

Vaillant, G.E., 1982. The historical origins and future of Sigmund Freud's concept of the mechanisms of defense. *International Review of Psycho-Analysis*, *19*, pp. 35–50.

Westerling, H., 2009. *A dark trace: Sigmund Freud on the sense of guilt*. Leuven, Belgium: Leuven University Press.

Winnicott, D.W., 1964. *The child, the family and the outside world*. London: Routledge.

———, 1965. *The maturation process and the facilitating environment: Studies in the theory of emotional development*. London: Hogarth.

———, 1965. Ego distortions in terms of true and false self. In: Winnicott, D. W., ed. *Maturational processes and facilitating environment*. New York: International Universities Press. pp. 140–152.

Chapter 8

An evolutionary psychological and adaptive defenses view of relations between markets and morality

I. Introduction

As we continue on the explication of morality in Smith's work, we will follow up on the link in his writing between markets and morality. In linking morality to markets, we turn to the literature in evolutionary psychology. We review the developmental processes that are necessary to participate in markets in a moral way. The foundational skills, capacities, defenses and internal mechanisms necessary to participate in the world of markets and its morality are often assumed. Foremost among these skills is delayed gratification, which allows for reflective and abstract thinking, the ability to resist temptation to satisfy immediate needs at the expense of others and to communicate desires and intentions in clear language. Krebs (2011) argues that

> ... mechanisms that give rise to a moral sense evolved to help early humans solve the adaptive problems that constrained their ability to reap the benefits of sociality.

> (p. 3)

Boehm (2008) traced the origin of morality to the adaptive problems created by hierarchal social orders. These adaptive problems that gave rise to morality originated from the competitive inclinations to dominance and the resulting social conflicts. At least within markets, humans introduced moral structures to address such problems.

The ability to delay immediate gratification is a building block of self-control and is correlated with measures of success and social adjustment (Krebs, 2011). Often, a high price is paid when self-control is lacking. Large human brains seem to increase our capacity to cope with primitive urges in socially acceptable ways (Krebs, 2011). Research suggests that people use a number of strategies to delay gratification in favor of long-term goals (Mischel, Cantor and Feldman, 1996). The neural mechanisms underlying control may differ as a function of the stage of processing at which control must be exerted and the type of information being processed. Delayed gratification is considered to be one of the most important components of cognitive control (Eigst et al., 2006).

Most forms of self-control and delayed gratification are described as prudential in Smith's view because urges are controlled to improve one's ability to maximize long-term gains. "To qualify as moral, the purposes that self-control serves and the goals that people use it to achieve must be moral" (Krebs, 2011, p. 87). There are, of course, several aspects of self-control. For example, Mischel, Cantor and Feldman (1996) identified five main correlates of gratification delay: (1) intelligence, (2) ego control, (3) orientation towards the future, (4) achievement of aspiration, and (5) social responsibility. In addition, there is a great deal of variation in people's awareness of their internal standards across situations. High-order cognitive abilities to regulate behavior have been the focus of psychological research on self-control. For example, children become more able to delay gratification and control their impulses as their sophisticated mental mechanisms evolve. From a bio-evolutionary perspective, genetics play an important role. Survival abilities and reproduction increase as humans and animals inherit genes that interact with the need to regulate urges, desires and motivational systems. Self-control varies across individuals. The individual differences can be attributed to the mismatch between mechanisms that evolved in ancestral environments and the demands and opportunities of their environments (Burdham and Phelan, 2000). According to evolutionary accounts, environmental demands play an important role in selecting and activating evolved mechanisms. Since self-control is necessary for most moral virtues, it is foundational to morality.

An important extension of the capacity for delayed gratification and the development of morality is the effect that such capacities and behaviors have on building trust. When we consider the effects/affects that morality has on markets and markets have on morality, probably one of the most important factors that allows markets to thrive is trust. One need not look any further than the daily financial trades and watch the ebb and flow that comes as a result of trust or the lack thereof in the current market.

Adaptive defenses, which were discussed in Chapter 6, describe the means for individuals to adopt morality so that it can be used both personally and interpersonally. Over time, consensually adopted understandings develop into a moral structure that attempts to define the ideal interactions between people, and defenses are the action mechanisms that help to implement morality within the person.

We examine these above-mentioned issues in Smith's work and the groundbreaking breadth and scope of his theoretical position in the TMS. His meticulous and systematic interweaving of social philosophy and economic theory allow us to examine the interactive dynamics in his treatment of markets and morality from the perspective of evolutionary psychology and the adaptive defenses that are necessary for their application.

This chapter is organized as follows. In Section II, evolutionary psychology and adaptive defenses are described. Section III is a presentation of interactions between morality and markets. In Section IV, we put all this together and analyze relationships among markets, morality adaptive defenses and evolutionary psychology. A discussion is presented in Section V.

II. Adaptive defenses and evolutionary psychology

Adaptive defenses were covered in Chapter 6, so here we will only briefly review them for the reader. Moral behavior necessitates that individuals contain their immediate emotional impulses and desires for gratification, and reduce the intensity of the frustration that arises from not immediately gratifying those needs. Adaptive defenses are the mechanisms needed to accommodate the immediate tension and discomfort brought about by exerting the pro-social behaviors necessary to enable civil behavior. Adaptive defenses also facilitate the capacity to assimilate complex sets of behavior that go into moral structure.

The behavior that is necessary to apply Smith's work on morality would not be possible if the human species had not also grown the capacity to do so. When Smith was writing about morality, it was assumed on his part that humans had the ability for "self-command". This is an assumption that is not always true in light of the human shortcomings that make themselves known when it comes to morality.

Evolutionary psychology

Evolutionary psychology provides a perspective on how morality develops in the context of human evolution. Evolutionary psychologist Krebs (2011) views morality as a way of people advancing their interests through cooperative means:

> a set of ideas about how people who live in groups should behave in order to meet their needs and advance their interests in cooperative ways.
>
> (p. 27)

This definition implies that one of the requirements for morality is that people must to some extent resist the temptation to immediately satisfy their own interests at the expense of others. This further suggests that a social structure that fosters the adaptive interests of its members through cooperation is an important function of morality. Moral behavior is about how members of groups ought to behave, which is reinforced by social sanctions. Put another way, Haidt (2008) states that morality mediates unbridled selfishness, which makes social life and cooperative communities possible.

The development of morality from the perspective of evolutionary psychology is accomplished by examining the coevolution of personal/cultural innovations and genetics (Richerson and Boyd, 2005). First we will examine some of the personal/cultural adaptations and then the genetic components that go along with them.

The evolutionary psychology of morality speaks to the pragmatic needs of group living. Krebs (2011) states:

> . . . from the perspective of evolution, the key to understanding morality lies in identifying the adaptive functions that the mental processes that produce moral behaviors, moral norms, moral judgments, moral emotions and moral behavior evolved to serve.
>
> (p. 3)

He goes on to say humans could solve their adaptive problems that limited their ability to benefit from sociality by the evolution of a moral sense.

It follows then that human behavior that increases the cooperative possibilities between people also requires us to be aware of and exercise restraint of purely individual needs. Learning theory (Skinner, 1969) teaches us that such cooperative behavior in individuals must be rewarded within groups or cultures in order for it to continue. In particular, the behavior or set of behaviors that need to evolve within groups or individuals are those which allow for enough delayed gratification for them to reap the self-interested benefits of cultural morality. This necessarily means that structural forms must evolve which teach or otherwise acculturate the individuals within those cultures to reap the benefits of such civilizing processes. Behaving in mutually beneficial ways while resisting the temptation to advance one's own interests at the cost of the welfare of others and the social order of their group morality helps people to maximize their gains from cooperative social relations.

Krebs also discusses the evolution of primitive pro-social behaviors such as deference and self-control. These concepts are also important for morality as described by Smith, as individuals must defer to the impartial spectator's judgments and must show self-control. For example, self-control, such as gratification delay, is correlated with measures of success and social adjustment. Most forms of self-control are described as prudential because urges are controlled to improve one's ability to maximize long-term gains.

From the perspective of genetic evolution, one can infer that those genetic capacities that allow humans to make adaptations to communal living would enable a greater survival into group life than those who did not. Krebs (2011) puts it concisely by stating that early humans who inherited genes that design mechanisms that disposed them to behave in moral ways and endowed them with a sense of morality fared better in the struggle to survive and to reproduce than early humans who did not inherit such genes. At the same time, moral reasoning may be maladaptive even though it helped to serve adaptive purposes.

In addition to assuming that mental mechanisms produce moral behavior through the interaction of genes and the environment, evolutionary psychologists argue that mental mechanisms are products of evolution. Krebs (2011) also argues that from a psychological perspective, self-interest at the expense of others must be balanced with unselfishness as the necessary qualities for morality, and requires a degree of perceived fairness.

Uniquely human pro-social behaviors, such as deference, also have neurological sources. It has been suggested that the expansion of the human brain was largely a result of solving social problems that arose when early humans banded together to foster their mutual interests, which is relevant for the evolution of morality.

> Theories of brain evolution that emphasize the adaptive value to early humans of solving social problems are most relevant to evolution of morality.
>
> (Krebs, 2011, p. 190)

Flagrantly immoral behavior is more likely in people that had acquired prefrontal damage (Mendez, Anderson and Shapira, 2005). There is a biological bias in humans that leads them to behave in ways that reinforce moral codes and sustain cooperative exchanges. Krebs tells us that

> The mental mechanisms that give rise to moral emotions were selected in ancestral environments because they induced early humans to behave in ways that increased their inclusive fitness . . . the emotions experienced by early humans became refined and expanded as their brains evolved and the emotions experienced by human infants became refined and expanded as they develop.
>
> (p. 216)

The content of Smith's work points to ego (adaptive) defenses that are in the service of ego ideals, what Freud (1923) came to term the superego. These superego ideals, we have argued, are synonymous with Smith's moral structure.

III. Markets and morality

It has been often argued that Smith's economic man requires a moral man (see for example, Macfie (1967) and Young (1997)). In this section first we discuss how morality fosters markets, second how markets foster morality and finally how markets may undermine morality.[1]

Morality fosters markets

The argument that morality fosters markets in Smith's work has been documented by Paganelli (2009; 2013) and will be presented in this section. Smith's writings fall into two inter-related categories: morality fosters the market process by providing structure for its participants through the application of moral principles that need some form of justice to enforce them, and conversely, when there is an absence of morality and its structure, the value of such a structure becomes known.

Smith's writings look at how morality fosters markets and emphasizes as a part of that moral structure the need for justice. Smith is also quick to point out the consequences when there is a lack of morality in markets. Smith's contention is that justice is foundational to supporting the moral structure that fosters markets,

> Justice ... is the main pillar that upholds the whole edifice. If it is removed, the great, the immense fabric of human society ... must in a moment crumble to atoms.
>
> (TMS, p. 101)

Without justice, a society is not a human society. Individuals would be "like wild beasts ... and a man would enter an assembly of men as he enters a den of lions" (TMS, p. 102). So, when morality is ignored, the system of justice that commerce alone generates becomes a system of brute justice.

For Smith the basic need that motivates and shapes morally driven behavior is the innate desire for the approbation of others. There are two sources for approbation in Smith's writings that pertain to the issue of morality fostering markets: one is approbation that comes as the result of good moral conduct, and the other comes from a "parade of wealth". The approbation that comes from good moral conduct tends to support and foster markets through the general support that a moral structure maintains for markets to grow within. In the absence of desire for approbation that comes from good moral conduct, and the presence of the desire for approbation from the status associated with wealth, moral structure no longer fosters markets. This is because when possession of wealth dominates, individuals may take great moral risks due to the great admiration of men of fortune. One is more likely to behave in morally questionable ways when the gain in approbation that comes wealth is high (Levy, 1999).

From markets to morality

We have just looked at how virtues may foster markets and we will now look at how markets foster virtue, along with a continued discussion of how markets may undermine virtues. For a more thorough discussion of these two views, see Hirschman (1982). In the review below we refer to the most salient aspects of the arguments in regard to markets and virtues and how they may undermine virtues.

Markets foster morality

According to Smith, among civilized nations (commercial societies), virtues are more cultivated. One of the perspectives Smith had was that commercial societies are fundamental for fostering moral capital (Rosenberg, 1990). This is because self-interest is inherently corrupting and the expansion of vocational spheres leads to just and honest behavior. Furthermore, it is only under competitive conditions that commercial society can be an effective builder of moral capital, as noted by Rosenberg, because wealth alone is inherently corrupting (see also Rasmussen, 2013).

In his work, Smith emphasized that those virtues that develop as a result of repeated commercial dealings with one another become the basis of trust that others will not cheat and that they generate probity and punctuality, which are principle virtues of a commercial society. Dealers choose to lose rather than lose the trust of others (LJ).

Capitalism fosters development of self-command, because individuals can further their goals by furthering the goals of others. Both parties benefit from exchange.

> Thus, an individual can simultaneously be under the constant pressure of competition to practice self-command and be humanitarian. . . . The privileged caste, not subject to competitive pressures, cannot develop self-command.
>
> (Herbener, 1987, p. 282)

The importance of self-command is expressed in the following statement of Smith:

> Self-command is not only itself a great virtue, but from it all the other virtues seem to derive their principal lustre.
>
> (TMS, p. 284)

According to Smith, it is the combination of self-command and superior reason that lead to prosperity under capitalism. Virtues develop in an environment where there is role switching (Herbener, 1987).

Within capitalistic interactions, there is incentive to pursue business profits instead of pursuing only pleasure. The increased importance of the commercial class increases parsimony and frugality in the society. Profit increased by industry creates a passion for it and pleasure to see an increase in a man's fortune. This is the reason commercial society increases frugality, an important aspect of prudence. Smith sees frugality as having public benefits: ". . . every frugal man a public benefactor". In a mercantilist system, instead, prudence does not develop, since those who have the favor of the state gain wealth. In a more capitalist system, the virtue of ". . . prudence is of the bourgeois"

(McCloskey, 2006). By imitating virtuous individuals, the society becomes more virtuous.

Smith strongly contends that in a market system virtue is rewarded:

> What is the reward most proper for encouraging industry, prudence, and circumspection? Success in every sort of business. And is it possible that in the whole of life these virtues should fail of attaining it? Wealth and external honours are their proper recompense, and the recompense which they can seldom fail of acquiring.
>
> (TMS, pp. 193–194)

In the literature, other mechanisms through which markets foster morality are discussed. For brevity, but for completeness, we will only refer to some of them. Commercial economy also instils habits of attention to detail, orderliness, reliability and precision (Rosenberg, 1990). According to McCloskey (see for example 1994 and 2006), markets yield a long list of "bourgeois virtues", which includes honesty and trustworthiness. In the bulk of transactions, the bourgeois must talk to each other, which defines business reputation, and the economy depends on trust. Smith asserts that men possess a certain disposition to indolence (Rosenberg, 1964). The growth of commerce and industry introduces new consumer goods. This in turn provides a major incentive to overcome indolence and indifference. Paganelli (2013) argues that the conditions of the poor are improved due to the wealth generated in commercial societies fostering moral behavior.

Market society undermines morality

As we have alluded to earlier, Smith and those who have commented since he first spoke of it were also well aware of detrimental effects brought about by commercial societies. Smith recognizes that attainment of large amounts of wealth is likely to corrupt even though the desire for affluence is a fundamental propelling force of every mankind. He says that this corruption occurs because

> . . . a man of a large revenue, whatever may be his profession, thinks he ought to live like other men of large revenues; and to spend a great part of his time in festivity, in vanity, and in dissipation.
>
> (WN, p. 814)

Wealth has the potential to circumvent the evolutionary capacities, such as self-command and trust, because the incentive for cooperative behavior decreases.

Hirsch (1976) argues that markets undermine moral values. "As individual behavior has been increasingly directed to individual advantage, habits and instincts based on communal attitudes and objectives have lost out. The weakening of traditional social values has made predominantly capitalist economies more difficult to manage" (p. 118). He points out that the emphasis on self-interest makes cooperation more difficult, which is needed for the functioning of the system.

Other links, which we will briefly refer to, are the following. Monopoly or special privilege destroys primary economic virtues of the capitalist class due to being released from the forces of a competitive market place.

Smith put a great emphasis in the WN on the division of labor and how it is enhanced with the expansion of markets leading to increased productivity. Yet, at the same time Smith was also aware of some negative consequences of this process, such as making workers "stupid" and "ignorant". Rosenberg (1990) argues that this is a depleting source of moral capital in a commercial society, as was recognized by Smith (see also Pack (2006) on the impact of commerce on character).

Smith also argues: "Another bad effect of commerce is that it sinks the courage of mankind, and tends to extinguish martial spirit" (LJ, p. 331). (See Tegos (2013) for an elaboration of this point.) Under a free polity, a citizen becomes a soldier only for self-defense (Winch, 1978). Commerce leads not to virtues but manners (Pocock, 1985). Rosenberg (1990) highlights that the main function of family is to provide for security, which can be provided by state in a commercial society, and families no longer have the incentive to stay together.

IV. Markets and morality: the integration of evolutionary psychology, self-command, adaptive defenses and delayed gratification

Over the course of evolutionary social development, defenses allowed for the development of what has come to be referred to as delayed gratification. From an evolutionary psychology point of view, a requirement for morality is that people must first have the capacity to resist the temptation of immediately satisfying their own needs at the expense of others. This is a very significant lynchpin that links evolutionary psychology and adaptive defenses. The genetic and behavioral capacity that allowed humans to delay the immediate gratification, and enabled social cooperation and group living, was reinforced by its social utility. This fostered the intellectual capacity for reflection and the growth of moral structures that could serve the specific needs of individuals and groups.

Markets increase the probability of cooperation that evolves due to the evolutionary development of the individual psyche within both groups and cultures. This evolution, which is directly related to participation in markets, requires delayed gratification. Delayed gratification developed through evolution and includes the use of adaptive defenses that enable an individual to participate in mutually cooperative market interactions. This is because with these capacities one is able to contain unbridled self-interest.

The emotional tension that is generated between the individual's desire to immediately gratify his own needs and the needs of the consensual or moral structure are where adaptive defenses come in. The management of the tension is facilitated by defenses that allow the individual to rationalize or restrain his need for gratification. This ability for restraint then lays the groundwork for the moral virtues that Smith has so clearly laid out, and more directly for the self-command, trust and consistency that facilitate markets.

Self-command, as referred to by Smith, and delayed gratification are intimately related. Without self-command, it is not possible to have delayed gratification. Indeed, reciprocally, delayed gratification then goes on to reinforce the use of self-command. Evolutionary psychology shows how the capacity to resist the immediate satisfaction of individual needs at the expense of others allows individuals to advance their interests in cooperative ways. The ability to delay gratification and gain self-command allows for the development of morality and increases the potential for cooperative sociability.

Self-command and the capacity for delayed gratification in the most immediate sense make adaptation possible. For example, the long-term goal of having enough food for a cold winter requires the ability to plan for the future and look beyond the immediately gratifying circumstances of plenty. It is part of our evolutionary history, even for mammals, to save and store for the future, which involves adaptive defenses for unforeseen circumstances. The mastery of the capacity for delayed gratification and the cognitive ability to imagine into the future are necessary for this and countless other civilizing tasks of a similar nature.

Self-command is viewed as moral by philosophers such as Smith, and is seen as prudential when it serves morality. Social norms of individuals within groups influence the standards people adopt for their conduct. Writing on the importance of self-command, Smith states: "The most perfect knowledge, if it is not supported by the most perfect self-command, will not always enable him to do his duty" (TMS, p. 279). Furthermore, Smith states:

> In the steadiness of his industry and frugality, in his steady sacrificing the ease and enjoyment of the present moment for the probable expectation of the still greater ease and enjoyment of a more distant but more lasting period of time, the prudent man is always both supported and rewarded by the entire approbation of the impartial spectator, and of the representative of the impartial spectator, the man within the breast.
>
> (TMS, p. 252)

It is readily acknowledged that the foundation for self-interest and even greed has been basic to our species and its survival:

> for our ancestors in a harsh world, greed paid off in the only currencies that matter to genes – survival and the ability to have offspring. From them, we have inherited greediness that manifests itself today as a desire to accumulate money and possessions.
>
> (cited by Krebs, p. 93)

The civilization of such basic survival needs builds the capacity for markets. In the TMS, Smith considers the attainment of wealth (bettering one's condition) and greatness as "grand and beautiful and noble". Their attainment is well worth "all the toil and anxiety which we are so apt to bestow upon it" (TMS, p. 214). In the WN it is argued that the motive to better our condition prompts us to save. Smith argues that capital is slowly accumulated by "private frugality and good conduct of individuals, by their universal and uninterrupted effort to better their own condition" (WN, p. 345). We should recall here that the prudent man is frugal. Through savings, thus there is moral basis for economic growth (see also Fitzgibbons, 1995 on this point). As Smith puts it: "Capitals are increased by parsimony, and diminished by prodigality and misconduct" (WN, p. 337).

Delayed gratification in terms of financial savings leads to capital accumulation that is an essential element of commercial progress and expansion of markets. Thus, we can say that this aspect of morality fosters markets. In turn, markets foster morality, since expansion of markets increases investment opportunities, giving incentives for further savings. It is, of course possible that investment opportunities undermine delayed gratification and lead to greedy behavior. Those individuals for whom the capacity to delay gratification has been compromised, or who have been irresistibly tempted by rewards in the market place, face challenges to their moral capacity and are the most vulnerable to this type of behavior.

Trust

The evolutionary capacity for trust is the extension of the ability to delay gratification. The development of adaptive defenses leads to consistent enough behavior in relation to others for trust to develop. Trustworthiness presupposes self-control. From an evolutionary psychology point of view, the development of trust is essential for cooperative behavior. Individuals must trust that others will not put their own interest first at the expense of other individuals. Adaptive defenses have a role in the development of trust as well. For example, when individuals trade with each other, intellectualization (in the ability to conceptualize the trade) and rationalization (the ability to rationalize the potential risk/benefits) are used as defenses that allow each individual to participate in trade. Repeated interactions between these traders lead to the building of trust. The desired need is for the product that their neighbor is willing to trade for. Each needs a reasoning capacity on how to make the trade, the relative value and the ability to rationalize why this should take place in an agreed upon way and in an orderly fashion. At least two defenses are necessarily employed here; intellectualization and rationalization, which allow each participant in the trade to contain their immediate need, make the proper arrangements and deliver their goods to each other. These defenses act in the service of delayed gratification, and with repeated interactions over time build a level of trust. To extend this even further, the trusted delivery of goods allows both participants to expand their markets to others.

Bruni and Sugden (2000) suggest that Smith gives a theory of rational trust, where rational trust means trust can be recommended to rational beings. Smith himself highlights the importance of trust.

> Humanity does not desire to be great, but to be beloved. It is not in being rich that truth and justice would rejoice, but in being trusted and believed, recompenses which those virtues must almost always acquire.
>
> (TMS, p. 194)

He continues to say that:

> Frankness and openness conciliate confidence. We trust the man who seems willing to trust us. We see clearly, we think, the road by which he means to conduct us, and we abandon ourselves with pleasure to his guidance and direction.
>
> (TMS, pp. 398–399)

In relation to trust, Smith also states: "We are mortified when we happen to deceive other people, though unintentionally, and from having been ourselves deceived" (TMS, p. 398).

Smith also wrote on informal trust. He states that cheating neighbors would make him lose. In addition, probity and punctuality emerge as a result of self-interest, not due to national character (LJ).

Thus, in commercial societies, trust is prevalent because damage to one's reputation as untrustworthy would lead to the loss of business. Where contracts are not comprehensive enough, and monitoring compliance with them is prohibitively expensive, people will seek out trustworthy trading partners.

Fukuyama states that even though contracts allow strangers to work with one another, the process works much more efficiently when trust exists. For economic output (expansion of markets), honesty and trust, which are public goods, are necessary. Evensky (2011) amplifies the role of trust in Smith and states that there are two kinds of energy in Smith's system that underlie trust. One is the energy that drives individuals towards "bettering their conditions". The other is the role of laissez-faire that is the source of "unbounded freedom", which is essential in unleashing individual energy. However, this energy can only be unleashed when trust exists.

If over time individuals and institutions prove to be trustworthy, we trust. In a market system, if trust decreases, the "transaction costs associated with protecting ourselves from the risk of immoral and unethical behavior rise" (Evensky, 2011, p. 250). Transaction costs are lowered to the degree the regulation of markets increases trust. When trust is lower, the transaction costs will be higher and the market will be constrained. Smith supports government involvement

to stabilize trust in the markets. However, government alone is not a sufficient constraint in an expanding commercial system. Civic ethics are essential.
Citizens trust each other, and the governing bodies, to discourage destructive
behavior of those few who do not adhere to ethical behavior in commercial
free-market systems.

Capital is a necessary element of commercial progress; and once again trust
is essential for capital. There is an incentive to accumulate capital to the degree
there is trust that the accumulated wealth will be secure. "The constraints of
civic ethics and positive law are the only barriers that stand between one's
wealth and its loss to unconstrained greed" (Evensky, 2011, p. 254). The security
of both accumulated capital and circulating capital are essential. The latter adds
a new dimension of trust because it passes through the hands of others. While
government and regulation are important to implement law that surrounds
transactions, the foundational ethos of trust among the participants is a core
component of capital in the market place.

Frequent dealings in the market place may foster trust if an individual comes
to believe that the trading partner is trustworthy. To conduct its business in
the long-term and to have long-term gains, each trading partner must act in
trustworthy ways. Those with the least ability to delay gratification are the most
vulnerable to the corrupting effects of the market place and would become
untrustworthy. As we argued above, if gratification is not delayed and immediate needs are put ahead of others, there needs to be a disincentive by the members of the society and reward for being trustworthy.

Delayed gratification and trust

As has been implied in the sections above, cooperative human interaction, particularly in economic interactions, requires the ability to exercise delayed gratification. Delayed gratification facilitates the capacity to participate in markets
and build the moral understandings that create trust. In realizing the benefits
of cooperative behavior in markets, markets have the reciprocal potential of
reinforcing cooperative morality, and therefore strengthen it. The increase of
cooperative behavior over time develops trust in both cooperative behavior and
in the markets that cooperative behavior fosters.

The rewards of cooperative morality and delayed gratification in the market
place increase the incentive for greater and greater rewards. As collective trust
grows in the market place, this also increases the hope and possibility of reward.
In contrast, because of the enticement for rewards in the markets, there is a
challenge by some to undermine morality. Those individuals for whom the
capacity to delay gratification has been compromised are the most vulnerable
to the temptations of immediate rewards at the expense of ethical constraint.
When the consensual morality is breached, it weakens the trust that people
have in the markets, often causing a pullback or diminished participation. In

order for continued participation, a renewed trust and fair play needs to be re-established. Some form of justice needs to be applied to re-assert the authority of the collective morality. The re-assertion of such justice has been evidenced by the response of governmental authority to the exploitative events occurring in the markets these last several years.

V. Discussion

We have looked at the factors that go into how morality affects markets and how markets in turn affect morality. While it is clear that the growth and elaborate development of market structures over time have required a great deal of moral integrity, it is also clear that the temptations brought about by short-term gains and the accumulation of wealth can have a corrupting effect or morality as well.

The evolutionary development of morality runs parallel to the development of market place skills. Adam Smith's elaborate structure of morality and the ability to apply it is the result of a great deal of evolutionary human development. The development of the foundational capacity for delayed gratification is at the base of the development of any moral virtue. Without the capacity to delay the satisfaction of instinctual and emotional needs, the capacity for interactions that consider other's needs and mutual self-interest would be impossible. Delayed gratification co-evolved with adaptive defenses. Delayed gratification and adaptive defenses also made possible those behaviors that Smith termed "virtuous", and they became the foundation for the development of morality.

Smith's system of morality represents an important apparatus that governs interpersonal interactions as they relate to the market place. The desire and need for "approbation", as Smith called it, along with the pragmatic need for interpersonal trust and trust in the market place, gives explanation for how morality has been maintained socially. As these behaviors are practiced over time, a greater degree of trust is established in the market place.

The practice of the virtuous behaviors is made possible by the "self-command" that his moral structure is based on, and can only be accomplished by the aid of adaptive defenses that allow the individual to deal with the frustration that comes as a result of the restraint of immediate desires.

While Smith's moral structure and the psychological mechanisms that underlie it lend understanding to the reciprocal development of markets and morality, it also reveals the vulnerability in the market place to exploitation. At least in the short run, those who would attempt to exploit the established structures and resultant trust often do so by indulging in immediate gratification. History has however established that the interactive relationship between markets and morality have expanded both our human evolution and the evolution of markets, even with the ever-present temptations for exploitation.

Note

1 On wealth and virtue, see Hont and Ignatieff (1983). On relations between virtues and
competition, see Wells and Graafland (2012).

References

Boehm, C., 2008. Purposive social selection and the evolution of human altruism. *Cross-Cultural Research*, 24, pp. 319–352.
Bruni, L. and Sugden, R., 2000. Moral canals: Trust and social capital in the work of Hume, Smith and Genovesi. *Economics and Philosophy*, 1, pp. 21–45.
Burdham, T. and Phelan, J., 2000. *Mean genes*. New York: Perseus Publishing.
Eigst, I., Zayas, V., Mischel, W., Shoda, Y., Ayduk, O., Dadlani, M., Davison, M., Aber, L. and Casey, B.J., 2006. Predicting cognitive control from preschool to late adolescence and young adulthood. *Psychological Science*, 17(6), pp. 478–484.
Evensky, J., 2011. Adam Smith's essentials: On trust, faith, and the free markets. *Journal of History of Economic Thought*, 33(2), pp. 249–267.
Fitzgibbons, A., 1995. *Adam Smith's system of liberty, wealth, and virtue: The moral and political foundations of the wealth of nations*. Oxford: Oxford University Press.
Freud, S., 1923. *The ego and the id: The standard edition of the complete psychological works of Sigmund Freud*, Volume XIX (1923–1925).
Freud, S., 1930. Civilization and its discontents. In: Strachey, J., ed. *The standard edition of the complete psychological works of Sigmund Freud, Volume XXI*. London: Hogarth Press. pp. 57–146.
Griswold, C.L., 2006. Imagination: Morals, science, and arts. In: Haakonssen, K., ed. *The Cambridge companion to Adam Smith*. Cambridge: Cambridge University Press.
Haidt, J., 2008. Morality. *Perspectives on Psychological Science*, 3(1), pp. 65–72.
Herbener, J., 1987. An integration of The Wealth of Nations The Theory of Moral Sentiments. *The Journal of Libertarian Studies*, VIII(2), pp. 275–288.
Hirsch, F., 1976. *Social limits to growth*. Cambridge, MA: Harvard University Press.
Hirschman, A.O., 1982. Rival interpretations of market society: Civilizing, destructive or feeble. *Journal of Economic Literature*, 20(4), pp. 1463–1484.
Hont, I. and Ignatieff, M., 1983. *Wealth and virtue: The shaping of political economy in the Scottish enlightenment*. Cambridge: Cambridge University Press.
Krebs, D.L., 2011. *The origins of morality: An evolutionary account*. New York: Oxford University Press.
Levy, D., 1999. Adam Smith's kattalactic model of gambling: Approbation from the spectators. *Journal of History of Economic Thought*, 21, pp. 81–91.
McCloskey, D. N., 1994. Bourgeois virtue. *The American Scholar*, 63(2), pp. 177–191.
———, 2006. *The bourgeois virtues: Ethics for an age of commerce*. Chicago: University of Chicago Press.
Macfie, A.L., 1967. *Individual in society, papers on Adam Smith*. London: George Allen and Unwin.
Mendez, M.F., Anderson, E. and Shapira, J. S. R. N., 2005. An investigation of moral judgment in frontotemporal dementia. *Cognitive and Behavioral Neurology*, 18(4), pp. 193–197.
Mischel, W., Cantor, N. and Feldman, S., 1996. Principles of self-regulation. The nature of willpower and self-control. In: Higgins, E.T. and A.W. Kruglanski, eds. *Social psychology: Handbook of basic principles*. New York: Guilford Press. pp. 329–360.

Nieli, R., 1986. Spheres of intimacy and the Adam Smith problem. *Journal of the History of Ideas, 47*, pp. 611–624.

Pack, S.J., 2006. Adam Smith and Marx. In: Berry, J. C., M.P. Paganelli and C. Smith, eds. *The Oxford handbook of Adam Smith*. Oxford: Oxford University Press. pp. 523–538.

Paganelli, P.M., 2009. Approbation and the desire to better one's condition in Adam Smith: When the desire to better one's condition does not better one's condition and society's condition. *Journal of the History of Economic Thought, 31*(1), pp. 79–92.

———, 2013. Commercial relations: From Adam Smith to field of experiments. In: Berry, J. C., M. P. Paganelli and C. Smith, eds. *The Oxford handbook of Adam Smith*. Oxford: Oxford University Press. pp. 333–347.

Pocock, J. G. A., 1985. *Virtue, commerce and history: Essays on political thought and history, chiefly in the eighteenth century*. Cambridge: Cambridge University Press.

Rasmussen, D.C., 2013. Adam Smith and Rousseau: Enlightenment and counter- enlightenment. In: Berry, J. C., M.P. Paganelli and C. Smith, eds. *The Oxford handbook of Adam Smith*. Oxford University Press. pp. 54–76.

Richerson, P.J. and Boyd, R., 2005. *Not by genes alone: How culture transformed human evolution*. Chicago: Chicago University Press.

Rosenberg, N., 1964. Neglected dimensions in the analysis of economic change. *Bulletin of the Oxford University, Institute of Economics and Statistics, 26*(1), pp. 59–77.

———, 1990. Adam Smith and the stock of moral capital. *History of Political Economy, 22*(1), pp. 1–17.

Skinner, B.F., 1969. *Contingencies of reinforcement: A theoretical analysis*. New York: Appleton Century-Cropts.

Tegos, S., 2006. Adam Smith: Theorist of corruption. In: Berry, J. C., M. P. Paganelli and C. Smith, eds. *The Oxford handbook of Adam Smith*. Oxford: Oxford University Press. pp. 353–371.

———, 2013. Adam Smith: Theorist of corruption. In Berry, J. C., M. P. Paganelli, C. Smith, eds. *The Oxford handbook of Adam Smith*. Oxford: Oxford University Press.

Wells, T. and Graafland, J., 2012. Adam Smith's bourgeois virtues in competition. *Business Ethics Quarterly, 22*(2), pp. 319–350.

Winch, D. 1978. *Adam Smith's politics: An essay in historiographic revision*. Cambridge: Cambridge University Press.

Young, T.J., 1997. *Economics as a moral science*. Lyme: Edward Elgar Publishing Limited.

Chapter 9

On dependency

I. Introduction

In this chapter, we focus on Smith's views on human relationships, in particular as they concern his approach to dependencies in the WN. We examine Smith's views from a psychoanalytic perspective. The results reveal that Smith considers *dependence* on others a problem and sees the solution to this problem in impersonalized interdependence. Our analysis results further indicate a central tension between dependence and independence in Smith's writings. The *personal dependency patterns* he exhibited in his life, through a reading of his biographies, also suggest a tension between dependence and independence in his life. Benefitting from psychoanalytic literature, it is proposed that developing the ideas in the WN was part of Smith's creative solution to this tension. In particular, his solution to one individual's dependence on another was through a system of impersonalized interdependence. In other words, it is argued that Smith defended against his personal dependence through his economic theorizing.

Most economists view economics as a field that develops through applications of "the scientific method" described in mainstream notions of the philosophy of science. Many social scientists, including certain economists who are not in the mainstream, have criticized the limited nature of this approach to economics. For example, the great economist Schumpeter (1954, pp. 3–4) has argued that the subject matter of economics is a historical process and that its implicit intellectual history should be made explicit. Philosopher Harding (1995) has criticized mainstream economics research on the grounds that economists lack recognition of the embedded values in their assumptions, such as those that describe men as rational, self-interested individuals. In addition, there are a few studies on how the psychology of researchers enters into economic theorizing. Focusing on researchers as a group, Weisskopf (1949) argues that the conflict an individual feels between his/her ideas and the group's is defended against by making an intellectual compromise. Feiner (2003) suggests that the market functions as a "perfect substitute" for the mother to meet all needs and wants. Feiner (2003, p. 188) argues economists elevate markets institutions as a "defense against anxieties provoked by the guilty feelings associated with infantile rage at mothers/markets for not being perfect".

Adding to these constructive criticisms, it is noted here that latent meanings of texts are not analyzed in mainstream economics. Thus, starting from the premise that the emotional and unconscious basis for thought and action influences the development of a field of academic inquiry, latent content analysis is applied to the fundamental opening chapters of one of the most influential texts in economics, *The Wealth of Nations* by Adam Smith.

One of the essential ways psychoanalysis can be applied is by seeking ". . . the function of the unconscious in human behavior as evidenced by life styles . . . creativity and sublimations . . . writing . . . human action and inhibition" (Loewenberg, 2007, p. 15).[1] Following this lead, latent content analysis is applied to the study of the first three chapters of the WN. In order to be able to examine this work, we use strategic principles of listening;[2] the suspension of individual biases or presuppositions is also an important feature of psychoanalytic listening[3] in favor of the present materials, which include listening for affect, imagery and figurative language – words that appeal to the senses, metaphors, etc., what is implied in observable choices and contingencies, repetition, as it indicates a latent unconscious scenario and gaps in the material.[4]

The WN is chosen because Adam Smith is widely recognized as the father and founder of contemporary economics and the WN is considered a seminal text. The chapters analyzed here are on the division of labor and are among the most widely studied pieces of work by Smith (see for example Rosenberg, 2003).[5] On the surface, Smith's analysis of the division of labor focuses on the productivity gains that result from it. Smith's important insights about the technological superiority of division of labor and specialization have become one of the pillars in economics.

This analysis reveals that Smith views personal dependence on others to meet one's needs distasteful. Smith argues that people never reach a stage of independence from others. How, then, do men survive in a world where they do not have the capacity to be independent, yet dependency is unacceptable? Smith sees the solution to this problem in a system of socially distanced faceless contracting. Individuals who are able, due to the division of labor and specialization, to produce more than they need of a particular good, offer their produce in exchange for that of others by appealing to others' self-interest. Thus, the market exchange that is entered voluntarily is a system that enables people to meet their needs through other people via impersonalized interdependence. In this analysis, people's dependence on each other is unmentioned; in rare instances when such dependency comes into the text, it does so only implicitly, and the topic remains unexplored.

In order provide a broader exploration of Smith's views on dependency, the views on *social dependency* and *personal relatedness* reflected in his LJ and TMS are also analyzed. Furthermore, through a reading of his biographies, the *personal dependency patterns* he exhibited in his life are identified.

From LJ and TMS, it is deduced that while he disdained some forms of dependence, he cherished others. In particular, Smith shows a strong antagonism towards the unequal dependence of one social group on another (LJ).[6] Domination is in human nature, he argues. He also expresses a belief that domination and dependency corrupt human character. In his writings on personal dependence (in TMS), Smith shows a great regard for the value of family and friendships for personal happiness. He argues that a man's affections naturally fall upon his immediate family.[7]

The picture that emerges so far is that Smith idealized independence in the WN, exhibited a strong disdain towards unequal social dependence in LJ, yet had a high regard for personal relatedness in his writings in the TMS. This picture suggests a central tension between relatedness and independence in Smith's writings. To shed light on the potential roots of this tension, his personal life is examined. The most salient aspects of Smith's life that are learned from his biographies are that Smith's father passed before Smith's birth and that he lived with his mother throughout her life, until she passed at the age of 90, only several years prior to Smith's passing. Smith did not develop any romantic partnerships beyond having had loving or affectionate interactions with a couple of women. At the same time, he had enduring male friendships. For his financial needs, Smith initially depended on family income and later on rich businessmen, gentry, intellectuals and aristocrats for teaching positions and his pension. Thus dependency patterns Smith exhibited in his life also suggest a tension between dependence and independence. In this chapter, it is proposed that his solution to one individual's dependence on another was through a system of impersonalized interdependence among equals through market transactions, as my analysis of his chapters on the division of labor illustrates. In other words, I argue that Smith defended against his personal dependence through his economic theorizing.

Consistent with the results of this analysis, it has been noted by Kuiper (2002) that dependency has been a complicated issue for economists, since being dependent on others requires power differences, relations between non-homogenous individuals. These issues do not neatly fit in the optimal outcomes analysis of market processes. Thus, dependency has been placed outside the framework of economic analysis. Kuiper concludes that in economics, dependency is seen as a social problem and its solution is provided through economic exchange.

One may argue that Smith was only writing about economic relations in a capitalist system. However, even in a capitalist system transfer of goods between people takes place not only through faceless transactions in the market place. They also take place between individuals with close ties with one another, such as within the family, close friends, members of extended family and close knit communities. That Smith chooses only to focus on impersonalized interdependencies in the WN is noteworthy.

There is, of course, a vast amount of scholarly work on Adam Smith. A very informative and useful review is contained in Haakonssen (2006). Since the novelty of this work is an application of psychoanalytic reading of the aforementioned work by Smith, there is not an immediately relevant literature to review.

Some important qualifications are necessary. This chapter has a limited scope as described above. It is neither an analysis of the entirety of the WN, nor an analysis of Smith's entirety of works. This chapter also has a limited scope in that the social, historical context of Smith's works are not analyzed, except for brief references to the Scottish Enlightenment. Finally, it should also be noted that this study is not about whether Smith viewed humans as benevolent or self-interested, but it concerns his views and attitudes on dependency as reflected in his writings and his life.

In the rest of the chapter, the following organization is used. Section II, which focuses on the chapter on the division of labor in the WN, analyzes the idealization of impersonal interdependence that Smith exhibits in that text. Section III, on his attitude towards social dependence, and Section IV, on his attitude towards personal dependence, reflect the strong sentiments with which he wrote about these forms of dependence, as well as the apparent intensity with which he experienced them. In that section, first, a synopsis of Smith's personal relations, based upon his biographies as well as some of his own writings, is provided. Later in the same section, a psychoanalytic interpretation of his struggle with dependence in his personal life is discussed. Concluding remarks are contained in Section V.

II. A psychoanalytic reading of the division of labor

The WN shows the usefulness of the market economy. Smith's analysis of markets is based on trade between self-interested individuals. Smith further argues that the pursuit of self-interest would benefit the whole society. Self-interested competition within a free market would keep the prices low, and the market would guide the production of the right amounts of a whole variety of goods and services. An essential component of Smith's analysis of markets is his treatment of the division of labor. The chapters on the division of labor are places where his attitudes towards dependency are most apparent. Thus, next an analysis of Smith's chapter on the division of labor is presented.

II.1. Chapter I: "Of the Division of Labour"

In this chapter, people's dependence on each other is unmentioned; in the rare instances when dependence comes into the text, it does so only implicitly, and the topic remains unexplored. For example, Smith describes the operations of a manufacturing firm where division of labor takes place. With the division of labor, every man is dependent on each other's produce, but this is not acknowledged in the text. Second, in the discussion of how inventions occur, the potential for an invention that arises through cooperation of workers is not considered. Therefore, workers' dependency on each other's work during an invention process is not taken into account. The process of exchange of extras makes each person depend on the products of others. However, Smith's characterization of this exchange erases people's dependence on each other or reduces it to socially distanced impersonalized transactions.

This chapter opens by stating that "the greatest improvement in the productive powers of labour and the greater part of the skill, dexterity, and judgment with which it is anywhere directed, or applied, seem to have been the effects of the division of labor" (WN, p. 13).

Smith's interest in productivity was a shared one during the Scottish Enlightenment. Scots were poor. They believed that if the country were to prosper, the economy needed to improve, men would have to be trained and science would have to be used to solve problems. There were intense debates about conditions that may lead to economic growth. Both the mercantilist and free-trade solutions were being debated. Scots argued for more efficient industries, larger markets and more investment.

Smith observes division of labor in those industries or manufactories where workmen can be collected in the same workhouse and viewed by a spectator. To explain the process of the division of labor and the resulting gains from it, Smith gives his famous pin factory example: "One man draws out the wire, another straights it . . . making pins is, in this manner, divided into about eighteen distinct operations" (WN, p. 15). Smith goes on to state that one worker could probably make only 20 pins per day, while if 10 people divided up the 18 steps required for making a pin, they could make a combined 48,000 pins in one day. The description of pin making is written with a meticulous focus on the number of pins that can be produced. Smith takes more than one page of the 12-page chapter to elaborate on this example, perhaps to preserve Smith's status as scientific observer.

Placing value on scientific work was an important aspect of the Scottish Enlightenment. Sir Isaac Newton had a significant influence on the Scottish Enlightenment. Both institutional factors, such as the creation of new teaching positions, and individual initiatives were instrumental in the rise of Newtonianism in Scotland (Wood, 2003, p. 102). As Wood (2003) explains,

> Natural knowledge and mathematics were increasingly presented as polite forms of learning and gentlemanly accomplishments, which meant that the study of natural sciences could be seen as exemplifying the values now thought to be appropriate to academe. Newtonianism, in turn, benefitted from this shift, because it too was construed as a branch of knowledge fit for a polite gentleman.
>
> (p. 103)

It is also argued that Newton's success in his discovery of the natural laws of motion had a significant impact on Adam Smith's efforts to discover the general laws of economics (Hetherington, 1983).

While Smith is relentlessly arguing that the division of labor increases productivity, however, he leaves out important aspects of the reality of pin factories that do not suit his argument. For example, the work conditions are sanitized, portraying workers as equals. As is well known, however, various groups of workers, adults, apprentices and children were discriminated by the tasks they were assigned, children being assigned the worst tasks.

One also wonders whether the dichotomy between specialization and the separate crafting of each individual pin is a false one. Marglin (1974) argues that indeed it is. Furthermore, implicit in Smith's description of the pin factory is that one man depends on the other's work. However, dependency and its potential implications – which may involve, for example, conflict that could lead to a reduction in productivity, feelings such as envy or gratitude that may impact the work environment or workers' relations to one another – are not addressed.

Smith generalizes his argument to other manufacturing industries where labor can be subdivided into different tasks. He makes comparisons across different industries and across different countries. Though the argument may largely be valid, the multitude of examples provided, the length of the text devoted to them (two pages of a 12-page chapter) and the sweeping generalizations are notable. There appears to be a strained effort to convince the reader of the "universal truth" of the argument made.

Smith then turns to a discussion of how the division of labor results in improved productivity. One of the arguments Smith makes is that the division of labor propels invention. His imagery is that of one man focusing on a single object (WN, pp. 20–21). Though this image fits certain instances of invention, it is the only one brought up in the text – at the cost of raising the possibility of a group of workers jointly working on an invention. Thus, some important potential dependencies are not considered, but only the one that is consistent with the argument being developed in the text.

Another argument of this chapter is that the division of labor leads to "universal opulence". The extension of the universal opulence to the "lowest" ranks of people assumes power- and conflict-free social relations of exchange. This is another place in the chapter where people are dependent on each other's produce and the ability to exchange to benefit from the opulence of the society. Again, the exchange process is described as an idealized situation in which all men are equal except for the difference in the amount of their product arising from the division of labor. They enter into exchange with one another out of their free will in a harmonious society. More important is the fact that people are interdependent through what Smith depicts as an impersonal exchange in the markets.

II.2. Chapter II: "Of the Principle Which Gives Occasion to Division of Labour"

In this chapter Smith argues that a man is able to produce surplus goods to offer to others because of his increased productivity due to division of labor.

Ironically, we again end up in a world in which human beings depend on each other. The dependence, however, is impersonalized, sanitized, and reduced to market exchange among equals.

One of the key building blocks for the arguments in this chapter is stated in the first paragraph:

> division of labour, from which so many advantages are derived, is not originally the effect of any human wisdom. It is the necessary . . . consequence of a certain propensity in human nature . . . the propensity to truck, barter and exchange one thing for another.[8]
>
> (WN, p. 25)

The assertion that the propensity to truck, barter and exchange is unique to humans is developed with the following words:

> It is common to all men, and to be found in no other race of animals, which seem to know neither this nor any other species of contracts. Two greyhounds, in running down the same hare, have sometimes the appearance of acting in some sort of concert. Each turns her towards his companion. . . . This however, is not the effect of any contract, but of the accidental concurrence of their passions in the same object at that particular time. Nobody ever saw a dog make a fair and deliberate exchange of one bone for another with another dog.
>
> (WN, pp. 25–26)

The most curious aspect of this statement is that animals are portrayed as having passions and acting on them, whereas men are characterized as relating to each other through contracts. Of course, men have passions, and animals exchange things, though we may not think of them as forming contractual arrangements. Ants and bees, for example, exchange things with others in their communal living.

According to Smith, animals and men also differ in that animals, when grown to maturity, are independent of each other, whereas men have constant need for the help of others, but they cannot expect this from their benevolence alone. The contrasts he draws between animals and men continue being important to Smith's depiction of how men and animals get what they want. Animals, he asserts, get what they want from other animals or men by gaining their favor. Men, by contrast, do not have time to do this on every occasion. A man will succeed in getting what he wants from other men "if he can interest their self-love in his favour, and shew them that is for their own advantage to do him what he requires of them" (WN, p. 26). "Give me that which I want, and you shall have this which you want, is the meaning of every such offer", Smith insists,

> and it is in this manner that we obtain from one another the far greater part of those good offices which we stand in need of. It is not from the

> benevolence of the butcher, the brewer, or the baker, that we expect our
> dinner, but from their regard to their own self-interest.
>
> (WN, pp. 26–27)

According to Smith, a man never talks to others of his own needs, in other words, but of their advantages. "Nobody but a beggar chuses to depend chiefly upon the benevolence of his fellow-citizens" (WN, p. 27), Smith asserts. Men get what they want from each other "by treaty, by barter, and by purchase" (WN, p. 27).

There are a couple of striking aspects to the arguments related in the paragraph above. First, men are portrayed as unlike animals in being dependent on each other. However, many animals live in groups for their survival, depending on each other. Second, what is absent from this depiction is noteworthy. The argument would suggest that neither men nor animals take what they want by force or by using power. There are no conflicts in the process of getting what either an animal or a man wants. Smith's depiction of men as getting what they want only by an appeal to the self-love of others leaves out many possibilities: men can also get what they want through family, informal networks, gifts, reciprocity or others' benevolence. In other words, men have the possibility of depending on each other through personal relations, not only through impersonalized market exchange.

How do people then obtain things to offer to others in order to get what they want? To provide an answer to this question, the text turns to the division of labor:

> As it is by treaty, by barter and by purchase, that we obtain from one another the greater part of those mutual good offices which we stand in need of, so it is this same trucking disposition which originally gives occasion to the division of labour. In a tribe of hunters or shepherds a particular person makes bows and arrows. . . . He frequently exchanges them for cattle or for venison. . . . From a regard to his own interest, therefore, the making of bows and arrows grows to be his chief business . . . thus the certainty of being able to exchange all that surplus part of the produce of his own labour, which is over and above his consumption . . . encourages every man to apply himself to a particular occupation.
>
> (WN, pp. 27–28)

As it is in this chapter, it was common to compare animals and humans during the Scottish Enlightenment. Distinctions between animals and humans were made to reach conclusions regarding human sociality and socialization. It was believed that we could learn something about humans by studying the animal world. It was also noted that humans required extensive nurture, unlike animals; some animals would be able to join a herd within hours of birth, whereas the new human baby could not. Another distinction noted between animals and humans was the ability of humans to reason. However, reason could not be the basis of human sociality as, it was argued, it took time to develop.

It was argued that the parent–child bond among humans was more durable than that among animals and that it was this durability that led to familial and kinship ties that extended beyond mere instinct. Once the child established a durable bond with his parent, he could develop friendships and loyalty. The Scottish thinkers also argued that the human "frame was composed of passions that were the basis of our relations with others, our mores, our conventions and our morality: to understand the frame one must understand the mores, and vice-versa" (Garret, 2003, p. 83). Human frames were believed to have been created to harmonize with other humans. Eventually, the durability of parent–child bonding would grow into a habit, becoming second nature. Thus, habit would be a significant source of sociality and social coherence. This, of course, is argued to be an important source of slow changes in institutions. As Berry (2003) puts it, "Since customs are creatures of time, then time, that is gradual alterations in the sentiments of people, is what changes them" (p. 249). Thus, Scots were cautious about the speed of progress in social relations (see Berry, 2003, for a broader discussion of sociality and socialization during the Scottish Enlightenment).

III. Smith's views on dependence and social relations

In Smith's other writings, there is an acknowledgment of unequal dependence. Specifically, in Smith's view, domination is in human nature, and most humans despise treating others as free persons. He was deeply hostile towards the dependency the nobility imposed on their retainers and servile dependents. (See also Fiori and Pesciarelli, 1999; Lewis, 2000 and Perelman, 1989.) He believed domination and dependency undermined and corrupted human character and the moral stock of the society (Rosenberg, 1990). Smith saw self-interest inherently corrupting in societies where great wealth created hierarchy. Different social structures imposed on self-interested men, however, could have a powerful impact in mediating the corrupting nature of dominance and dependency. He saw commercial society as a powerful force that prevents unequal social dependency, giving rise to liberty and the security of individuals.

Writing on domination, Smith tells us that,

> the love of domination and authority over others, which I am afraid is natural to mankind, a certain desire of having others below one, and the pleasure it gives one to have some persons who he can order to do his work rather than be obliged to persuade others to bargain with him, will forever hinder this [the employment of free labor in the Scottish mines] from taking place.

(LJ, p. 192)

He later returns to this subject in the WN:

> The pride of a man makes him love to domineer, and nothing mortifies him so much as to be obliged to condescend to persuade his inferiors. Wherever the law allows it, and the nature of the work can afford it, therefore, he will generally prefer the service of slaves to freemen.
>
> (WN, p. 388)

Smith speaks of a "tyranic [*sic*] disposition which may almost be said to be natural to mankind" while describing slavery (LJ, p. 452).

Smith thought sustained moral character could be provided by a market or commercial society. In his words,

> Nothing tends so much to corrupt and enervate and debase the mind as dependency, and nothing gives such noble and generous notions of probity as freedom and independency. Commerce is one great preventive to this custom.
>
> (LJ, p. 333)

Smith returns to this subject in the WN by highlighting how commerce contributed to the rural society through introducing "the liberty and security of individuals" (WN, p. 412) and by relieving them of servile dependence:

> . . . commerce and manufacturers gradually introduced order and good government, and with them, the liberty and security of individuals, among the inhabitants of the country, who had before lived in a continual state of war with their neighbors, and of a servile dependency upon their superiors. This though it has been least observed is by far the most important of all their effects.
>
> (WN, p. 412)

Scots also thought about freedom and its meanings. Control and power in Scotland were manifested in both the formal mechanisms of the church and state as well as in patronage. Patronage gave local elites extensive powers, though patrons were few in number because Scotland was governed by a small number of merchants and landowners. (See Emerson, 2003) for a broader discussion of the context of the Scottish Enlightenment.) Scots saw change in power relations as a slow process. Smith, for example, argued that the destruction of feudal power would be brought about by the "silent and insensible operation of foreign commerce and manufacturers" (WN, p. 418) and by the changes in the form of "property and manners". "These changes were", Garret (2003) states,

> almost entirely positive, the emancipation of social inferiors, women, slaves and children from their barbarous conditions in rude times through the emergence of liberal societies and governments.
>
> (p. 80)

IV. Smith and personal dependence

In this section, first, a synopsis of Adam Smith's biography is presented. The goal here is to delineate the salient aspects of Smith's experiences with personal dependency; the personal aspects of his life are discussed below. Later in this section, some possible interpretations of Smith's dependency patterns are presented.

IV.1. A synopsis of Smith's family history and personal relationships

There are volumes of biographies on Adam Smith. Among these biographies, I find Stewart (1793/1858), West (1969), Ross (1995) and Weinstein (2001) most useful in providing information on Smith's life; thus the synopsis provided below is based on them. The content of these biographies is mostly centered on Smith's works. Because the information on his personal life is not nearly as rich as the information on his works, the synopsis will suffer from the constraints imposed by the available information. The scantiness of information on Smith's life is, of course, not surprising. In his circles, it was important to keep one's own personal affairs private as well as to protect the privacy of those with whom one had intimate personal relations.

Let us first recall some pertinent information we provided in the introduction to this book. Adam Smith's father died about six months prior to his birth. The senior Smith had been a customs officer at Kirkcaldy and named several of his friends as guardians for the young Adam Smith. These men were participants in the early stages of the Scottish Enlightenment, to which Adam Smith became a major contributor.

Smith's family could afford good accommodations for Smith throughout his years of schooling because the elder Smith died a fairly rich man, leaving a large income and some property behind. Smith continued being dependent on family income through his teens and adulthood. Throughout his life Smith was frequently dependent on rich businessmen, gentry, intellectuals and aristocrats for teaching positions, his pension, and his appointment as a customs officer.

Margaret Douglas, Smith's mother, was from a powerful, landowning family. As we indicated in the Introduction, she was a Stoic woman with firm religious values. She believed in controlling one's emotions through self-command, a personal discipline that she clearly passed on to Smith.[9] Based on her portrait by C. Metz (Kirkcaldy Museum of Art) (Ross, 1995, p. 310), Ross views her as an austere woman. Ross states that "when Smith writes in *WN* of the two systems of morality, on the one hand the liberal and on the other the strict and austere (v.i.g.10), it is perhaps appropriate to think of his mother as upholding the values of the second" (p. 309).

Margaret Douglas was left a widow with a newborn after a marriage of only about three years. According to his biographers, Smith was constitutionally a sickly child and his health prevented him from participating in the activities of his peers. Douglas Stewart wrote, "The weakness of his bodily constitutions prevented him from partaking in their more active amusements . . ." (Stewart (1793/1858, p. 270). Ross (1995) speaks of Margaret Douglas as a remarkable mother who brought Smith through an illness-ridden childhood, with the help of the guardians appointed in his father's will. While raising Smith, his mother had not only the support of Smith's guardians but also of her family. Ross (1995) suggests that Smith's mother was able to compensate for the absence of Smith's father through her close kinship and family bonds. Stewart (1793/1858) states that as a child, Smith "required all the tender solicitude of his surviving parent. She was blamed for treating him with an unlimited indulgence" (p. 1). Besides creating a stable environment for her sickly child, Margaret Douglas is also known to have encouraged him to become a distinguished scholar. According to Ross (1995), "There is every indication that he responded to his mother's care by loving her deeply and seeking to please her, not least in achieving distinction in his career as a professor and a man of letters" (p. 17).

Smith's mother was a Stoic woman. An aspect of the Stoic doctrine that is important in Smith's upbringing is the central tension between independence and dependence. On the one hand, nature has its rules that all creatures follow and on which they depend. On the other hand, rational creatures can show independence, choosing certain actions that they consider moral and rejecting others.

Smith never married. His most influential relationship was with his mother, to whom he kept returning to through his life. Smith lived with his mother until her death in 1784, only six years before his own passing in 1790. The depth of his feelings towards his mother is very eloquently expressed in a letter he wrote upon her death:

> That the final separation from a person who certainly loved me more than any other person ever did or ever will love me; and whom I certainly loved and respected more than I ever shall either love or respect any other person, I cannot help feeling, even at this hour, as a very heavy stroke upon me.
>
> (cited by Ross, 1995, p. 358)

Another important woman figure in Smith's life was his cousin Janet Douglas. She joined his household in 1754 and was his housekeeper. There are indications that his cousin partly filled the gap in his life after his mother's death. When she was dying, Smith wrote, "She will leave me one of the most destitute and helpless men in Scotland" (cited by Ross, 1995, p. 401).

As much as Smith depended on these two women, not only did he remain a bachelor all his life, but he also did not develop any lasting romantic relationships. There were only a few women who gained his affections. We are told that Smith was in love as a young man with a beautiful and accomplished woman. However, unknown circumstances prevented their marriage. Reportedly, he beamed at her company later in life, though only with kindness rather than with any romantic interest (Ross, 1995, p. 402). One may wonder whether Smith's appearance might have been an impediment to his involvement with women: he was a physically unattractive man with a funny walk. The known facts, however, suggest otherwise. For example, although actress and novelist Mme. Riccoboni thought him as ugly as a devil, she is said to have been won over by the goodness of his heart. "She was writing", Ross records, "that she liked Smith very much, wishing the devil would carry off all the *gens de letters* and bring back Smith" (p. 210). Ross adds, "It is feared that the biographer can do little more with the topic of Smith's sex life than contribute a footnote to the history of sublimation" (p. 214).

At the same time, it seems that Smith had wishes about being a father. Ross (1995) quotes a letter in which Smith writes,

> not only to shew it some of my young friends, in the mean time, but to leave it a legacy to my family and Posterity, if it should ever please God to grant me any, as an example of inflexible probity which they ought to follow on all occasions.
>
> (p. 257)

Despite his lack of any lasting romantic relationship, Smith had numerous male friendships, starting in his childhood. Above all he was beloved for his character. Through all accounts of his character and personality, Smith is described as a good, kind and even-tempered man who was beloved by many for these characteristics.[10] He was known for relying on signs of sympathy or the lack of it to gauge the effect of what he was saying. He was legendary for his absentmindedness.[11] At times, this led him to exhibit embarrassed manners in the company of strangers; however, Smith was extremely communicative. Ross (1995) quotes Carlyle, who shared a membership with Smith at the Poker Club, saying that,

> he was the most absent man in Company that I ever saw, Moving his Lips and talking to himself, and Smiling, in the midst of large Company's. If you awak'd him from his Reverie, and made him attend to the Subject Conversation, he immediately began a Harangue and never stop'd till he told you all he knew about it, with the utmost Philosophical Ingenuity.
>
> (p. 142)

Smith's sickly nature continued through his adulthood. His physicians diagnosed him with hypochondriasis, as Smith continually experienced exhaustion, low spirits, bad appetite, skin disease, involuntary shaking of the head, pains in the limbs and violent colds. "He would often be forced to stop writing because of sudden bouts of illness. . . . By all accounts, including his own, his poor-health impinged on his work time" (Weinstein, 2001, p. 9). At times, Smith's health appears to have interfered with his social and personal relationships. Stewart (1793/1858) quotes a letter from Hume (1772) to Smith:

> I shall not take any excuse from your state of health, which I suppose only a subterfuge invented by indolence and love of solitude. Indeed, my dear Smith, if you continue to hearken to complaints of this nature, you will cut yourself out entirely from human society, to the great loss of both parties.
>
> (p. 25)

Smith, however, had numerous lifelong friends, some of whom were "the most famous minds of his time, including, but not limited to Edmund Burke, Benjamin Franklin, Adam Ferguson, Turgot, and Voltaire. His greatest friend, and perhaps his greatest influence was David Hume" (Weinstein, 2001, p. 8). He felt a great affection for Hume. They are known to have advised each other on personal, philosophic and professional matters. In Hume's obituary, which Smith wrote in the form of a letter, he spoke of his friend in the most glowing terms. He concluded by writing,

> I have always considered him, both in this lifetime and since his death as approaching as nearly the idea of a perfectly wise and virtuous man, as perhaps the nature of human frailty will permit.
>
> (Weinstein, 2001, p. 19)

Smith's writings suggest that he considered friendships and family very important for happiness (Griswold, 1999; Nieli, 1986). Man's affections naturally fall upon his immediate family, according to Smith. In his view, man has a natural great affection for his family from habit and past acquaintance. He knows their situation, and he is also in a position to have an effect upon them. In Smith's words,

> Wealth and external honours are their proper recompense, and the recompense which they can seldom fail of acquiring. What reward is most proper for promoting the practice of truth, justice and humanity? The confidence, the esteem and love of those we live with. Humanity does not desire to be great, but to be beloved. It is not in being rich that truth and justice would rejoice, but in being trusted and believed, recompenses which those virtues almost always acquire.
>
> (*TMS*, p. 194)

Smith expresses his belief that a prudent man is always capable of friendships and steady faithful attachments (TMS, p. 251). The most virtuous attachment, which is the happiest form of attachment, is based, according to Smith, upon the love of virtue (TMS, p. 264).

His affections towards his friends were equally returned by them. Ross (1995) quotes a letter from a friend of Smith's written one month prior to Smith's passing in July 1790: "Poor Smith! We must soon lose him; and the moment in which he departs will give a heart-felt pang to thousands" (p. 404). Stewart (1793/1858) also writes that Smith

> will be long remembered by a small circle, with whom, as long as his strength permitted, he regularly spent an evening in the week; and to whom the recollection of his worth still forms a pleasing, though melancholy bond of union.
>
> (p. 38)

IV.2. Psychoanalytic suggestions about Smith's personal dependency

In this section, potentially relevant suggestions towards a psychoanalytic formulation of Smith's dependency patterns are discussed. Of course, this section is necessarily speculative because of the limited information we have about Smith's personal relationships and about the characters of his primary attachment figures.

Three pertinent experiences have resulted in shaping some very significant attitudes in Smith. These experiences are: he was a sickly child and a hypochondriac in his adult life; his father died prior to his birth; he lived with his mother for most of his life until her death in her 90s and did not have any romantic partners. These experiences not only shaped his character but also significantly affected his perceptions. We also assume that the experiences that he did not have also influenced his understandings of himself and the world. He excluded significant aspects of human nature within himself and in his writings about the market place. This is particularly true of his attitudes towards independence and dependence.

There is considerable evidence that Smith was a sickly child. This would undoubtedly bring with it intense feelings of helplessness, powerlessness, frustration, anger and an acute sensitivity to power differentials. It has been noted earlier that these types of feelings are notably missing from his discourse. The denial of such feelings is consistent with obsessive dynamics that deny such human passions and isolate his affects from the realm of human discourse.

There are many references to an "All-powerful Being" in Smith's TMS, which is his treatise on moral code. Law and order are most often associated with power and authority. We often endow the father with power and authority as an inherited part of our psychological makeup (see for example, Etchegoyen (2001) and Fanogy and Target (2002)). This was first noted by Freud (1913). Smith, however, saw the Deity not only as punishing but also as benevolent. In the TMS, he writes,

> The happiness of mankind, as well as of all other rational creatures, seems to have been the original purpose intended by the Author of nature, when he brought them into existence.
>
> (TMS, p. 193)

Thus, it is possible that Smith was referring to an idealized all-powerful father with a yearning for his protection and the harmony that might be created by him. His idealization of independence might be a defense against this longing. Having grown up without a father, he would have been left with many unconscious fantasies about who his father was and what this world of men might be about.[12]

One of Smith's constructs that extends his denial of human emotions is in his disavowal of human differences. Viewing others as equal diminishes a need to depend on them and avoids envy and competitiveness that would come as a result of individual differences. Such differences would emphasize one person's attributes or abilities over another. Recognition of differences would also bring to light dependency needs, which further bring with them longing, frustration, anger and envy. His having grown up without a father might highlight the unique dependency needs that a child would have on a father. His not having had a father would deprive him of the experience of being dependent in an unequal power oriented relationship and its attendant emotional reactions.

It appears that lacking a father, Smith may have been left with a longing resulting in a deep wish for a connection with men. It is conceivable that Smith's male friends fulfilled the role of his father in his life. We know that his friends included the most famous minds of his time. A point that raises curiosity on this subject concerns how he was described by his friends. His male friends frequently depicted him as generous and kind. One may wonder whether his generosity towards men in his life stemmed from his longing for a father. In other words, his generosity might have been a subliminatory defense against this longing. He further defended against this longing by idealizing his needs in relation to other men to defend against his natural longing for a father and for human love with a woman other than his mother.

The absence of Smith's father might also have played a crucial role in Smith's lifelong dependence on his mother. First, the absence of his father is likely to have made it possible for Smith's mother to have greater than usual influence. His inability to separate from his mother might also suggest that Smith did not experience father surrogates, despite the presence of guardians appointed by his father and of his mother's close ties to male kinsfolk (such as her brother). Furthermore, his mother might have failed to potentiate a relationship with a father, even if in fantasy, in his father's absence. Perhaps, she could not separate from Smith to allow him space for a triadic representation.

When we speak about Smith's mother, we are touching a confluence of issues ranging from her character and the circumstances of his birth to his not having a father and its implications for the oedipal struggle. We don't know much about Smith's mother other than that she had a strong character, she had strict values and she held the view that one's emotions should be kept regulated. At the same time, she has been described as overindulgent of Smith. Her husband's passing before Smith's birth, combined with Smith's sickly nature, might have generated or heightened anxieties about mothering in her. Given what we know of her character and circumstances at Smith's birth, a question that arises is if she was able to respond in consistently containing and mirroring manners towards her infant. If indeed she failed to mirror or contain him at times and was at other times overindulgent, Smith would have found himself in an environment where the effects of his behavior were unpredictable. He would have been left with un-soothed feelings such as anxiety, fear and a desire for comfort. It is possible that his lifelong hypochondriasis was consciously or unconsciously a way he knew to gain his mother's affections.

It is also of no small importance to note that for Smith in his father's death he wins the oedipal conflict by default. Not only does this bring with it additional unconscious guilt, it once again does not allow Smith to experience the identification with the father and its resultant learning. In this circumstance what is lost is not only the opportunity for father to son bonding but also the modeling of the independent/dependent relationship between his mother and father.

Smith does not have any recorded romantic partnerships with women. There is, of course, the possibility that Smith had romantic partnerships that are not known to us. We don't know if he had an attraction to men, a possibility that might have emerged from his being without a father to provide a model of masculine identity for him. Given the importance of keeping one's personal affairs private at the time, either of these possible situations would, of course, have been kept as secrets. Smith's continual return to his mother may suggest that he idealized her. It is possible that his idealization of his mother did not allow any room for other intimate partnerships in his life. It appears that Smith met his needs for closeness through a relationship with his mother instead of meeting them through an adult romantic partnership. His relationship to his mother and its exclusive dependencies do not appear to have allowed him the experience to forge a real life relationship with an autonomous woman and the experience of forging a new relationship with all its attendant struggles, joys and emotional learning experiences.

The above discussion suggests that Smith experienced an un-integrated pattern in his relationships with women, vacillating between dependence and avoidance. This collision of two separate world views is expressed not only in Smith's personal relationship patterns but also in his writings. As my analysis of the WN demonstrates, in that text, Smith idealizes impersonalized interdependence. In contrast, in the TMS, he idealizes personal dependency.

How does someone deal with disturbingly intense and widely ranging experiences of human dependency? There is no doubt that Smith was a genius. It seems that he used his genius to defend against the un-integrated collision of idealized versus devalued dependency through creative solutions. It thus seems that his admiration of impersonalized interdependence, reflected in his theorizing in the WN, was a solution for him. Putting it in different terms, we may conceive that the glorified state of independence in the WN was a reaction formation to his lifelong dependence on his mother and financial dependence on his benefactors. It is therefore suggested that Smith turned the dependency he experienced in his personal life into its polar opposite in writing the WN.

Denying his reality of lifelong dependence on his mother and benefactors, Smith appears to have idealized independence.

V. Concluding remarks

Smith glorified an economy where impersonalized transactions among self-interested individuals take place. He idealized markets, arguing that market expansion would lead to economic prosperity. The argument he makes is that larger markets create greater opportunities for exchange. Increased opportunities for trade lead, in turn, to a greater division of labor and thus improve productivity and economic growth. Smith's idealization of markets as sites of impersonalized interdependence among participants was rooted in his lifelong struggle with dependency. In the denial of the reality of his personal dependence, he conceived of markets as institutions that would lead to independence and hence to prosperity.

The importance of analyzing the works and lives of leaders in their fields has to be undertaken. In doing so, we not only understand a man and his work but also how an entire field develops and ideas survive. Freud (1921) suggests that the groups that can subsist are those that can identify themselves, not only with one another, but with a leader. Thus, he asserts that man is not a herd animal but a horde animal led by a chief. Adam Smith was and continues to be such a chief. Whether we individually agree with his ideas on economics or not, they continue to influence our everyday lives.

In closing, it is suggested that a general analysis of dependency needs and their effect on one's chosen beliefs about economics and how those has shifted over time would be an important topic to be further explored.

This chapter was published by Ozler: "Adam Smith and dependency", *Psychoanalytic Review, 99*(3), pp. 334–358, June 2012.

Notes

1 For example, "Freud offered his bold cultural hypotheses as cultural inventions and in 1934 planned to subtitle his book on Moses 'a historical novel'" (Loewenberg, 2007, p. 20).

2 Thus, at its foundation, psychoanalytic methodology requires listening. The suspension of individual biases or presuppositions is also an important feature of psychoanalytic listening in favor of the present materials. "So, listening has to do with various sources of information, and listening ultimately implies organization – being open to chaos and uncertainty, being unconsciously receptive and sensitive, but it also means knowing how to organize the material and how to understand it. . . . You can identify a series of steps if you want: unencumbered listening, understanding, new fragmenting, synthesizing, formulating, interpreting, and validating – and then starting the whole or part of the process again" (Langs, 1978, pp. 10–11).

3 In Bion's words, "The rock on which the analysis comes to shipwreck is the obstruction of the memories and desires of the psychoanalyst" (1967, p. 126).

4 Loewenberg's list also includes sexuality and gender identifications, attitudes towards property and wealth, consistent personal and interpersonal styles, demeanor, and activities, fantasy, humor, evidence of ambivalence, action or inhibition, frustrations, and their

tolerances, aggression and hostility, rationalizations, splitting, that is, polarizing and dividing the world, symbolic politics and anxiety, earlier traumas, narcissism, crisis, life space,
such as attitudes towards time, competition, nature, rivalry and death (Loewenberg, 2007,
pp. 109–111).

5   For overviews of the WN, see Özler and Kuiper (2007; 2008).
6   For a discussion of Smith's views on social dependence, see Perelman (1989).
7   Nieli (1986) argues that in Smith's system of "natural connections", there is a sphere that
expands outwards from nuclear family to extended family to friends and finally to the
national level.
8   Smith indicates that this propensity might arise from "original principles of human
nature" or from "reason or speech" (WN, II.ii.2).
9   Smith himself placed a great value on the regulation of emotions, reflecting his upbringing with Stoic morals. Smith writes, "Self-command is not only itself a great virtue, but
from it all the other virtues seem to derive their principle luster" (TMS, p. 284). Smith
saw early childhood as a period of overwhelming emotions "when an indulgent . . . parent must pit one violent feeling in the child against another . . . to restore their charge's
even temper" (Ross, 1995, p. 21). However, he believed there was no such indulgent partiality at school and that the school years were therefore crucial in character formation.
10 A couple of anecdotes evidence exceptions to his even temperament. On one occasion,
"Johnson . . . attacked Smith for praising Hume and called him a liar, whereupon Smith
retorted that Johnson was a son of a bitch" (Ross, p. 192). Smith was also said to be a
"most disagreeable fellow after he drank some wine" (Ross, p. 251).
11 A widely cited anecdote tells us that while "he was talking warmly on his favorite subject, the division of labour", he "forgot the dangerous nature of the ground on which he
stood" and fell into a pit – a noisome pool (Ross, p. 152).
12 Smith's well known phrase of the "invisible hand", which reconciles individual and
social interests, might be a reference to his absent father.

References

Berry, C.J., 2003. Sociality and socialization. In: Brodie, A., ed. *The Cambridge companion to the
Scottish Enlightenment*. Cambridge: Cambridge University Press. pp. 243–257.
Bion, W., 1962. Learning from experience. In: *Seven servants*. New York: Jason Aronson.
pp. 1–111.
Emerson, R., 2003. The contexts of the Scottish Enlightenment. In: Brodie, A., ed. *The
Cambridge companion to the Scottish Enlightenment*. Cambridge: Cambridge University Press.
pp. 9–30.
Etchegoyen, A., 2002. Psychoanalytic ideas about fathers. In: Trowell, J. and A. Etchegoyen,
ed. *The importance of fathers*. New York: Taylor & Francis Inc., pp. 20–41.
Fanogy, P. and Target, M., 2002. Fathers in modern psychoanalysis and in society. In: Trowell, J.
and A. Etchegoyen, ed. *The importance of fathers*. New York: Taylor & Francis Inc., pp. 20–41.
Feiner, S.F., 2003. Reading neoclassical economics: Toward an erotic economy of sharing. In:
Barker, D. and E. Kuiper, eds. *Toward a feminist philosophy of economics*. London: Routledge.
pp. 180–193.
Fiori, S. and Pesciarelli, E., 1999. Adam Smith on relations of subordination, personal incentives and the division of labor. *Scottish Journal of Political Economy, 46*, pp. 91–106.
Freud, S., 1913. Totem and taboo. In: *The standard edition of the complete psychological works by
Sigmund Freud, XIII* (Translated by J. Strachey. 1960). London: Hogarth Press. pp. 1–162.
———, 1921. Group psychology and the analysis of the ego. In: *The standard edition of the
complete psychological works by Sigmund Freud, XVIII*. (Translated by J. Strachey. 1955). London: Hogarth Press. pp. 88–92.

Garret, A.V., 2003. Anthropology: The "original" human nature. In: Brodie, A., ed. *The Cambridge companion to the Scottish Enlightenment*. Cambridge: Cambridge University Press. pp. 79–93.

Griswold, C.L., 1999. *Adam Smith and the virtues of Enlightenment*. Cambridge: Cambridge University Press.

Haakonssen, K. ed., 2006. *The Cambridge companion to Adam Smith*. New York: Cambridge University Press.

Harding, S., 1995. Can feminist thought make economics more objective?. *Feminist Economics*, *1*(1), pp. 17–32.

Hetherington, N.S., 1983. Isaac Newton's influence on Adam Smith's natural laws in Economics. *Journal of History of Ideas*, *44*, pp. 497–505.

Kuiper, E., 2002. Dependency and denial in conceptualizations of economic exchange. In: Gerschlager, C. and M. Mokre, eds. *Exchange and deception. A feminist perspective*. Dordrecht: Kluwer Publishers. pp. 75–90.

Langs, R., 1978. *The listening process*. New York: Jason Aronson.

Lewis, L.J., 2000. Persuasion, domination and exchange: Adam Smith on the political consequences of markets. *Canadian Journal of Political Science*, *33*(2), pp. 273–289.

Loewenberg, P., 2007. *Decoding the past: The psychohistorical approach*. Brunswick, NJ: Transaction Publishers.

Marglin, S.A., 1974. What do bosses do? The origins and functions of hierarchy in capitalist production. *Review of Radical Political Economics*, *6*, pp. 60–112.

Nelson, J.A., 1992. Gender, metaphor, and the definition of economics. *Economics & Philosophy*, *8*(1), pp. 103–125.

Nieli, R., 1986. Spheres of intimacy and the Adam Smith problem. *Journal of the History of Ideas*, *47*, pp. 611–624.

Özler, S. and Kuiper, E.J., 2007. Psychoanalytic analysis of texts by Adam Smith (1723–1790). *Journal of American Psychoanalytic Association*, *55*(1), pp. 305–309.

———, 2008. On dependency and the market: A psychoanalytic reading of Adam Smith's wealth of nations. Manuscript, UCLA, Los Angeles.

Perelman, M., 1989. Adam Smith and dependent social relations. *History of Political Economy*, *18*, pp. 503–520.

Rosenberg, N., 1990. Adam Smith and the stock of capital. *History of Political Economy*, *22*(1), pp. 1–17.

———, 2003. Adam Smith and the division of labour: Two views or one? *Economica*, *32*(126), pp. 127–139.

Ross, I. S., 1995. *The life of Adam Smith*. Oxford: Clarendon Press.

Schumpeter, J.A., 1954. *History of economic analysis*. E. Boody, ed. London: Routledge.

Stewart, D., 1858. *Account and the Life and Writings of Adam Smith LL.D.* In: Sir Hamilton, W., ed. *Collected works*. Edinburg: T. Constable and Co. Vol. 10, pp. 1–98. (Original work read at the Royal Society of Edinburgh, 1793)

Weinstein, J.R., 2001. *On Adam Smith*. Belmont, CA: Wadsworth.

Weisskopf, W.A., 1949. Psychological aspects of economic thought. *The Journal of Political Economy*, *57*(4), pp. 304–314.

West, E.G., 1969. *Adam Smith*. New York: Arlington House.

Wood, P., 2003. Science in the Scottish enlightenment. In: Brodie, A., ed., *The Cambridge companion to the Scottish enlightenment*. Cambridge: Cambridge University Press. pp. 94–116.

Chapter 10

On friendship

I. Introduction

In this chapter, we will examine Smith's work on friendship and then look at it from several psychoanalytic perspectives. As we will describe in the next section, Smith saw the satisfaction of the human need for connectedness and friendship as being fundamental for wellbeing. He saw this need as a significant component of sympathy, and it is because solitude is "horrifying" that we seek out contact with others. We will further examine the motivations that Smith sees as the force behind friendship: Does Smith view friendship as something that we seek out in some pragmatic way to serve our self-interest by avoiding the dread of being alone? Or does he see it coming from a genuine desire to be related to others and experience the pleasure of that "fellow feeling"? Or perhaps there is some combination of both.

Smith observes that where there is love and friendship, society flourishes and people are happy. That being said, it also appears from his writings that Smith's notion of friendship points to its pragmatic usefulness. To follow this line of inquiry, friendship appears to be prescriptive to alleviate discomfort. This perspective views friendship as the result of an evaluative thought process that seeks to fulfill a personal deficit, and does not necessarily seek out intimate contact or the valuing of another person based on a generative feeling towards that person. Put another way, friendship appears in some of Smith's work as an objectified need that must be met to alleviate suffering rather than something that one takes pleasure in and seeks out. He also tells us that a prudent man is capable of friendship and that the most virtuous friendships are based on a mutual love of virtue. This latter understanding would lend support to the notion that friendship is something of an objectified function. Rather than seeking out the pleasure of friendship, friendship is used to avoid the pain of isolation.

In the secondary literature, an argument made is that friendship is based on love. Griswold (1999) and Uyl and Griswold (1996) state that an important component of the TMS is friendship.[1] They argue that

> The Theory of Moral Sentiments is generally about love: our need for love and sympathy, love as friendship, self-love, the love of praise and praiseworthiness, the love of beauty.
>
> (pp. 609–610)

An example of this that Smith gives is "the chief part of human happiness arises from a consciousness of being beloved" (TMS, I.ii.5.2). They argue that sympathy in the broadest sense is mutual affection, thus friendship is enduring mutual affection for Smith. Mutual friendship is agreeable to the impartial spectator, and Smith is entirely approving of love among family members. Since the conduct we approve in ourselves is also that which we approve of in others, friends are our other selves. The key to seeing friends as other selves and linking friends with virtue is self-approbation. A long acquaintanceship and much experience are necessary for friendship in addition to virtue.

We will review Smith's position and analyze the nature of friendship that is being described. Is it love (the genuine desire to be related to another) or usefulness (the desire to protect and control our wellbeing) or some interesting combination of both? He seems to offer examples and reasons for both. Such an analysis enables us to investigate what was included and what might be missing in Smith's description of friendships. Without saying so he seems to be including both, starting from the pragmatic virtuousness of friendship and then citing the beneficial effects of friendship upon the human condition. His starting point seems to be similar to his understanding of others' needs from enlightened self-interest. However, it is also clear that the larger implications of Smith's impersonalized interdependence, which we described in Chapter 9, are very important to the expansion of human interactions.

To contextualize our work, we then review the literature on friendship in commercial societies that is based on Smith's work. The debate in that literature is on whether commercial societies are conducive to warm friendships or more cool distant relationships. Our view is that even though one can find elements of both in Smith's work, the work on the whole when it comes to commercial societies implies cool friendships.

We analyze Smith's work from a psychoanalytic perspective. We see an idealized view of love and friendship in Smith's work. This idealization is based on seeing friendships from the view point of good/bad and right/wrong. Those who live up to these ideals are included and those who do not are excluded. For example, he does not include some dynamics in human relationships that are examined in the psychoanalytic literature. These include the absence of love, guilt and reparation, a mechanism to accommodate the positive and negative feelings and mature dependence. Our goal in doing this is not to criticize Smith from modern psychoanalytic perspectives. Rather, in using the understandings generated by the contemporary psychoanalytic literature, we aim to argue that on the whole friendship in the TMS is based on cool interactions that involve usefulness of friendships.

II. Smith on friendship

Smith puts generosity, humanity, kindness, compassion, mutual friendship and esteem together. He goes on to say that when all of these social and benevolent affections are expressed

> in countenance or behaviour, even towards those who are not particularly connected with ourselves, [they] please the indifferent spectator upon almost every occasion.
>
> (TMS, p. 47)

Smith tells us that these emotions, even when they are excessive, are never regarded with aversion. "There is something tender agreeable even in the weakness of friendship and humanity" (TMS, p. 49).

Smith values conversations with friends as well as strangers by saying that "The conversation of a friend brings us to a better, that of a stranger to a still better temper" (TMS, p. 178). From this perspective, he sees friendship as a human need, and that deprivation from friendship is an atrocity. Even the "rudest vulgar man" feels the affections of friendship and the harmony that it brings. Friendships are useful; our friend expresses sympathy with our joy, and he enters our resentments, which we are anxious to communicate. Even when one fails due to his own fault, he can generally depend on the sympathy of his friends. There is a consensual validation in friendships.

> Where the necessary assistance is reciprocally afforded from love, from gratitude, from friendship, and esteem, the society flourishes and is happy. All the different members of it are bound together by the agreeable bands of love and affection, and are, as it were, drawn to one common center of mutual good offices.
>
> (TMS, p. 100)

This quote supports the hypothesis that Smith sees friendship coming from a genuine love and desire to be related as a primary motivation. He goes on to express that the impartial spectator is pleased when mutual friendship and all the benevolent affections are expressed. When the impartial spectator approves our conduct, we are in friendship and harmony with all mankind.

> The man within the breast decides when friendships ought to yield gratitude and security. In what cases friendship ought to yield to gratitude, or gratitude to friendship, in what cases the strongest of all natural affections ought to yield to a regard for the safety of those superiors upon whose safety often depends that of the whole society; and in what cases natural affection may, without impropriety, prevail over that regard; must be

left altogether to the decision of the man within the breast, the supposed impartial spectator, the great judge and arbiter of our conduct.

(TMS, p. 267)

With the approval of the impartial spectator, we feel secure and worthy of high regard. When we are excluded from friendships, we are excluded "from the best and most comfortable of all social enjoyments" (TMS, p. 286). We have the greatest sympathy for friendship.

On the other hand, he speaks in a way that also sees friendship as being utility based, for example when he indicates that our joy is enlivened when our friends express sympathy with our joy. Yet, we are more anxious to communicate our disagreeable passions, such as resentment, because we gain more satisfaction from it in comparison to when we share our disagreeable feelings.

We can venture to express more emotion in the presence of a friend than in that of a stranger, because we expect more indulgence from the one than from the other.

(TMS, p. 242)

However, this utility is limited. Smith also tells us that when in adversity we should not seek the sympathy of intimate friends but go into the "day-light of the world and society". We are told to do the same thing when we have good fortune as well.

In this way, it seems that Smith idealizes friendships and wants to keep them for certain types of interactions and not others. Friends bring tranquility and sedateness to our minds. We excuse a person who treats his weak friends with kindness and humanity. We can express emotions in the presence of a friend more readily than in the company of strangers. "There is something agreeable even in the weakness of friendship and humanity" (TMS p. 49). Friends also give us more sympathy than common acquaintances. We share our friends' joy, and we listen to them with gravity when they face a misfortune. Smith says that we expect more indulgence from a friend.

According to Smith, an attachment that is

founded altogether upon esteem and approbation of his good conduct and behavior confirmed by much experience and long acquaintance is by far the most respectable.

(TMS, p. 264)

These attachments that are based on natural sympathy are not rendered habitual for convenience and can exist only among men of virtue.

The attachment which is founded upon the love of virtue, as it is certainly, of all attachments, the most virtuous; so it is likewise the happiest, as well as the most permanent and secure. Such friendships need not be confined to a single person, but may safely embrace all the wise and virtuous, with whom we have been long and intimately acquainted, and upon whose wisdom and virtue we can, upon that account, entirely depend.

(TMS, p. 264)

Friendship for Smith is also qualified and has a prescriptive attitude. People should treat a weak friend with humanity and kindness. We should treat the friends who fail with generosity. Yet, even in the "noblest and the best of minds", the one who succeeds will be treated with more affection, even if the difference is little. Smith tells us what kinds of friendships are respectable:

But of all attachments to an individual, that which is founded altogether upon the esteem and approbation of his good conduct and behaviour, confirmed by much experience and long acquaintance, is, by far, the most respectable . . . persons to whom we attach ourselves are the natural and proper objects of esteem and approbation; can exist only among men of virtue. Men of virtue only can feel that entire confidence in the conduct and behaviour of one another, which can, at all times, assure them that they can never either offend or be offended by one another.

(TMS, p. 265)

This reference to friendship seems to have an evaluative thought process. In this instance Smith talks about internal states without referring to feeling states. In this way, he seems to objectify friendships and exclude real subjective feelings states even though Smith seems to be referring to feeling states in the following example:

When we bring home to ourselves the situation of his companions, we enter into their gratitude, and feel what consolation they must derive from the tender sympathy of so affectionate a friend. And for a contrary reason, how disagreeable does he appear to be, whose hard and obdurate heart feels for himself only, but is altogether insensible to the happiness or misery of others!

(TMS, p. 29)

Clearly Smith speaks of both the pragmatism of friendship and of the presence of love and its special accommodations in friendship. We will go on to further examine the permutations of friendship that Smith speaks of and examine them in the light of both Smith's dual understanding of friendship and from the psychoanalytic reflections on friendship in the following sections.

III. Friendship in commercial societies

In what follows we review the most relevant literature to give context to Smith's notion of friendship in commercial societies. There is a debate about whether Smith saw commercial society as conducive to warm friendships or as one that is based on cool strangership. Silver (1997) coined "strangership" as a neologism to indicate that interactions with strangers are a counterpart to being friends. As described by Silver (1997), the old meaning of a stranger being unfriendly has been replaced.

> ... the modern 'stranger' in well-ordered civil society [is] one who participates in the same society as oneself, who shares common ground in the literal and metaphorical sense of the phrase, and with whom there exists a pervasive possibility of becoming acquainted and allied.
>
> (p. 54)

Hill is one of the leading advocates of interpreting personal relationships in commercial societies as a form of "strangership", as exemplified in her 2011 article, among her other works (especially see, Hill, and McCarthy, 2004; Hill, 1996; Hill, 2010). Hill (2011) emphasizes that commercial society led to "new forms of amicable *strangership*" (p. 111). Hill and McCarthy (2004) argue that "the new "strangership" described by Smith is not warm, but rather, cool-friendship enhancing. According to the authors, Smith expressed no regrets about friendships being based on benefice and being replaced by the virtues of prudence and justice. Mechanisms of solidarity of traditional societies are replaced by the pursuance of self-interest within a division of labor that promotes exchange relationships. The commercial relationships are impersonal but polite and amicable. Friendships, though less intense, can now be extended to most anyone because one often comes into contact with many others through exchange relationships.

Cropsy (1957) states that commercial society glues people together through commercial relationships. According to Ignatief (1984), the dynamism to achieve progress can be only in a society of strangers mediated through indirect social relations. Paganelli (2010) argues that in commercial societies, the opportunities to interact with strangers lead to distance in personal relationships.

Smith describes the change in the nature of friendship that takes place in the highly quoted following passage:

> Among well-disposed people, the necessity or conveniency of mutual accommodation, very frequently produces a friendship not unlike that which takes place among those who are born to live in the same family. Colleagues in office, partners in trade, call one another brothers; and frequently feel towards one another as if they really were so. Their good

agreement is an advantage to all; and, if they are tolerably reasonable people, they are naturally disposed to agree. We expect that they should do so; and their disagreement is a sort of a small scandal. The Romans expressed this sort of attachment by the word necessitudo, which, from the etymology, seems to denote that it was imposed by the necessity of the situation.

(TMS, p. 263)

In Hill's and McCarthy's (2004) interpretation, the above paragraph does not refer to the demise of necessitudo. Instead, it refers to the way it has evolved into a commercial phenomenon. They state that Smith views warm friendships as chosen. Sympathetic relationships which have their origins in the desire to have a concordance of sentiments with others, especially the impartial spectator, are

> not to forge warm friendships, but rather to generate amicable strangerships. . . . Strangers are neither friends 'from whom we can expect any special favour or sympathy' nor 'enemies 'from whom we cannot except any special favour or sympathy at all'.
>
> (Hill and McCarthy, 2004, p. 5)

The new culture of strangership is impersonal, rational, voluntary, dispassionate and rule-governed, but polite and amiable. It is universalistic not exclusivist.

According to Berry (2010), in Smith's conceptualization of commercial societies there is a deep interdependence among the members of commercial society, which is also beneficial for the society as a whole because through division of labor it generates opulence for the society as a whole. Unprecedented levels of mutuality were developed through voluntary exchange. As Berry tells us:

> . . . since . . . in commercial society 'every man is a merchant' this further entails that a commercial society's coherence – its social bonds – does not depend on love and affection. You can co-exist socially with those to whom you are emotionally indifferent.
>
> (2010, p. 9)

We need the assistance even of those people we don't know, and in a commercial society we mostly live with strangers.

Along the same lines, in Chapter 9 we argued that in Smith's conceptualization interactions among individuals in the WN took the form of impersonalized interdependencies. This conceptualization is based on viewing Smith as having defended against his lifelong dependencies on his mother, and later his cousin and other benefactors.

Silver (1990; 1997) has a very different interpretation of friendship in Smith. He views that the above quote on necessitudo is a morally superior form of friendship because it is voluntary and based on natural sympathy instead of being constrained by necessity. To make this argument he states that the new form of friendship in commercial societies ". . . reflect[s] a new universalism in civil society, as does the market in the economy". He insists that Smith does not advocate an exchange theory of personal relationships. According to him, Smith's theory of personal relations is not based on self-interested exchange but on sympathy, and the new forms of personal relations cannot be addressed by market exchange (1997). In this view, sympathy helps form new friendships that spare society from hostile and suspicious relationships towards others and thus form a civil society.

Of course, Smith was also aware that even in commercial societies intimate friendships could develop. As quoted, for example in Berry (2010), Alvey (2005) and Young (1997), Smith states that "Commerce, which ought naturally to be, among nations, as among individuals, a bond of union and friendship . . ." (WN, p. 493). Commerce, thus, can convert trading partnerships, even strangers into friends (Alvey, 2005, p. 257). This, of course, does not mean that this was the predominant form of relationship that commercial society entailed according to Smith.

Bruni and Sugden (2008) use the term "sociality" to refer to relations between individuals that are based on some degree of intimacy, concern for the other, concern for the group and non-instrumentality. According to the authors, even though market relations cannot be conceptualized as friendships, by creating

> . . . a space in which friendship, constructed as an intimate and chosen relationship between equals, can exist. In this sense, the market allows us to pursue and express sociality; but is not itself a locus of sociality.
>
> (p. 45)

Their primary argument is that . . . market interactions [are] instances of wider class of reciprocal relationships in civil society, characterized by joint intentions of mutual assistance (p. 35).

At the other end of the spectrum, the view is that with the advent of commercial society there was a movement towards impersonal, individualistic, self-interested relationships, and that relationships were atomistic. Polanyi (1944) refers to a "certain isolation" in market societies as the view held by orthodox economists. That Adam Smith held this view is in part based on the following statement expressed by Stigler (1971): "The *Wealth* of *Nations* is a stupendous palace erected upon the granite of self-interest" (p. 265).

Particularly in his writings on commercial societies, Smith demonstrates a sensitivity to the "necissitudo" in impersonal exchanges. He does not rule out the possibility of some type of friendship in circumstances where self-interest dominates, however "strangership" is more often the circumstance of commerce.

IV. Friendship in psychoanalytic literature

Surprisingly, there has been little written on friendship in the psychoanalytic literature. Friendship in psychoanalytic parlance is a special form of object relation (relation to others). In our presentation below, we will describe important and relevant literature that is applicable to friendship and describe how it relates to Smith's views that we have described above. Our purpose is not to pass judgments on Smith's views from the psychoanalytic literature that followed his time. Rather, we are striving to highlight the salient aspects of human relationships that have been relevant since humans came to existence. Our goal is to identify the strengths and limitations of the friendships that Smith conceives.

Psychoanalytic theory pertinent to friendship

For Freud (1921; 1930), friendship is a manifestation of aim-inhibited sexuality. Friendship therefore is a sublimation of the sexual instinct that is channeled into interpersonal interactions. His view dominated psychoanalytic thinking over many years. Others after him offered up understandings that served to both extend and revise this view.

Klein (1937) built a strong argument that relationships in our adult life are shaped by our very early interactive experiences. Her work pointed out the ambivalence and complexity that make up friendships and close intimate relationships are affected by the many strong and opposing emotions that they elicit. Klein postulated that the baby both desires her mother and hates her; she is the first object of love and hate. Love is elicited when attachment is consonant to the baby's needs and feels well contained by the mother. Alternately, the baby becomes dominated by the impulses to destroy the person she desires most when frustration, hate and aggressive feelings are aroused. Throughout our lives, as in the baby's mind, love and hate are experienced, and this becomes a challenge in human relationships.

Klein further elucidated that when we experience hate towards a person we love, we feel guilty. The fear of losing the loved one becomes active when the conflicts between love and hate arise in the baby's mind. The resulting guilt enters as a new element into love, becoming an inherent part of love and influencing it markedly both in quantity and quality. We then make reparations in our unconscious phantasy for the injuries that we imagined doing in phantasy. In all human relationships making reparation is a fundamental element of love.

The very strong attachment towards the mother paradoxically also drives the child away from the mother because it leads to a fear of dependence. There is a conflict between the desire to give up the mother and the desire to keep her forever. These conflicts lead the child to develop the capacity to transfer love to others to replace the first loved ones. This is very important for the development of human relationships. The love for parents remains but love for other people is added. The child's conflicts and guilt arising from the attachment and the dependence on the first people she loves lessens with a wider circle of love. The conflict between love and hate do not disappear, but are transferred to others though in a lesser degree. The guilt feelings that arise due to hateful feelings towards others create a drive to make reparations. These early experiences and skills are transferable to interactions in later friendships.

Klein's work within psychoanalytic thought was augmented by the work of Fairbairn (1941), who introduced the notion that libido (instinctual sexual energy) is not primarily pleasure seeking, but is object seeking (seeks out others); unlike what was advanced by Freud (1921), "the psychological introjection of objects and, in particular, the perpetuation of introjected objects in inner reality are processes which by their very nature imply that libido is essentially object seeking" (Fairbairn, 1946, p. 70). Freud did not alter his libido theory, however there are places where he refers to libido as object seeking implicitly. He even makes it explicit by saying that "Love seeks for objects" (1930), even though he did not go so far as to elaborate this understanding the way Fairbairn did.

Parallel but not identical to Klein, in 1946 Fairbairn argued that the very early dependent and exclusive relationship with the mother matures into a complex system of relationships in all degrees of intimacy. In 1940, Fairbairn wrote about mature dependence. He described mature dependence as "a capacity on the part of the differentiated individual for cooperative relationships with differentiated objects" (p. 145). Individuals accept and relate to the integrity of others. Mature dependence is not the same as independence, because the capacity for relationship implies dependence to some degree. According to Fairbairn, there is a gradual developmental path from the total dependence of the newborn to mature dependence of the adult person. An individual necessarily depends on relationships with others because psychic dependence is not attainable in isolation.

Winnicott (1960a) extended, expanded and greatly elaborated on the work of Klein and argued that infant and maternal care together form a unit. He wrote that "there is no such thing as an infant", in other words there would be no infant without maternal care. The infant makes the journey from absolute dependency to relative dependence and then to independence. This develops in parallel to moving to the reality principle from the pleasure principle and from autoerotism to more mature object relations. In the phase of absolute dependence, the infant cannot know about maternal care. He does not have control over what is badly done and what is done well. At the relative dependence stage the infant becomes aware of the need for the details of maternal care. Finally, when the infant moves to independence, the infant develops the capacity for doing without actual care.

For healthy development of an infant, "good enough" mothering is necessary. The good enough mother "makes active adaptation to the infant's needs, an active adaptation that gradually lessens, according to the infant's growing ability to account for failure of adaptation and to tolerate the results of frustration"

(Winnicott, 1971, pp. 13–14). The good-enough mother repeatedly meets the omnipotence of the infant and to some extent makes sense of it. A true self begins to have life, through the strength given to the infant's developing ego by the mother's implementation of the infant's omnipotent expressions (Winnicott, 1960b, p. 145). In the extreme, when the mother's adaptation is not good enough at the start the infant might be expected to die physically, because the attachment to the external other is not initiated and the infant is cut off and isolated from maternal care (p. 146).

Mothers have three functions to facilitate a healthy development (Winnicott, 1962; 1965). (1) Holding is an important element of maternal care. Holding includes a range of activities by the mother from the literal physical holding and touching of the baby to following minute by minute changes in the infant's physical and psychological growth and development (Winnicott, 1960). It is based on holding in mind the infant's mental state. With the presence of the holding environment, aggression and love are integrated. Ambivalence is tolerated, and concern, acceptance and responsibility emerge (Winnicott, 1963). (2) The holding environment leads to the establishment of personalization. When the baby is not overwhelmed, the handling of the baby is adaptive. (3) Winnicott (1971) distinguishes object relating and object usage. In object relating, the subject is described as an isolate in object relating. Object usage is described in terms of acceptance of the object's independent existence, while relating is described in terms of the individual subject. But in object usage, the object, if it is to be used, must be a part of shared reality, in other words, must be real, not a bundle of projections. As part of the reality principle, the capacity to use objects must be developed by the subject, which is part of the maturational process. In moving to object usage, the subject destroys the object (it becomes external), then the object might survive the destruction by the subject. The subject says both "I love you" and "I destroyed you". If the object survives, the subject can now use the object. With the survival of the object, the subject starts to live a life in the world of objects. The mother becomes real and separate who can be used separately not just omnipotently.

Transitional objects constitute early friends (Winnicott, 1971). The object might be a doll, blanket or a pet. Transitional object serves as an early friend. It is an external adjunct to an inexperienced and tender ego. The sequence starts with the relationship of the infant to the mother, that then migrates to the use of transitional objects as a displacement and finally, after the mastery of inner inadequacies and conflict, there is a return to human relationships, including friendships. A significant milestone in this process of establishing outer relationships is the child learning to be alone, which paradoxically leads to the capacity to establish friendships (Winnicott, 1958). He states, "It seems that I attach great importance to this relationship, as I consider that it is the stuff out of which friendship is made" (p. 33).

Rangel (1963) is one of the few psychoanalysts that focused on friendship. He takes basic psychoanalytic understandings and studies them interactively and coined the term "intersystematic". He takes up where the theoretical work of Fairbairn left off by expanding the scope of the possibilities that are potentiated by friendship. Rangel hypothesizes that friendship is foundational to potentiating, mirroring and developing human capacities. Rangel examined instinctual and genetic development, and expanded on the role of complex structural and inter-systemic maturity. From this perspective, friendships serve as a major organizer of one's environment. Friendships are the fruition of structuralized, integrated and intersystemic relationships along with love and interpersonal development.

In friendships, multiple functions operate dynamically. Friends satisfy both sexual and aggressive instinctual drives, both primary and drive derivative. Friendships serve to regulate and meet homeostatic needs of the organism. Usually when we speak of friendship, it is a friendship based on positive and constructive affects. That being said, friendship also includes the generation of and mediation of aggression both within the individual and in the interpersonal interactions between friends. As such, friendships represent not only the derivatives primarily of erotic and libidinal components of the instinctual system of life, they are also important in the growth of our interpersonal capacities and the mastery of aggression and the affects of traumatic experiences.

Rangel sees a reciprocal interaction between the inherited ego apparatuses, instinctual drives and the environmental influences. Each follows independent developmental and maturational courses. The role of friendship can be placed within the continuously operating energetic exchange and operating network of influences. Friendships exert and receive multiple channels of communication, which serve both external and internal psychic ends. Along with love, friendships represent the realization of structuralized, integrated, intersystemic and interpersonal development. They become enduring with structuralizing.

Liking and having a regard for a person are essential components of friendships. The affects in friendships are more sustained, durable and even productive. Friendships are influenced by the external environment and the inner psychic development history, and have the potential to enhance adaptation through ongoing interaction.

Even though Kernberg (2011) writes about passionate love, several points he makes are relevant for any type of close relationship, including friendships. He points out the importance of "interest in the life project of the other". This interest is a source of personal enrichment. This brings a depth to joint explorations of intellectual interests, such as art. Identification with the values and interests of the other become one's own commitments and aspirations. Another important element is trust. Trust that the other will tolerate and understand one's frailty, one's uncertainty, allows one to be open on such things as conflicts and weaknesses. Forgiveness and being able to forgive the other, even in the face of major conflicts, adds an important dimension to close relationships. Deeply felt gratitude for the presence of the other and the closeness experienced, as well as acceptance of the uncertainty about future developments that might lead to changes in the relationship are elements of humility. Another important consideration is mature dependence, which involves the capacity to allow oneself to be taken care of by the other, without a sense of guilt and shame. Mature relationships also require the acceptance of the other as a free agent.

V. An analysis of friendship in Smith's works from a psychoanalytic perspective

Smith speaks of friendship and love from a somewhat idealized perspective. On the one hand, he has an optimistic perspective on love, life and friendships. Yet within his structure there is no real accommodation of the difficulties that come from human interaction. His idealization takes the form of good/bad, inclusion/exclusion and right/wrong. So, those who live up to the ideals are included and those who do not seem to be excluded. In fairness, his inclusion of friendship as an important component of life and development is a significant contribution. He laid out the gross structure of his understanding, and the elaboration of the more practical and developmental psychological matters are the work of more modern psychologists.

As Klein (1937) has commented, love, hate, guilt and reparation are aspects of human relations that are a significant part of human development and make possible the practical living of friendships. Winnicott, similar to Klein, speaks at length of the co-existence of love and destructive feelings, the accommodation of which are necessary for the ongoing care of human interactions. These important aspects about everyday relationships are not present in Smith's work. He speaks about love but not about the ambivalence in love, because he does not hold a perspective that recognizes hate or other negative feelings that are always present even in loving relationships. Smith's perspective did not include a practical accommodation for guilt or reparation in his characterization of love.

Smith shares a commonality with Fairbairn in viewing people as object seeking (seeking out others in relationship) because they find complete solitude horrifying. Fairbairn went on to elaborate and differentiate mature dependence from total dependence. These differentiations are limited in Smith because he has not elaborated on how individual differences and needs are accommodated. Also, mature dependence implies a dependence of some sort. However, as we have argued in Chapter 9, Smith does not elaborate on dependency at least in part because he seems to be defended against such dependency.

Smith shares with Kernberg the value of joint intellectual interests in relationships: "When we have read a book or poem so often that we can no longer find any amusement in reading it by ourselves, we can still take pleasure in reading it to a companion" (TMS, p. 17). Kernberg goes on to elaborate on the issue of trust. In particular, he offers that we trust that the other will tolerate and understand one's frailty and limitations as an important element of friendship. Smith does speak of friendship as bringing an "indulgence" and includes "love and gratitude". It is not clear if it included in the most virtuous of friendships based on the mutual love of virtue. It is also not clear whether the acceptance or tolerance of another's frailty are included. Smith does make references to gratitude for the presence of the other and the tolerance of a friend's limitations. Finally, Kernberg also elaborates on mutual dependence, and the capacity to allow oneself to be taken care of by the other, which once again was not a part of Smith's conceptualization.

Rangel's work on friendship elaborates on the many life serving functions that are brought about by good friendships. Smith certainly points to the value and need for friendship, while the more specific elaboration of the process and benefits are for more current theorists.

Psychoanalytic work does not include reflections on "strangership" or "impersonalized interdependence" that are a part of commercialized relationships. It can be conjectured that psychoanalytic commentary would include many of the aforementioned attributes such as love, hate, guilt and reparation, which to a modified extent still play an unconscious role even in impersonalized interactions.

VI. Discussion

Smith describes several qualities that are a part of friendship. He recognizes that some forms of friendship come from a genuine personal desire for friendship, even if it is to avoid the dread of being alone. He also elaborates about the needs of commerce, in which his more objectified view of friendship, with all its prescriptive detail, certainly has utility value. In answer to the question posed in the introduction, whether Smith sees friendship in terms of its ability to avoid the pain of isolation or as a genuine pleasure to seek out the friendship of another, the answer is that he certainly sees both, and it is our further observation that the preponderance of his work places a stronger emphasis on avoiding the pain of isolation both personally and in commerce.

Consistent with his many achievements, Smith conceptualized new forms of relatedness that served the growing needs of an era of human interaction that was necessitated by commercial relationships. He laid claim to a territory that was no doubt influenced by his own strengths and limitations, and formulated a new way of relating across a vast frontier of immediate, national and international relations. These new relationships were often based on mutual self-interest and the "necessitudo" for the tasks at hand in commerce. We also see the unintended consequences of such interactions as explicated by the numerous contributors that have written on this issue. We realize the many possibilities in human, commercial and international relations that are opened by such "strangership". As the result of long-term interactions, there is indeed the possibility of appreciation and friendship over time. Even larger is the possibility of coming to understand and accommodate great differences among individuals, communities, national and international partners. This mechanism for opening interactions no doubt stays mostly in the impersonal area but creates the possibility of larger understandings, connections and genuine friendships that may come out of what was originally an impersonal mechanism.

While this new form of interaction is not the same as what Kernberg alludes to in his examination of intimate relationships, it is not too great a stretch to imagine that many of the principals that he alludes to can also apply in this more impersonal sphere. First of all, these relationships are relationships of choice as are close intimate partnerships. There is the choice made to pursue these interactions. There is interaction based upon mutual interests that may include a growing interest in the other as a result of the mutual valuing of issues within commercial interactions. There is also an acceptance of the limitations or frailties that are implied in those interactions that do not preclude ongoing interaction, rather it is accommodated as a part of the relationship.

Note

1 The authors note that Thomas Read states "Sympathy seems to me to be inseparably connected with Love Affection and Esteem. I cannot possibly love a Man without being pleased with every good that befalls him and uneasy at his misfortune. [. . .] If you ask me why I take so much concern in his good or bad fortune it is because I love him" (Cited by Norton and Stewart-Robertson, 1980).

References

Akhtar, S., 2009. Friendship, socialization, and the immigrant experience. *Psychoanalysis, Culture & Society, 14,* pp. 253–272.

Alvey, J.E., 2005. Economics and religion: Globalization as the cause of secularization as viewed by Adam Smith. *International Journal of Sociology, 32*(3), pp. 249–267.

Berry, C.J., 2010. Adam Smith's moral economy. *The Kyoto Economic Review, 79*(1), pp. 2–15.

Bruni, L. and Sugden, R., 2008. Fraternity: Why the market need not be a morally free zone. *Economics and Philosophy, 24*(1), pp. 35–64.

Cropsy, J., 1957. *Polity and economy: With further thoughts on the principles of Adam Smith.* Indianapolis, IN: St. Augustine Press.

Emerson, R.W., 1926. *Friendship in essays, first and second series.* New York: Palgrave Macmillan, pp. 114–130.

Fairbairn, W. R. D., 1941. A revised psychopathology of the psychoses and psychoneuroses. *International Journal of Psychoanalysis, 22,* pp. 250–279.

———, 1946. *Schizoid factor in the personality: Psychoanalytic studies of the personality.* London: Tavistock Publications Limited.

Freud, S. 1921. Group psychology and the analysis of the ego. In: *Standard edition.* London: Hogarth Press Vol. 18, pp. 65–144.

———, 1930. *Civilization and its discontents.* In: *Standard edition.* London: Hogarth Press. Vol. 21, pp. 57–146.

Griswold, C.L., 1999. *Adam Smith and the virtues of enlightenment.* Cambridge: Cambridge University Press.

Grotstein, J., 1989. Of human bondage and human bonding: The role of friendship in intimacy. *Contemporary Psychotherapy Review, 5,* pp. 5–32.

Hill, L., 1996. Ferguson and Smith on "human nature", "interest" and the role of benefice in market society. *History of Economic Ideas, IV*(1–2), pp. 353–399.

————, 2010. Adam Smith's cosmopolitanism: The expanding circles of commercial stranger ship. *History of Political Thought, XXXI*(3), pp. 449–473.

————, 2011. Social distance and the new stranger ship in Adam Smith. *The Adam Smith Review, 6*, pp. 111–128.

Hill, L. and McCarthy, P., 2004. On friendship and necessitude in Adam Smith. *History of Human Sciences, 17*(4), pp. 1–16.

————, 2011. Social distance and the new strangership in Forman-Brazilia, F (Ed). Adam Smith. *The Adam Smith Review*, 6, pp. 111–128.

Ignatieff, M., 1984. *The needs of strangers*. New York: Picador Press.

Jones, E., 1942. The concept of a normal mind. *International Journal of Psychoanalysis, 23*, pp. 1–8.

Kernberg, O.F., 2011. Limitations to the capacity to love. *International Journal of Psychoanalysis, 92*, pp. 1501–1515.

Klein, M., 1937. *Love, guilt and reparation*. New York: The Free Press. pp. 344–369.

Norton, D.F. and Stewart-Robertson, J.C., 1980. Thomas Reid on Adam Smith's morals. *Journal of History of Ideas, 41*(3), pp. 381–389.

Paganelli, M.P., 2010. The moralizing role of distance in Adam Smith: The Theory of Moral Sentiments as possible praise for commerce. *History of Political Economy, 42*(3), pp. 425–441.

Polanyi, K., 1944. *The great transformation: The politics and origins of our time*. Boston: Beacon Press.

Rangell, L., 1963. On friendship. *Journal of the American Psychoanalysis Association, 11*, pp. 3–54.

Schulman, R., 2009. Commentary on friendship. In: Akhtar, S., ed. *Good feelings: Psychoanalytic Reflections on positive attitudes and emotions*. London: Karnac Books. pp. 267–274.

Silver, A., 1990. Friendship in commercial society: Eighteenth-century social theory and modern sociology. *American Journal of Sociology, 95*(6), pp. 1474–1505.

————, 1997. Two different sorts of commerce-Friendship and strangership in civil society. In: Weintrub, J. A. and K. Kumar, eds. *Public and private thought and practice: Perspectives on grand dichotomy*. Chicago: University of Chicago Press. pp. 43–74.

Stigler, G.J., 1971. Smith's travels on the ship of state. *History of Political Economy, 3*(2), pp. 265–277.

Uyl, D. J. D. and Griswold, C.L., 1996. Adam Smith on friendship and love. *The Review of Metaphysics, 49*(3), pp. 609–637.

Winnicott, D.W., 1958. The capacity to be alone. In: *The maturational process and the facilitating environment*. London: Karnac Books Ltd. pp. 29–36.

————, 1960a. The theory of parent-infant relationship. In: Winnicott, D.W., ed. *The maturational process and the facilitating environment*. London: Karnac Books Ltd. pp. 37–55.

————, 1960b. Ego distortions in terms of true and false self. In: Winnicott, D. W., ed. *The maturational process and the facilitating environment*. London: Karnac Books Ltd. pp. 140–152.

————, 1962. The theory of parent infant relationship: Further remarks. *International Journal of Psychoanalysis, 43*, pp. 238–245.

————, 1963. Communicating and not communicating leading to a study of certain opposites. In: Winnicott, D.W., ed. *The maturational process and the facilitating environment*. London: Karnac Books Ltd. pp. 179–192.

————, 1965. Ego distortions in terms of true and false self. In: Winnicott, D. W., ed. *Maturational process and the facilitating environment*. London: Karnac Books Ltd.

————, 1971. Transitional objects and transitional phenomena. In: Winnicott, D.W., ed. *Playing and reality*. New York: Tavistock. pp. 1–34.

Young. J.Y., 1997. *Economics as a moral science: The political economy of Adam Smith*. Cheltenham: Edward Elgar Publishing.

Chapter 11

A Jungian interpretation of the place of women in Smith's works

1. Introduction

Adam Smith's attitude towards morality and his attitude towards women reflect his ambivalence between instinctual nature (capacities we are born with) and the "self-command" that is necessary for the achievement of a virtuous moral structure. Smith viewed women as being identified with the instincts, and while this allows them to have humanity, it requires no self-command. Smith sees men as having the capacity for generosity because they are able to exercise self-command above and beyond humanity, which requires no self-command. Throughout his work, Smith consistently viewed the achievement of moral virtue through self-command as a great advancement, and values this achievement over instinctual life because it requires the exercise of effort and self-command.

We will consider Smith's attitude towards women from the perspective of C. G. Jung. Jung studied and wrote on a broad spectrum of psychological experiences and issues, and their implications for the psychological conditions that affect both men and women. We chose Jung's perspective because while he recognized differences between men and women, he did not discriminate between them as being better or worse. He saw both men and women as being capable of development. In particular, we will examine his understanding of the contrasexual aspects of "anima" and "animus", or the masculine and feminine qualities that are present in both men and women, to point out what seems to be missing in Smith's assumptions about men and women.

We conclude that at best Smith had an ambivalent attitude towards women and instinctual life, and this view mirrored the cultural attitudes of his time and was reflected in his writing on morality. For example, he identifies generosity as being a male attribute that requires self-command. Alternately he identifies humanity as an instinctual capacity that we are born with as an attribute of women, which does not require self-command. In his moral theory Smith puts a premium on self-command and elevates a man's capacity over a woman's. As such there is a premium of self-command over instincts, generating an implicit bias. Moreover, Smith's theory of moral judgment did not speak to the possibility that morality and self-command were intertwined with the instincts.

To give context to Smith's attitudes towards women, we review the salient cultural attitudes towards women during Smith's time. We review the feminist approaches of the time, which Smith was familiar with, as well as review the attitudes of Rousseau and Hume, his contemporaries. We will then review Smith's attitude towards women through his references in the TMS, WN and LJ. In particular, we explore Smith's attitude towards women by looking into the gendered and hierarchical distinction that Smith makes between humanity and generosity. Finally, after giving a brief description of Jung's concepts that are relevant for our undertaking, we will compare and contrast Jung's views with Smith's and we will recognize the strengths and limitations in Smith's theorizing.

II. Views of some of Smith's contemporaries on women

In this section we give a brief overview of contemporary feminist influences of the time and highlight the prevailing views on women on Smith's writings. In addition, we review the perspectives of Smith's contemporaries, Rousseau and Hume. These examples cast light on the cultural influences that are mirrored in Smith's writings.

Early feminist waves and the Scottish context

During the Scottish Enlightenment, the discussion of women's issues was just beginning.[1] That being said, at an everyday cultural level, there was little movement in real women's lives. We will look at the work of Sebastiani (2013) and Kuiper (2006) for this section. There were challenges to male hegemony throughout Western history (Offen, 2000). Several features of feminist discourse were listed: (1) the possibilities within women's roles were being enlarged, (2) male supremacy was being criticized, and (3) the conditions for women could be changed for the better (Akkerman and Stuurman, 1988).

While women played an intellectual role in Parisian salons, they remained excluded from clubs in Edinburgh and Glasgow. However, even in Scotland, women's status and visibility was on the rise. Women and men had equal access to salons in France in the 18th century. Women from the aristocracy who organized these salons invited guests like Diderot, Hume and Voltaire. Scientific academics were, however, closed to women (Noble, 1992). Women became respected members in advanced societies. During 1789–1793 in France, women had the opportunity to state their views.

During the 18th century, the position of women in Britain was slowly evolving. Economic developments led to the rise of the nuclear family. Workshops outside the house became prevalent, where tasks done by women at home earlier were being done where men and women initially worked together. Later, however, women were excluded from these workshops with the rise of the bourgeois ideology of the non-working housewife. Even though girls' education was being discussed and better education was being advocated for, there was not much change.

Feminist pamphlets, poems and books were being written from the mid-17th century onward. These were written by both lower-class women as well as by educated women with "good breeding". During this period of the Enlightenment, women's issues were a part of the exploration of societal issues (Offen, 2000). Women writers known as "Blue stockings" became more visible around the 1750s. They were telling women "to be assertive, take the lead, wait for no man, write, create, do not flinch from flouting custom" (Ferguson, 1985 cited in Kuiper, 2006, p. 43). These writings advocated better education for women (Wollstonecraft, 1792). It was also emphasized that men's jobs should be open to women and women's jobs should not be taken over by men.

Kuiper (2006) gives an excellent overview of two texts written by women during this period, both of which emphasize the changes in contemporary images of women: "... the role of women that began in the seventeenth century, towards a representation of women's lives that was increasingly based on their own experiences" (Kuiper, 2006, p. 43). Kuiper (2006) states that although she did not find any direct evidence of Smith being familiar with these two texts, she argues that Smith encountered this discourse on a number of occasions. According to the author Smith was also in direct contact with French, English and Scottish feminists.

The net result was that women became a symbol of commercial society in the 18th century, incorporating the ethos of conversation and transaction. As time went on, there was a distinctively feminine role in the consumer goods market and the community of taste. Men became more humanized and the relationship between men and women began to shift towards love, rather than mere instinctual reproduction. In this area women were relegated to monogamous marriage in family relations and the private sphere.

Society would rise towards perfection by the inclusion of women.

> The process of material development and the refinement of manners were so closely linked to the condition of women that a balanced relationship between the sexes became emblematic of progress itself. It was through this relationship that human sociability, initially merely potential could develop.
> (Sebastiani, 2013, p. 138)

Hume

Hume was a friend of Smith. As pointed out by O'Brien (2009), Hume's concern with internalization of morals in the family was his starting point in addressing issues concerning women.[2] In his "A Treatise of Human Nature" (1888) (Treatise from here on), Hume's view was that women's chastity was key to making society work. In the section entitled "of chastity and modesty" in the Treatise, Hume considers these two attributes as duties which belong to the "fair sex", similar to Smith who viewed the lack of chastity as the greatest offence. The foundation of these virtues is not in nature, rather, "such notions arise from education, from the voluntary conventions of men, and from the interest of society" (Hume, 1888, p. 570). These virtues of women are necessary to care for men's offspring. Shame was seen as the restraint against women's infidelity, as well as praise for chastity. This alone, however, is not sufficient because "All human creatures, especially of the female sex" more easily overlook "remote motives in favour of any present temptation" (Hume, 1888, p. 571). An important solution to this problem is education: "Education takes possession of the ductile minds of the fair sex in their infancy" (Hume, 1888, p. 572). Once established, the rule of this kind extends to old age (Hume, 1888).

The situation was seen as different for men:

> Tis contrary to the interest of civil society, that men shou'd have an entire liberty of indulging their appetites in venereal enjoyment: But as this interest is weaker than in the case of the female sex, the moral obligation, arising from it, must be proportionally lower.
>
> (Hume, 1888, p. 573)

In "Enquiry Concerning the Principles of Morals" (1751), Hume makes a distinction between "barbarous" societies and "civilized" societies regarding women. In the former, women are subject to male tyranny and outside the rules of justice. In civilized societies, on the other hand, through a process of sexual negotiation, women gain a measure of justice and public rights (Hume, 1751, p. 191).

In the essay "Of the rise and Progress of the Arts and Sciences" (1742), which suggests that male supremacy is best expressed through gallantry rather than tyranny, he states:

> As nature has given *man* the superiority above *woman,* by endowing him with greater strength of mind and body; it is his part to alleviate that superiority, as much as possible, by the generosity of his behaviour, and by a studied deference and complaisance for all her inclinations and opinions.
>
> (p. 133)

In the "History of England" (1808–1810), Hume claims that a prejudice against women is not a product of bigotry, but natural. He states some traits that characterize women: "womanish submission", timidity, bashfulness, excessively affectionate nature, jealousy and amorous gallantries.

Hume, at times, makes favorable comments about women, stating that "this sovereignty of man the man is real usurpation". According to him this destroys equality. He goes on to say:

> We are, by nature, their lovers, their friends, their patrons: Would we willingly exchange such endearing appellations, for the barbarous title of master and tyrant?

(1874–1875, p. 192)

Sebastiani (2005) highlights that in the shift of Europe from a subsistence economy to an international market, women were placed in a central role. "They came to represent 'commerce' as an economic and intellectual exchange" (p. 77). Hume (1752) wrote that men enter into the society of conversation, in an urban world, leaving their solitary existence behind. Men became more sociable and developed their humanity by "conversing [with women] and contributing to each other's pleasure and entertainment" (p. 271), and the two sexes engaged in a sociable manner. Virtuous women educated civil men. In "The Rise and Progress of the Arts and Sciences" (1742), Hume also stated that the company of virtuous women was the best school of manners.

Hume seems to signal an evolving perspective of mutual interdependence between men and women, while representing a prevailing attitude of differences. As in Smith we find an ambivalent attitude towards women in Hume's writings. On the one hand, he sees chastity as being fit for women, talks about womanish submission and on the other hand, he seems to speak against domination of women.

Rousseau

Rousseau, with whom Smith was acquainted, has a considerable body of work on the natural role of women and the relations of the sexes.[3] Rousseau advocated for the necessity of the differences between men and women to maintain the cultural balance and integrity. Unlike some other commentators of the time, he did not see this as being determined by nature but as a human construct for the purpose of cultural stability.

Along this line, it is well documented that Rousseau advocated different education for women, teaching them to be submissive and dependent, to lead different lives than men. Women were seen as mothers and wives confined to the private sphere with no direct access to power, and they were made for the delight of men. The restrictions to women's education were seen as following the commands of nature. Educating women like men would lead to a degeneration of all order in society and would be against the laws of nature. Women who were educated along the lines that Rousseau suggested were worth more to themselves and society. Men, on the other hand, were prepared to be soldiers and citizens, trained in a craft and were allowed to express their desires and thoughts. Educating women like men would lead women to aggressively pursuing their own desires, and men would no longer defer to their timidity. He writes, "decide to raise them like men. The men will gladly consent to it! The more women want to resemble them, the less women will govern them, and then men will truly be the masters" (Rousseau, 1979, p. 363). For Rousseau, the feminine virtue of a civil society is the natural passivity and timidity in sexual relations.

However, for Rousseau it is not nature that differentiates sexes. Because of what Rousseau considers beneficial and necessary, sex differences should be encouraged, enforced and created. He saw men being instinctively repelled by women who paid more attention to books than their children, and they would "die an old maid". As Wexler (1976) points out, education should make men more able to control their sexual urges, and strength is the most desirable of their virtues.

On the difference between moral potential between men and women, he saw

> The Supreme Being wanted to do honor to human species in everything. While giving man inclinations without limit, He gives him at the same time the law which regulates them, in order that he may be free and in command of himself. While abandoning man to immoderate passions, He joins reason (la raison) to these passions in order to govern them. While abandoning woman to unlimited desires, He joins modesty ("la pudeur") to these desires in order to constrain them.
>
> (Rousseau, 1979, p. 359)

As pointed out by Lange (1981), a woman restrains her behavior while man controls or governs his. According to Rousseau, while women should be passive and weak, men should be strong. It is because of the common aim of reproduction, the different biological contributions of each sex are required.

Women are able to care for themselves and their children. Yet, women are assumed to be weaker than men, and division of labor arises from living together.

> The habit of living together gave rise to the sweetest sentiments known to men: Conjugal love and paternal love. Each family become a little society all the better united because reciprocal affection and freedom were its only bonds; and it was then that the first difference was established in the way of life of the two sees, which until this time had had but one. Women became more sedentary, and grew accustomed to tend the hut and the children, while the men went to seek their common subsistence.
>
> (Rousseau, 1964, pp. 146–147)

The sexual division of labor is a reflection of the essential difference between sexes. He views that it is "touching" when women stay at home and do their domestic duties and make their husbands happy. On the other hand, woman outside her home "displays herself indecently". At the same time, he states that if men were to stay home and do the occupations that come with it, they would become crippled because they would be feminized and weakened.

He goes on to say that the qualities of chasteness, modesty and timidity are in society's interest. Modesty, decency, timidity are the natural and cardinal virtues of women. He argues that male headed families are a social institution. He views that social equality between the sexes creates a danger to civic virtue.

According to Rousseau, it is the environmental factors that play a role in mental capacities. He explicitly states that there are two classes: those who think and those who do not, and states that these two classes are made up of men and women. Women have abilities: they are talented, well-read, intelligent, cultured and eager to learn. Their traditional role does not prevent them from exercising reason. However, he sometimes states that "higher" rational capacities are beyond women. But more importantly, he believes that women should not perform rational operations. He thinks that because men and women are interdependent, it is useful to educate the sexes differently. In the name of mutual dependence, he promotes sexual differentiation. He does not advocate complete and free development of women's rational capacities.

According to Rousseau, men exclude women from power, preferring the stupidest man to the wisest woman. It is men who prevent women from governing. He states that "had injustice not deprived them [women] of liberty, and the opportunity to manifest these qualities to the world", they would have more "love of virtue" and "noble mindedness" than men. Women could have carried out "heroism and courage to greater heights", and they would have been able to distinguish themselves (Sur les femmes, cited by Kofman and Dukats, 1989, p. 124).

It appears that on the whole Rousseau put women in a devalued position, even though he states that it is men who exclude women from power.

With the backdrop of Smith's feminist contemporaries, Hume and Rousseau, it is not difficult to imagine the assumptions that Smith attributed to women and their roles within his cultural context.

III. Women in the TMS

We contend that even though Smith is somewhat ambivalent on the whole, he gives women a secondary value and that their contributions are taken for granted because their behavior is derived from human instinct rather than the result of "self-command". The secondary literature has also argued that the TMS is gendered and women are devalued in most of his writing (see, for example, Harkin, 1995; 2013; Rendall, 1987). The following quote has often been referred to as a dividing line drawn by Smith separating women and men drawing a distinction between the capacity for morality between men and women:

> Generosity is different from humanity. Those two qualities, which at first sight seem so nearly allied, do not always belong to the same person. Humanity is the virtue of a woman, generosity of a man. The fair-sex, who have commonly much more tenderness than ours, have seldom so much generosity. That women rarely make considerable donations, is an observation of the civil law. Humanity consists merely in the exquisite fellow-feeling which the spectator entertains with the sentiments of the persons principally concerned, so as to grieve for their sufferings, to resent their injuries, and to rejoice at their good fortune. The most humane actions require no self-denial, no self-command, no great exertion of the sense of propriety. They consist only in doing what this exquisite sympathy would of its own accord prompt us to do. But it is otherwise with generosity. We never are generous except when in some respect we prefer some other person to ourselves, and sacrifice some great and important interest of our own to an equal interest of a friend or of a superior. The man who gives up his pretensions to an office that was the great object of his ambition, because he imagines that the services of another are better entitled to it; the man who exposes his life to defend that of his friend, which he judges to be of more importance; neither of them act from humanity, or because they feel more exquisitely what concerns that other person than what concerns themselves.
>
> (TMS, pp. 222–223)

This quote from the TMS reveals Smith's contention that humanity is the primary domain of women and generosity is the primary domain of men. It also asserts an attitude that values the superiority of generosity over humanity. Specifically, he sees the moral virtues that have been developed through "self-command" as being more valuable than those abilities that are a part of human nature instinctually. Smith then further differentiates these two capacities by assigning them to specific genders; he sees generosity as the primary domain of men and humanity as the primary domain of women.

In much of the literature we review, this distinction between generosity and humanity is interpreted in two ways: (1) generosity is seen as a greater virtue over humanity because it requires the willful exercise of "self-command", and (2) Smith's general attitude that men are associated with generosity and women are associated with humanity. Both humanity and women are given a subordinate status. On the other hand, in our reading of the TMS, there are also several places where Smith puts humanity and generosity at the same level, not elevating one over the other.

Smith recognized that both humanity and generosity are necessary; however, he further genders the distinction by claiming that men can find this balance. But, he does not see women as exhibiting the same capacity. Rendall (1987) argues that on the one hand Smith continually refers to the necessity of balance between generosity and humanity, and according to Smith, "the contest between the two principles" (TMS, p. 289) ideally would bring a balance between generosity and humanity for men. On the other hand, he sees women as only having one side of this balance, humanity. In addition, Rendall argues that Smith sees women as not having the sufficient self-command and courage, and therefore "there was little suggestion that women might acquire the virtues of public life" (Rendall, 1987, p. 59). Harkin (2013) argues that Smith identifies risk-taking with masculine generosity, while he identifies sympathy with feminine, which is something less than risk-taking.

Smith furthers his argument that he sees virtues as having a gendered basis in the following quote from the TMS:

> The soft, the gentle, the amiable virtues, the virtues of candid condescension and indulgent humanity, are founded upon the one: the great, the awful and respectable, the virtues of self-denial, of self-government, of that command of the passions which subjects all the movements of our nature to what our own dignity and honour, and the propriety of our own conduct require, take their origin from the other.
>
> (TMS, p. 29)

Rendall (1987) comments on this quote by saying that gentle virtues and self-command are gendered, the gentle virtues belonging to women and self-command belonging to men. Harkin (2013) goes on to argue that "amiable" virtues and "great" virtues have two different sources based on the type of effort made by the spectator. The first is entering into the sentiments of the sufferer, which is a simpler process. "[T]he soft, the gentle, the amiable virtues" are the result of this effort. On the other hand, "the great, the awful and respectable" virtues are a result of the greater effort that requires imagining the spectator's feelings and moderating the expression of sufferings. Harkin (1995) states that amiable sentiments are feminine and the awful sentiments are masculine. The author also argues that Smith puts a greater value on the latter.

Contrary to these arguments, Clark (1993) states that it is clear in Smith's treatise that this description is a dynamic framework that establishes how society and the individual can reach approximate equilibrium. Analyzing the quotes provided above, the author concludes that women also need self-command and men humanity through daily life, arguing the following:

> The impulses that all humans, regardless of sex, have both to sympathize with others' sufferings and to soften the expression of their own out of consideration for others' probable responses, provide a general framework for understanding the causal and occasional 'genderings' of these phenomena that appear in the treatise. Both humanity and self-command are

generic attributes before they take shape in any specific way for one sex or the other.

(p. 343)

This view holds that humanity and self-command hold an equal place and they are mutually dependent on each other.

It is argued in Alvey (1993) and Justman (1993) that there is genderedness in the TMS. The TMS supports the view that men are rational and women are emotional. Women have excessive desires that they can't control: they are "vain", "frivolous" and "luxurious". Men are involved with public affairs, while women are confined to the domestic arena. Justman, however, is aware of the complexity of Smith's views. In his more nuanced argument, he points out that Smith argues that most men in commercial societies take the characteristics of women, making the point that trade involves relationships and a sensitivity to human interactions. "[T]he male of Smithian society has more in common with his own image of woman than . . . Adam Smith himself, cares to admit" (p. 19). Justman also states that greatly praised virtues of propriety, prudence and modesty are also attributed to women. (See Alvey (1993) for a critical assessment of Justman's views, where he states that Justman's views are more complicated than just delivering "a contemporary feminist denunciation of the dead, white man" (p.167).)

A related issue to this discussion is whether sympathy is masculinist or not. Cole (1991) argues that Smith's description of sympathy is a masculinist one, mutual sympathy belongs to 18th century men and that Smith implies women cannot aspire to it. The author argues that men in the TMS rise above the two interchangeably used terms of "weakness" and "effeminacy". Women have an automatic sympathy, or a "natural' sensibility. Their sympathy is at worst "womanish lamentations" and at best, "exquisite humanity". The feminine form of sympathy is "pre-verbal and pre-social, a passive response to suffering unshaped by social norms. Yet, because it is so, woman or more precisely, the 'feminine' – can serve as the (a) moral body upon which Smith's entire system is erected" (p. 116). Harkin (1995) counters Cole's argument by stating that sympathy is not a male phenomenon. Instead sympathy, which is essentially a feminine tendency, requires a certain mechanism of control. While Marshall (1986) views Smith as hostile to the moral agency of women, Kay (1986) has the view that Smith relegated sympathy based on a female sensibility to a devalued status. According to Harkin (1995), sympathy is a lesser virtue due to women's failure to view things as the impartial spectator would and their failure in transforming their feelings into deeds. As such it is argued that sympathy or humanity is an inadequate basis for morality, "too easily aroused and too cheaply indulged to be much respected" (p. 180).

Kuiper (2003) argues that the TMS's content is masculine. Her view is that women are absent in the TMS, and Smith takes a distance from women. According to Kuiper, the impartial spectator constitutes an identification with the father within. She argues that different editions of the TMS show two shifts. The first is increasingly identified with the father, the second is a move away from humanity towards self-command. Folbre (2009) argues that Smith's emphasis on masculine morality links him to his Enlightenment predecessors, and that in Smith's system women were placed outside reason, and that for Smith women are absent. Harkin (2013) points to the infrequent references to women in the TMS. She states that when they are mentioned it is to illustrate some delusion or vice, or women's inability to distinguish what is praiseworthy from what is praised.

Contrary to most of the literature, Clark (1993) argues that the language of virtues in general and humanity are not as gendered as it is argued in the rest of the literature. In every commercial society, humanity is a defining virtue, and both male-female, public-private boundaries are transcended by humanity. Women's virtues do not hold an inferior place in morality. The author argues that self-command and humanity are mutually dependent on each other in civil society as a whole and within the individual. They are also complementary. "[T]hey are bound together in a kind of a double helix of reciprocity" (p. 344).

Furthermore, the author argues that "women are not excluded from moral agency, nor do their characteristic virtues hold an inferior place on a hierarchy of moral excellences" (p. 339). According to Clark (2014), Smith made women central to the modernist project: "If anything, indeed, his concept of self-command appeared as an antique Stoic virtue juxtaposed to the female inflected virtue of humanity" (p. 48). The author argues that according to Smith central to the commercial sociability was the latter.

In reviewing the works to this point, most of the literature, except for Clark (1993), have argued that Smith puts generosity in an elevated status relative to humanity, and in some places Smith puts humanity and generosity in the same sentence with equal value. For example, Smith states "Generosity, humanity, kindness, compassion, mutual friendship and esteem, all the social and benevolent affections, when expressed in the countenance or behaviour, even towards those who are not peculiarly connected with ourselves, please the indifferent spectator upon almost every occasion" (TMS, p. 47). He also considers generosity, humanity, justice and public spirit as the qualities "most useful to others".

Smith indicates that humanity and generosity both deserve love and admiration. About generosity, he tells us, "Magnanimity, generosity, and justice, command so high a degree of admiration that we desire to see them crowned with wealth, and power, and honours of every kind" (TMS, p. 195). Humanity is not a less admired quality than generosity: "What reward is most proper for promoting the practice of truth, justice, and humanity? The confidence, the esteem, and love of those we live with" (TMS, p. 193). How humanity and self-command are intertwined is further illustrated in the following statement: "The man who, to all the soft, the amiable, and the gentle virtues [humanity], joins all the great, the awful, and the respectable [self-command], must surely be the natural and proper object of our highest love and admiration" (TMS, p. 176).

Therefore, even though Smith states, "Humanity is the virtue of a woman, generosity of a man" (TMS, p. 222), he does not appear to be putting humanity in a lower status devaluing women, as has been argued in most of the literature.

Humanity is so important that those who don't open to humanity should be "shut out" from all affections. They would be in a society but it would be like living in a desert with nobody to care for them. Humanity may sometimes be excessive, but we regard it with compassion. Smith finds even the weakness of humanity agreeable. "We only regret that it is unfit for the world, because the world is unworthy of it . . ." (TMS, p. 49).

At other places, however, self-command is elevated. According to Smith, humanity does not require self-command but generosity does. Self-command is learned from the impartial spectator and is acquired from Nature. There is a considerable degree of admiration and esteem for those who exert self-command. There is a noble propriety in self-command. The exercise of self-command is learned from hardship, which no one puts themselves into willingly. Firmness of nerves is the best preparative for self-command. Furthermore, "Self-command is not only itself a great virtue, but from it all the other virtues seem to derive their principal lustre" (TMS, p. 284). At the same time, "Our sensibility to the feelings of others, so far from being inconsistent with the manhood of self-command, is the very principle upon which that manhood is founded" (TMS, p. 176).

Humanity and self-command develop under different conditions:

> In the mild sunshine of undisturbed tranquility, in the calm retirement of undissipated and philosophical leisure, the soft virtue of humanity flourishes the most, and is capable of the highest improvement. But, in such situations, the greatest and noblest exertions of self-command have little exercise. Under the boisterous and stormy sky of war and faction, of public tumult and confusion, the sturdy severity of self-command prospers the most, and can be the most successfully cultivated. But, in such situations, the strongest suggestions of humanity must frequently be stifled or neglected; and every such neglect necessarily tends to weaken the principle of humanity.
>
> (TMS, pp. 177–178)

Humanity is more cultivated among civilized nations and diminishes among "savages" because of the hardiness demanded of them. Masculine firmness of character is destroyed because of the "delicate sensibility" required in civilized nations.

In terms of how humanity and self-command are related to each other, Smith makes contrary statements. To illustrate this, let us remind ourselves of a quote we presented in the literature review section:

> The soft, the gentle, the amiable virtues, the virtues of candid condescension and indulgent humanity, are founded upon the one: the great, the

awful and respectable, the virtues of self-denial, of self-government, of that command of the passions which subjects all the movements of our nature to what our own dignity and honour, and the propriety of our own conduct require, take their origin from the other.

(TMS, p. 29)

Here Smith is saying that self-command is the basis of humanity. Yet, self-command originates from humanity. Elsewhere, however, he asserts that "The man of the most exquisite humanity, is naturally the most capable of acquiring the highest degree of self-command" (TMS, p. 177), putting humanity as an important source of self-command. This quote would appear to show that Smith is ambivalent about giving priority to humanity or generosity. Based on this discussion, we cannot conclude that humanity is devalued, or that generosity, which requires self-command, is elevated in the TMS. In this light, we view Smith's attitude about elevating or devaluing women as ambivalent, and not fully one-sided. Yet, given the importance Smith attributes to self-command in establishing morality, on the whole he devalues women.

Smith values women as having an important function foundationally and in their embodiment of humanity. He does not come out and specifically say that women are not capable of moral development. He speaks to his personal and collective belief that in general women do not develop the same moral capacity as men. While he sees men as being able to develop a balance of generosity and humanity, in the preponderance of his work he does not see women as capable of achieving the same balance.

III. Women in the WN

In the WN there are limited references to women's work and wages, and some aspects of women's work remain unanalyzed, like the link between the management of a household and political economy. For instance, Smith values the market and domestic morality of the family. He contends that a husband and a wife jointly must earn more than what is necessary for their own maintenance and he sees the household as having an important function in consumption, which leads to a benefit of public wealth, and yet does not discuss the sexual division of labor.

Smith's writing in the WN reflects the prevailing spirit of the times as it relates to men and women. Here Smith identifies work as a "male preserve" (Sutherland, 1995, p. 97). There are only few references to women earning wages or being involved in economic activity (see Pujol, 1992; Harkin, 2013). As pointed out by Pujol (1992) Smith does not refer to the link between the management of a household and political economy. The importance of a family's economic viability and women's work was something Smith was aware of, but as was common, seems utterly taken for granted and not singled out for its important integral necessity:

> A man must always live by his work, and his wages must at least be sufficient to maintain him. They must even upon most occasions be somewhat more; otherwise it would be impossible for him to bring up a family, and the race of such workmen could not last beyond the first generation. Mr. Cantillon seems, upon this account, to suppose that the lowest species of common laborers must everywhere earn at least double their own maintenance, in order that one with another they may be enabled to bring up two children; the labor of the wife, on account of her necessary attendance on the children, being supposed no more than sufficient to provide for herself....Thus for at least seems certain, that, in order to bring up a family, the labour of the husband and wife together must, even in the lowest species of common labour, be able to earn something more than what is precisely necessary for their own maintenance.
>
> (WN, pp. 85–86)

Another reference to women's work for wages is where Smith comments on the low wages of knitters and spinners in Scotland. Smith states that this is derived from "the principal part of their subsistence from some other employment" (WN, p. 134). Smith also states that:

> A great part of the extraordinary work, which is probably done in cheap years, never enters the publick registers of manufacturers. The men servants who leave their masters become independent labourers. The women return to their parents, and commonly spin in order to make cloaths for themselves and their families.
>
> (WN, p. 103)

Despite these limited references to women's employment, women are absent from organization and operations of capitalist economy.

There is also very limited reference to women's work within the household. Rendall argues that Smith creates an "increasingly clear cut division of spheres between economic world ... and the household" (Rendall, 1987, p. 71). Rendall states that Smith was writing at a time of restructuring where market economy was separated "from the domestic morals of the family" (Rendall, 1987, p. 45). During the period Smith wrote, the commercial world of the market economy was separated from the domestic morality of the family (Rendall, 1987). Women's participation in the industrial or market economy was made invisible. The household played an important role in morality.

> The pursuit of virtue was first to be relocated in the conjugal family. As an instinctual haven of the natural affections and "habitual sympathy", to

be contrasted with the market economy, and the social world, inspired by emulation, expediency, and the restrained pursuit of self-interest.

(Rendall, 1987, p. 71)

A woman's role was best reflected in this quote on their education, which seems to squarely put women in the familial and domestic realm, and is often referred to as the best known reference to women in the WN:

> There are no public institutions for the education of women, and there is accordingly nothing useless, absurd, or fantastical, in the common course of their education. They are taught what their parents or guardians judge it necessary or useful for them to learn, and they are taught nothing else. Every part of their education tends evidently to some useful purpose; either to improve the natural attractions of their person, or to form their mind to reserve, to modesty, to chastity, and to economy; to render them both likely to become the mistresses of a family, and to behave properly when they have become such. In every part of her life, a woman feels some conveniency or advantage from every part of her education. It seldom happens that a man, in any part of his life, derives any conveniency or advantage from some of the most laborious and troublesome parts of his education.
>
> (WN, p. 781)

Along with Smith's almost exclusive focus of women in the household in the WN, Rendall (1987) and Shah (2006) also pointed out that consumption was seen as an important role where "women were instead now to be consumers and transmitters of cultural norms, to the exclusion of productive responsibility" (Shah, 2006, p. 228). Women in households aided the economy by creating demand for consumer goods and commodities. Public wealth benefitted from the demand for goods, and this spending also led to increased employment.

Pujol (1992) and Shah (2006) also argue that sexual division of labor is not treated in the WN. It is argued that Smith was utterly blind:

> to the specific place women held in his day in industrial as well as agricultural production, not to mention the provision of domestic services. He is also blind to the use and manipulation of female workers in the transformation of the labour process and the introduction of technology which were taking place in manufacturing. The connections between sexual division of labour within the labor market and in society as a whole and the social division of labour are completely bypassed.
>
> (Pujol, 1992, p. 17)

Neither women's access to occupation nor any documentation of women's wages are discussed. In sum, even though there are limited references to women's work and wages, Smith recognizes at least some aspects of women's work.

IV. Women in LJ

In the LJ, Smith argues that it is the environment, nature and biology that shape gender relations. Biological differences were subject to historical change. His view is that women gained more respect in commercial societies in comparison to earlier societies, such as hunting. One reason for this, according to Smith, is the decline in high status of the military and a rise in trade and manufacturing. Smith also believed that men favored themselves, for example, by adopting double standards to adultery. The writings in the LJ reflect a progressive approach to women's role in domestic life and marriage.

The arguments for Smith's progressive attitude towards women are relative to some of the more institutionally oppressive attitudes of his time. Nyland (2003) argues that Smith had a progressive approach to women's role in domestic life and marriage. For example, Smith was also less committed to gender inequality as a theological or natural view as it was for Montesquieu (Harkin, 2013).

Smith argues that environmental factors, and biology, or nature, largely shape gender relations. The relative status of women was shaped by historical periods, and changing forms of subsistence (Nyland, 2003). Smith's view is that there was a rise in the respect given to women and marriage through the evolution form hunting societies to commercial societies, tying women's status to his four stage theory. The four stages were hunting, pastoral, agricultural and commercial stages (Meek, 1977).

Primarily by examining the nature of the marriage relationship, Smith discussed women's social status. He argued that marriage was necessarily a long-term relationship due to the length of time it takes for children to reach an age which would allow them to subsist by themselves. Long-term marriage was also necessary to provide children "with a sustained social environment in which they would be subject to the guidance of individuals who were their superiors and who would teach them self-discipline" (Nyland, p. 4).

Nyland (2003) gives a detailed discussion of the relation between women's status and the four stages. We highlight the salient aspects of this process here. In societies which were hunting, pastoral and agricultural, Smith argued that government strengthened the authority of the father, who had power over his entire family and slaves (LJ).

In the hunting stage of development where property and government are virtually absent, because women's physical capacity was not equal to that of men, and because of the limitations imposed on them by their reproductive roles, they did not have the respect men had. Women were not equal to men as warriors or hunters.

> The head of the family is the person on whom the others are all naturally in a great measure dependent for their support and defence.
>
> (LJ, p. 176)

Women's situation did not change much in pastoral or agricultural societies, since the high status of the warrior did not fundamentally change. Things started to change for women in commercial societies. A decline in the high status of the military due to an increase in trade and manufacturing contributed to an increase in women's status. The economic cost of warfare was significantly higher in commercial societies: "Trade, commerce, cannot go on, and they therefore will not go out to the wars" (LJ, p. 230). In addition, increased wealth, the ability of women to inherit wealth and the commodity culture all contributed to an increase in women's status. Smith also argues that the Church aided women by changing the earlier right of men to divorce their wives, while women could not divorce their husbands. The Church made divorce impossible for women and men. The economic position of women was enhanced as a result.

> This rendering divorces not easily obtainable gave the wife a more respectable character, rendering her in a great measure independent on the husband for her support. She was accordingly considered as a considerable member of the family, who had the same interest in the common stock as the master or the children; and from this it was that the wife after the demise of her husband came in for the same share as either of the other two parts of the family.
>
> (LJ, p. 47)

Smith's analysis of the historical changes in women's status in the development of culture showed great advancement from their previous conditions. Even though Smith considered men's greater strength as the source of their domination over women, he recognized that this was subject to historical change. Biological differences posed some limitations; however, Smith pointed to changes in this over time. Harkin (2013) is critical of Smith due to his lack of consideration of the lives of women, and the intimate emotional ties between wives and husbands, and other relatives. However, in these writings Smith's goal was to analyze the rights of individuals, of family and those who are a member of a society.

VI. Basic concepts of Carl Jung

We draw from Gabrinetti (2015) for this section. This brief presentation is to help facilitate a better understanding of the general concepts in Jung's work that are germane to the discussion of Adam Smith's work.

By way of introducing this section, the unconscious as it is referred to in this section and viewed from a psychoanalytic perspective is of great importance in its influence on the spirit of the times. The unconscious makes itself known through its influences on individuals, groups, cultural patterns, and as Jung pointed out, our collective human psychology. The unconscious exerts an important effect/affect on perceptions, attitudes and behaviors. This is particularly true with respect to those things that we are unconscious of, because they have the strongest influence on behavior. Thus it is of the greatest importance in the discussion of the psychology of Smith's time and for his attitude towards women. We will point out this influence later in this section.

Historically, Jung was one of Freud's earliest pupils. Their collaboration lasted between 1907 and 1912. The main point of their departure was over the nature of the unconscious. Freud understood the unconscious to be the result of unresolved conflicts that were repressed into unconsciousness. Jung didn't disagree that these contents were a part of the unconscious; however, Jung understood the breadth of the unconscious to be more comprehensive. His early laboratory research (1904, 1905, 1906, 1907) and later clinical writings (1917, 1928, 1936, 1943,1952, 1954) demonstrated that the unconscious not only included contents that were from the individual's immediate and personal conflicts, it also contained undeveloped individual potentials, general cultural content and inherited content that was the distillation of the human species. In addition to personal conflicts that came from outside life interactions, he saw that unrealized parts of the personality or "self" also want to be discovered and realized in consciousness. These contents make themselves known in patterns, symbols and imagery that carry with them a great deal of energy and fascination. Most importantly, these contents all influence consciousness. These include motifs of the heroic (Campbell, 1949), the great mother (Neumann, 1954), the child (Neumann, 1973) and the self (Henderson, 1990), to name just a few. Jung referred to these inherited inner patterns as archetypes. These archetypal patterns are brought into a person's life with strong instinctual/affective energy. Examples of this might include the kind of immediate love many parents feel for newborn children or the heroic patriotism that certain kinds of national experiences stir in some individuals. In addition, Jung also had a different attitude towards women, particularly in terms of their capacity for psychological development. Freud (1925) hypothesized that women had greater difficulties in the development of superego functions (conscience/morality) in relation to men. Jung (1968, 1980) wrote a great deal about men and women both having the capacity for development, and the capacity for men and women to realize their inborn potentials through what he referred to as the individuation process. Individuation is a lifelong process of interaction with the unconscious that facilitates the development of our unique inner potentials. This includes our capacity for moral development.

Jung referred to the part of the unconscious that contained the unresolved personal issues that Freud discovered as the personal unconscious. These contents are seeking to be made conscious and may cause conflicts with everyday consciousness when an individual is not willing or able to work with them. These would involve personal issues such as conflicts with people in our immediate lives like a spouse, friend or significant others that create emotional conflict. In addition to immediate daily conflicts, the personal unconscious would also include significant historical relationships such as with parental or other familial members that have ended up in the unconscious because of their difficulty and un-resolvability at the time. These unresolved contents still exert an "unconscious" influence on our daily lives and make themselves known through repeated conflicts that are experienced as difficult or even impossible patterns of struggle and suffering. For instance, an unresolved pattern of behavior with a parent can be lived out "unconsciously" by making a person act in ways that are similar to the parent that there is unresolved conflict with even though they don't like that behavior pattern in that parent.

The collective unconscious represents the shared accumulation of psychological capacities, potentials and instincts that are inherited from the history of all humans. Jung (1936) referred to inherited or historical unconscious as the collective unconscious, which contained archetypes, the capacity for individuation, the development of the self out of the collective unconscious and general human development throughout the lifespan. The term *analytic psychology* was used by Jung to describe his work and to differentiate it from Freud's.

The cultural unconscious represents the affectively charged cultural attitudes and norms that define patterns of behavior that significantly influence an individual's conduct. These would include a range of cultural customs, values and prejudices. It was Henderson (1990) who helped to refine the concept of cultural unconscious in Jungian thought. He states, "A great deal of what Jung called personal was actually . . . culturally conditioned" (p. 104). He adds: "part of the collective culture pattern transmitted through our environment before we were able to affirm its validity for ego-consciousness" (Henderson, 1967, pp. 7–8).

Henderson (1990) defines cultural unconscious as:

> an area of historical memory that lies between the collective unconscious and the manifest pattern of the culture. It may include both these modalities, conscious and unconscious, but it has some kind of identity arising from the archetypes of the collective unconscious, which assists in the formation of myth and ritual and also promotes the development of individuals.
>
> (p. 102)

The cultural unconscious referred to in this quote is located between the collective unconscious and the personal unconscious. It is a group or cultural level of the unconscious. A living continuity between the past and the present at the level of the group unconscious is manifested with reference to "an area of historical memory". An example of this would be the way a culture views the roles of men and women. These attitudes are often experienced as unreflected truths about how roles "ought to be".

Consciousness is the focus of an individual's general awareness and is usually referred to as *ego consciousness*. This is individually directed towards a person's outward life and awareness and towards inner life, imagination and needs. Well-developed ego consciousness and the capacity to accomplish life's tasks are essential to life function and wellbeing.

Jung's discovery of the *anima* and the *animus* were among his most relevant understandings for our present discussion. These represent the psychological counterpoints to our biological composition and are a part of our inherited unconscious. The feminine counterpart in men is the anima, and the masculine counterpart in women is the animus. The unconscious contains these capacities for what Jung referred to as the contra-sexual aptitudes and can foster a more complete development of the individual. Each person's potential is developed and expanded through a relationship with the anima or animus throughout the lifespan. These hypotheses serve to expand the development of the wholeness that is in potential in each individual.

The core of personality is the self and it grows out of an initial undifferentiated state from the collective unconscious, and this foundational source is the wellspring of ongoing development. The self represents the totality of the personality from which an individual grows and develops. The self includes inherent interests, aptitudes or even physical capacities that make for a distinctive blending of individual preferences and directions. The self is a unique set of capacities that may manifest internally as an interest or curiosity and can be creatively lived out in numerous ways. In the practice of analytic psychology, the unique capacities of the self, once they are recognized and valued within each person, generate the distinctive qualities of an individual. This includes the anima or animus potential that is inherent in the self of each individual.

As the experience of meaning and purpose begin to emerge as a conscious force in an individual's life, there is now the possibility of interaction with these deeper historical layers to the unconscious self. Jung (1968) called the interaction with the individual's conscious attitude or ego with the unconscious self over the lifespan *individuation*. Individuation is not a specific goal, but an ongoing life process. It is the ongoing interaction between the conscious ego and the unconscious that allows each individual to continue in their development throughout the lifespan.

The ego is this conscious capacity that is the necessary counterpart to the unconscious. Unlike the colloquial use of the word "ego", which usually refers to some form of personal inflation or self-aggrandizement, the ego in psychoanalytic terms refers to our conscious capacity to achieve mastery and the resulting competencies to direct our lives. For ongoing development, ego consciousness and competencies are required. We develop through our ability to realize our own needs, to interact with other people, recognize our desires and feelings and direct our efforts on our behalf for our outer and inner lives. Without well-functioning ego skills, life is very difficult. *Ego capacity* refers to a capacity for mastery in one's endeavors, competence and creative adaptation.

For the purpose of our current presentation, we will focus on ego capacity and the contra-sexual aspects to the individual's biological identity. Once again, in women there is the animus, which is the masculine counterpart, and there is the anima, or feminine counterpart in men. Jung saw the capacities of "masculine" and "feminine" as being differentiated from one's sexual biology. As such, these capacities can be developed in both biological men and women and allow for a wholeness that does not discriminate between men and woman as to their capacity to develop personally or morally.

VII. Synthesis of Jung and Smith on women

Cultural expectations of sex-role behavior have a strong influence on the perceptions of how people ought to behave. These expectations that emanate from the "cultural unconscious" (Henderson, 1967), often speak to a level of accumulated norms or un-reflected truths that may not reveal the current capacities and development within individuals in a given culture. In relation to Smith, we want to address the unconscious assumptions about the capacities within men and women, and to point out what is missing in Smith's assumptions about men's and women's capacities in general, and their capacity for humanity and generosity specifically.

Jung addressed wide-ranging capacities within men and women by addressing the "masculine" and "feminine" that are within each human being. He referred to the contra-sexual capacities as the anima in men and the animus within women. These were the complimentary capacities, or "the masculine and the feminine", within each biological male or female. He saw these capacities and qualities as being present in both biological men and women. Put another way, all of the attributes that heretofore were associated with male and female, are present in all humans, and can be developed. We will use Jung's understandings of anima and animus to address Smith's argument that the capacity for humanity and generosity were gendered.

From a Jungian perspective (and a general psychoanalytic perspective also), Smith's self-command is analogous to conscious ego competency, and this conscious capacity is key to any willful behavior. Jung would see this capacity as being aligned with the more animus or masculine abilities; however, he would not necessarily agree that such a capacity was gendered. As such, self-command is a capacity that can be developed in biological women as well. Culturally, virtues such as self-command, particularly in Smith's time, were generally assigned to biological men.

Equally, the anima or "feminine" is generally viewed to have qualities of emotionality, relatedness, generativity, i.e., fertility, feeling, dependency, vulnerability and the strength that comes from emotional relatedness. In particular, the feminine is often associated with these instincts, instincts that ground all humans in their foundational and visceral selves. This is no small matter. While advances in the Western world's rational and scientific areas have flourished, the literal root of life that makes all of this possible is often taken for granted, given a lesser value or gets ignored completely. In this respect, Smith and the contemporary culture of the time disregarded or gave a secondary status to what Jung later referred to as "the feminine".

It is important to keep in mind from a Jungian perspective that these qualities of the feminine are in both sexes and are a part of their wholeness. As such,
these qualities are not better or worse, more or less, they are simply part of
each individual's self and their realization results in the development of their
wholeness.

It is also worth noting that a paradoxical issue in Smith's foundational concept of sympathy as being a basis for morality is that it is built on relatedness
that was and is culturally more associated with the feminine. While this is culturally associated with "the feminine", sympathy from a Jungian perspective is
not confined to women specifically and can be developed in men also, as was
unconsciously assumed in Smith's theorizing.

When Smith spoke of the instincts, he did not make the link between the
energetic component of the instincts and the energy used to fund ego capacity
and self-command. As we argued in Chapter 4, without instinctual energy in
both men and women, there would be no energy to create morality, much less
provide a reason for its development. One of the primary reasons for morality
was in opposition to the unbridled acting out of instincts. Smith relegated the
instincts to a lower status because it took no self-command to achieve them, yet
without them there would not be virtue or morality because there would be no
foundational energy or tension to operate a higher order moral structure. There
is a tension between the conscious or unconscious instincts, and the conscious
morality that is being asserted to govern them. The instincts serve as the base
that gives morality its meaning and sets up the necessary tension that drives the
dynamic conflict to produce a moral system and to give it meaning and purpose.

It would also appear that Smith had a certain conflict in his own life with the
anima or with culturally defined feminine qualities. As we stated in Chapter 9,
ironically Smith was literally and absolutely dependent on his mother and then
later his cousin. Without them he could not have done the important work
that he in fact did. Yet, as with his theoretical writings, this kind of support is
assumed and not mentioned, much less valued. As we postulated in Chapter 9,
he defended against dependency on the feminine, and by default devalued it.

We postulate from a Jungian perspective that the capacities of generosity and
humanity are not in fact gendered, rather they are capacities of the self that
are available in both men and women. It can be argued that Smith's personal
unconscious was deeply affected by the cultural unconscious of his time (the
unconscious as manifested through the culture). We have also pointed out that
the attributes of the "feminine" that Smith relegated to women were devalued
during his era. Despite much progress in this area, to a lesser degree this conflict
is evidenced today with the feminine being undervalued. Smith's anima, which
embodies all the remarkable qualities of the feminine, was in his unconscious
exerting an influence through his use of sympathy as the foundational element
of his elaborate theory. However, due to his unconsciousness of this inner influence, it was not overtly valued.

VIII. Discussion

The spirit of the times in the 18th century that was represented in the cultural unconscious of that period evidenced an ambivalent relationship towards women. Smith's theory of morality celebrated the triumph of self-command over the instincts, and in so doing he also correlated the instincts with biological women. This line of thought continued into the 20th century, with Freud formulating that women did not have the same capacity as men to develop conscience. Jung countered that assertion by contending that both men and women were capable of ongoing individuation, which includes moral development.

It was as though women (and the presumption of their containment in the instincts) were assumed to be present and part of life, however, what they contributed was taken for granted and not given the same value as the more masculine striving for mastery and control. Smith saw women in the cultural context of this era. His contemporary Hume also showed ambivalence towards women, and Rousseau saw the differentiation between men and women as being expedient for cultural stability. Even though there is ambivalence in Smith's views on women, the net result is that women and their ascribed attributes were not given equal status alongside of masculine striving.

There is little evidence in Smith's theory that showed a conscious awareness of the underlying necessity for the instincts/feminine while constructing a morality to stand in opposition to unmitigated instinctual behavior. There is no question as to the importance of self-command, and the necessity for ego capacity in all human beings. What is missing in Smith's treatise is his reference to the source of self-command that originates in the instincts. In short, the conscious ego capacity to initiate "self-command" was purposely accomplished to regulate or stand in opposition to the unregulated living out of instinctual impulses that paradoxically supply the energy for moral thinking and action in the first place.

Smith valued the willful achievement of self-command because it attained something beyond the inborn instincts. The cultural attitudes of the time that specified that men and women did not have the same capacities made their way into Smith's theory. This did not allow for the recognition of the same capacity for "self-command" in both men and women.

Specifically, Smith did not seem to recognize that what drove his system or morality was instinctual energy to begin with. Jung saw the instinctual/archetypal self in both men and women, and saw the capacity for development in both. The advancement of ethical structure is *dependent upon the foundational instinctual energies in both women and men*. Smith relegated the fundamental instincts to a lower status because it took no self-command to achieve them, yet without them there would not be virtue or morality because there would be no foundational energy or tension to operate it. The instincts serve as the base that gives morality its meaning and sets up the necessary tension that drives the dynamic conflict to produce a moral system and to give it meaning and purpose by pointing to its absence.

In short, Smith's attitude, which was the contemporary attitude of his time, had morality differentiated from the instincts, and the instincts were more or less conflated with women. By extension women and instincts were objectified as something to be persevered against, by building a morality to govern the manifestations of purely instinctual behavior.

An important component for Smith is the capacity for self-command that became the principal virtue that enabled all the other virtuous behavior. There is no question that self-command (or ego capacity in psychoanalytic terms) is foundational to the development of any culture, morality or consciousness derived accomplishment. That being said, re-evaluating the important contribution that both instinct and women bring has only begun to come into consciousness and get addressed in the latter part of the 20th century and into the 21st century.

Jung addressed the cultural psychological tension between what he referred to as the animus "masculine" and anima "feminine" and valued both sides of this equation. From this perspective, what was missing in Smith's characterization of humanity and generosity was his making this a biological male/female issue, localizing these qualities in the biology of men and women and generally giving only men the capacity for their integration. Jung also valued the ego capacities of consciousness and self-regulation in relation to instinctual behavior, and that willful self-command was valuable and vital to the advancement of culture. At the same time, he also saw these capacities as the result of a self that was instinctually based and available to both genders.

When there is an *exclusive* valuing of these more "masculine" attributes, and a devaluing of instinctual and subjective experience, the robustness of the self's potential can get lost because this more one-sided attitude does not take into account the foundational instinctual life that manifests uniquely in each person. Jung would concur with Smith that such instinctual characteristics had culturally been relegated to women. However, unlike Smith, Jung felt that when both men and women were capable of valuing their psychological contra-sexual masculine and feminine, this allows humanity and generosity to be integrated, and with it wholeness and morality can be developed by both men and women.

Notes

1 Among the feminist contemporaries of Smith are: Mary Wollstonecraft, Catharine Cockburn, Elizabeth Burnett, Elizabeth Carter, Catherine Talbot and Catharine Macaulay.
2 See also Battersby (1981) and Baier (1979) for a discussion of women in Hume's works.
3 In synthesizing Rousseau's views, we draw from Wexler (1976), Weiss (1987), Lange (1981) and Kofman and Dukats (1989).

References

Akkerman, T. and Stuurman, S. eds., 1988. *Perspectives on feminist political thought in European history: From the Middle Ages to the present*. London: Routledge.

Alvey, J.E., 1993. Adam Smith on gender. *History of Economics Review, 26*, pp. 167–171.

Baier, A., 1979. Good men's women: Hume on chastity and trust. *Hume Studies*, 5(1), pp. 1–19.

Battersby, C., 1981. An enquiry concerning the human woman. *Philosophy*, *56*(217), pp. 303–312.

Campbell, J., 1949. *The hero with a thousand faces*. Princeton, NJ: Princeton University Press.

Clark, H.C., 1993. Women and humanity in Scottish enlightenment social thought: The case of Adam Smith. *Historical Reflections/Reflexions Historiques*, pp. 335–361.

———, 2014. Adam Smith on women: Nature, history and liberty. *Adam Smith Review*, 7, pp. 47–66.

Cole, L., 1991. (Anti) Feminist sympathies: The politics of relationships in Smith, Wollstonecraft, and more. *English Literary History*, *58*, pp. 107–140.

Dwyer, J.A., 1987. *Virtuous discourse: Sensibility and community in late eighteenth-century Scotland*. Edinburgh: John Donald Publishers.

Ferguson, M., 1985. *First feminists: British women writers, 1578–1799*. Bloomington, IN: Indiana University press.

Folbre, N. 2009. *Greed, lust & gender: A history of economic ideas*. Oxford: Oxford University Press.

Freud, S., 1925. Some psychical consequences of the anatomical distinction between the sexes. *Standard Edition*. London: Hogarth Press. Vol. 19, pp. 213–258

Gabrinetti, P.A., 2015. Analytic psychology. In: Neukrug, E.S., ed. *The Sage encyclopedia of theory in counseling and psychotherapy*. Thousand Oaks, CA: Sage Publications Inc. pp. 43–48.

Gregory, J., 1765. *A comparative view of the state of faculties of man with those of the animal world*. London: J. Dodsley.

Harkin, M., 1995. Smith's the 'Theory of Moral Sentiments': Sympathy, women, and emulation. *Studies in Eighteenth-Century Culture*, *24*(1), pp. 175–190.

———, 2013. Adam Smith on women. In: Berry, C.J., M.P. Paganelli and C. Smith, eds. *The Oxford handbook of Adam Smith*. Oxford: Oxford University Press. pp. 501–513.

Henderson, J. L., 1967. *Thresholds of initiation*. Middletown, CT: Wesleyan University Press.

———, 1990. *Shadow and self*. Wilmette, IL: Chiron Publications.

Hume, D., 1742. Of the rise and progress of arts and science. In: Miller, E.F., ed. *Essays, moral, political literary*. Indianapolis, IN: Liberty Fund.

———, 1751. Enquiry concerning the principles of morals. In: Selby-Bigge, L.A. and P. H. Nidditch, ed. *Enquiries concerning human understanding and concerning principles of morals*. Oxford: Oxford University press.

———, 1752. Of the refinement of the arts. In: Miller, E.F., ed. *Essays, moral, political literary*. Indianapolis, IN: Liberty Fund.

———, 1808–1810. *The history of England*. London: Scholey.

———, 1888. *A treatise of human nature*. New York: Oxford University Press.

———, 1874–1875. Of polygamy and divorces. In: Grose, T. H., eds. *The philosophical works of David Hume*. Iii. p. 234.

Justman, S., 1993. *The autonomous male of Adam Smith*. Norman, OK: Oklahoma University Press.

Jung, C.G., 1904–1907. *Experimental researches: Bollingen series*. Princeton, NJ: Princeton University Press.

———, 1917/1926/1943. *Two essays on analytical psychology: Bollingen series*. Princeton, NJ: Princeton University Press.

———, 1936, 1954. *Archetypes and the collective unconscious: Bollingen series*. Princeton, NJ: Princeton University Press.

————, 1968. *Aion: Researches into the phenomenology of the self: Bollingen series.* Princeton, NJ: Princeton University Press.

————, 1980. *Psychology and alchemy: Bollingen series.* Princeton, NJ: Princeton University Press.

Liangkang, N. and Xin, Y., 2009. Moral instinct and moral judgment. *Frontiers of Philosophy in China, 4*(2), pp. 238–250.

Kay, C., 1986. Canon, ideology, and gender: Mary Wollstonecraft's critique of Adam Smith. *New Political Science,* 7(1), pp. 63–76.

Kofman, S. and Dukats, M., 1989. Phallocratic ends. Hypatia. *French Feminist Philosophy, 2*(3), pp. 123–136.

Kuiper, E., 2003. The construction of masculine identity in Adam Smith's theory of moral sentiments. In: Barker, D. K. and E. Kuiper, eds. *Toward a feminist philosophy of economics.* New York: Routledge. pp. 145–160.

————, 2006. Adam Smith and his feminist contemporaries. In: Montes, L. E. S., ed. *New voices on Adam Smith.* New York: Routledge.

Lange, L., 1981. Rousseau and modern feminism. *Social Theory and Practice,* 7(3), pp. 245–277.

Marshall, D., 1986. *The figure of theatre: Shaftsbury, Defoe, Adam Smith and George Eliot.* New York: Columbia University Press.

Meek, R.L., 1977. *Smith Marx and after: Ten essays in development of economic thought.* London: Chapman and Hall.

Neumann, E., 1954. *The great mother: Bollingen series.* Princeton, NJ: Princeton University Press.

————, 1973. *The child.* New York: Harper & Row.

Noble, D.F., 1992. *A world without women: The Christian clerical culture of western science.* Oxford: Oxford University Press.

Nyland, C., 2003. Adam Smith, stage theory and status of women. In: Dimand, R. and C. Nylad, eds. *The status of women in classical economic thought.* Aldershot: Elgar. pp. 86–107.

Oakeshott, M., 1991. *Rationalism in politics and other essays.* Indianapolis, IN: Liberty Press.

O'Brien, K., 2009. *Women and enlightenment in eighteenth-century Britain.* Cambridge: Cambridge University Press.

Offen, K.M., 2000. *European feminisms, 1700–1950: A political history.* Stanford, CA: Stanford University Press.

Pujol, M.A., 1992. *Feminism and antifeminism in early economic thought.* Northampton: Edward Elgar Publishing Inc.

Rendall, J., 1987. Virtue and commerce: Women in the making of Adam Smith's political economy. In: Kennedy, E. and S. Mendus, eds. *Women in western political philosophy.* New York: St. Martin's Press. pp. 44–76.

Robertson, W., 1769. *The history of the reign of the emperor Charles V: With a view of the progress of civil society in Europe from subversion of the Roman empire to the beginning of sixteenth century.* London: W. and W. Strathan.

Rousseau, J.J., 1979. *Emile: Or, on education.* Translated by Bloom, A. New York: Basic Books.

————, 1964. *The first and second discourses.* Masters, R.D., ed. Translated by Masters, R.D. and Masters. J. New York: St. Martin's Press.

Sebastiani, S., 2005. "Race", women and progress in the Scottish Enlightenment. In: Knott, S. and B. Taylor, ed. *Women gender and enlightenment.* New York: Palgrave Macmillan. pp. 75–96.

————, 2013. *The Scottish enlightenment: Race, gender and the limits of progress.* New York: Palgrave Macmillan.

Shah, S., 2006. Sexual division of labor in Adam Smith's works. *Journal of History of Economic Thought*, *28*(2), pp. 221–241.

Sutherland, K., 1995. Adam Smith's master narrative: Women and the wealth of nations. In: Copley, S. and K. Sutherland, eds. *Adam Smith's wealth of nations*. Manchester: Manchester University Press. pp. 97–121.

Weiss, P.A., 1987. Antifeminism and woman's nature. *Political Theory*, *5*(1), pp. 81–98.

Wexler, V.G., 1976. Made for men's delight. *The American Historical Review*, *81*(2), pp. 266–291.

Wollstonecraft, M., 1792. *A vindication of the rights of woman*. London: Dover Publications Inc.

Chapter 12

Conclusions

Smith laid out a ground-breaking moral treatise that elaborated on the motivations for morality, how morality was developed and how it was perpetuated within a culture. In a pragmatic way, his work has withstood the test of time in that it accurately observed and articulated perspectives that were later elaborated upon by Freud and other psychoanalysts. In addition, his understandings about sympathy/empathy and how morality is transmitted have been empirically tested, making the transition from philosophical theory to direct psychological application.

We used several psychoanalytic perspectives to uncover the psychological content in Smith's work on morality. We elaborated on some of the salient issues in what we have identified as his moral psychology, its pragmatic applications and the strengths and limitations of these works. Since each chapter has a discussion or a conclusion section, our remarks here will be brief, touching the most salient elements of this book.

We concluded that Smith's approach to moral philosophy and the concepts he used were the forerunners to concepts and approaches that were later used in psychoanalytic theory. In particular, we uncover the components they share in common: instinct, self-command or ego capacity, sympathy/empathy and impartial spectator/superego. We go on to elaborate issues growing out of the application of moral philosophy, such as friendship and dependency, gendered attitudes in morality and the role played by defenses in the implementation of a moral system. Throughout, we examine the implications in the application of his moral system, the concerns that are revealed in the application of morality and where Smith's theory holds up in empirical research.

In Chapters 2 and 3, we argued that sympathy is a forerunner of empathy. They both have affective and cognitive dimensions and involve feeling something analogous to that of the other. Both processes require the ability to change situations with the other. In particular, both processes include being able to put ourselves in the other's situation through imagination. Second, the sympathetic process is intersubjective, as argued in Chapter 2. Both the sympathetic process and intersubjectivity in psychoanalysis are associated with mutual influence, mutual recognition and creating a shared meaning. Furthermore, in Chapter 3 we suggest that the evidence in the developmental psychology literature supports Smith's theory of morality based on the process of sympathy. Specifically, the evidence suggests that sympathy/empathy leads to pro-social behavior, as was indicated in Smith's theory.

In addition to sympathy being a forerunner of empathy, and the sympathetic process sharing common elements with intersubjectivity, as we argue in Chapter 2, Smith's impartial spectator is a forerunner of Freud's superego. We elaborate on the similarities and differences of these two concepts in Chapter 7.

An important aspect of Smith's work is the tension between self-command and passions or instincts. Smith puts a premium on self-command over passions. In Chapter 4 we pointed out that for the impartial spectator to be able to go along with the passions of the agent, self-command is required. In this way, morality is achieved through social coordination and self-command. This theme is also addressed in Chapter 11. Smith identifies instincts with women and self-command with men. He makes a gendered argument in saying that women have humanity, which comes from instincts with no requirement of self-command, and men have generosity, which requires self-command. He goes on to assert that while men have the capacity for greater self-command, women do not. Even though Smith puts humanity and generosity at the same level in some places, on the whole generosity is elevated above humanity. We examined this position from the work of C.G. Jung. We argue that from a Jungian perspective, instincts and self-command are not gendered, and that these two capacities that culturally may be associated with men and women are present in both genders. Further, Jung's perspective views men and women as both having the capacity for development or "individuation" that is not gendered when it comes to the development of self-command in relation to instincts. We discuss the need and integrative necessity for instincts and assert that without instincts there would be no self-command or the need for self-command.

In Chapter 6 we established that defenses are an integral but unseen part of Smith's theory and that they are necessary for adaptation. It is in this light that we use the term "defenses" as a necessary and important structural component to forming an attitude towards life. Through the use of defenses, individuals move from an instinctually unreflective state to a conscious state in relation to morality. This allows for consensual rules to be created and implemented, facilitating a stable moral structure that reifies defenses at a social level. This system of defenses in the TMS, like any other defensive system, has both strengths and limitations.

We take up morality and defenses in Chapter 7, where we compare Smith's approach to Freud's and to contemporary psychoanalysis. Both Freud and Smith recognize the civilizing nature of culture, even though they disagree on the origin of cultural norms. For Smith, moral laws are commands of the Deity, while for Freud they are more pragmatic. For Smith, the norms for moral behavior come from God and are implemented through the sympathetic process. As we argue in the Appendix of Chapter 7, Smith sees morality as a manifestation of the Deity's design, in which sympathy is the mechanism for the implementation of this design. For Freud, the development of morality in the development of civilization is the result of a practical evolution that allows for caring relationships and keeps us from doing harm to each other.

Freud and Smith agree that moral structure is a significant accomplishment in the face of instincts. For Smith, the implementation of moral behavior necessitates the impartial spectator and self-command, for Freud and later psychoanalysts, self-command or ego capacity is necessary and the superego carries out the duties of the impartial spectator. The impartial spectator is the arbitrator of cultural norms taught through family and culture, and the superego carries that same capacity within the personality for Freud.

We further elaborate on the pragmatic applications of cultural morality with the use of the literature on evolutionary psychology and adaptive defenses. In particular, we investigate the links between markets and morality in Chapter 8. Growing out of evolutionary psychology are the pivotal capacities for delayed gratification and trust in the complex human interactions that make possible the reciprocity between markets and morality. Delayed gratification and the development of trust evolve from the integration of adaptive defenses in relation to the impulsive demands of immediate instinctual needs. Delayed gratification, which is a moral virtue according to Smith, leads to savings furthering growth. Increased trust among participants leads to increased trade in the market place. Due to the realized benefits of trust being fulfilled in the market place, cooperative morality is enhanced.

Smith's attitudes towards personal relationships are addressed in Chapters 9 and 10. In Chapter 9 we argued that Smith characterized interactions among people as impersonalized transactions. From a psychoanalytic perspective, we suggest that this was a defense against his lifelong dependencies. In Chapter 10 we argued that Smith's ideas on friendship were a description of cool friendships based on an evaluative thought process, not on intimate interaction of feeling states. His perspective on friendship seems to be an extension of his discomfort with interpersonal dependency and closeness that we spoke of in Chapter 9. A limitation of this perspective is that it does not include mature dependence particularly because Smith did not develop the capacity to accommodate differences.

We believe that a psychoanalytic approach brings a broader and more functional perspective to the Smith scholarship. The psychoanalytic viewpoint has its origins in a pragmatic and applied discipline of psychotherapy. When evaluating Smith's theoretical work on morality from this perspective, the emphasis is on its potential for applicability and not just its ample philosophical elegance. Smith's work has been viewed as a philosophical treatise and a guiding narrative for morality, and for some, economic theorizing. We are approaching his work as a viable applied theory subject to research and critique. Along those lines we have identified several areas where we feel that this applied psychoanalytic perspective opens new areas for inquiry in Smith's scholarship.

In the first two chapters we identified sympathy as one of Smith's keystone understandings to explore. We explored its value in the creation of morality, and through the literature in developmental psychology show how sympathy/empathy is a key component in the formation of morality. We also elaborate on sympathy/empathy's role in mutual influence and the creation of shared meaning between people. This line of inquiry expands Smith's notion that the creation of morality is not based in isolated individuals, but places individuals within a socially embedded milieu needing intersubjective interactions to develop morality. This is an area of inquiry that still has many possibilities for future work in the Smith literature.

We further sought to apply Smith's theoretical structure to markets and morality. We brought together the work in evolutionary psychology and linked it with a further explication of adaptive defenses to discuss the interaction between markets and morality and how each affects the other. The psychoanalytic and psychological implications of the interactions between morality and markets are an open area for future inquiry.

Finally, we argued that Smith had at best an ambivalent attitude towards women in his works, which was also in line with the cultural attitudes of his time. We concluded that his view of instincts and self-command are gendered. This is no doubt an area that will continue to generate future research and speculation.

The role that human nature plays in the TMS and Smith's work in general is also an area that has yet to be examined from a psychoanalytic perspective. Even though there is some work on human nature described by Smith scholars, they are not from a psychoanalytic or psychological perspective (see for example, Berry, 2012, and Fleischacker, 2004). This area of inquiry would be of interest on its own and would no doubt be also relevant for linking the TMS to the WN.

While most economists have not read Smith's first book on morality, its psychological assumptions are the backbone of the WN. We have examined the psychoanalytic and psychological aspects of the TMS and argue that there are some properties of the TMS that are directly or indirectly relevant to the economics of the WN. Some principles laid out in the WN are derived from the themes in the TMS. As such, since this book focuses on the WN in addition to the TMS, it is relevant for economics. Below are some further ideas about the links between the two books.

Smith's approach in the TMS relies on pain and the pleasure principle (an important aspect of Freud's analysis). Wealth accumulation and the status obtained from it gives pleasure since it is admired, and avoids shame and pain, as argued in the TMS. In addition, the prudent man of the TMS is frugal and foregoes present enjoyment for the future, thus he saves. This is because in the TMS men have a desire to "better" their economic conditions due to the admiration and approval that comes from wealth accumulation. In the WN as well, men are portrayed as having a desire to "better" their conditions, and this desire comes from the "womb"; it is an instinct we are born with. Savings of the prudent man leads to capital accumulation and economic growth, which is Smith's principle interest in the WN. The wellbeing of the individual and the economy as a whole is improved due to the incentives of the prudent man.

Smith puts emphasis on "tranquility of the mind" as a great source of happiness in the TMS. He further argued that commerce flourishes in a tranquil society, where individuals conduct their businesses without unwarranted interference by others. A further area for research would be to examine the psychological foundations for a successful laissez-faire economy based on Smith's "tranquility of the mind".

Finally, Smith was also concerned with fairness, which he sees as a part of human nature. In the TMS, he states that in the "human breast" there is a consciousness of being punished for wrong doings, and "Nature" protects the weak. For Smith, in market situations a mixture of altruism and fairness also play a role, not only self-interest. He sees justice as a "main pillar" of a society and bases this on the natural sentiment towards fairness that people internalize through the impartial spectator. The interactions of fairness, justice and altruism represent another opportunity to research these connections from a psychoanalytic perspective.

References

Berry, C.J., 2012. Adam Smith's science of human nature. *History of Political Economy, 44*, p. 3.
Fleischacker, S., 2004. *On Adam Smith's Wealth of Nations: A philosophical companion*. Princeton, NJ: Princeton University Press.

Index

action 83–6
adaptive defenses: evolutionary psychology and 122–4; morality and 128–30; necessity of 79–80, 200
altruistic behavior 39–40
Alvey, J. E. 162, 181
anima 191
animus 191

Barnett, B. 112
Barret, W. 79
benevolence 73–5, 82, 92, 94
Benjamin, J. 10, 15, 25
Berry, C. 58, 162
Bion, W. R. 38, 111
Bolognini, S. 37
Brenner, C. 79, 114
Brissenden, R. F. 104
Brown, V. 22–3
Bruni, L. 131, 162
Burke, E. 149

Campbell, T. D. 56
Cantor, N. 121
Carlo, G. 39–40
Carlyle, T. 148
Carrasco, M. A. 77
Civilization and Its Discontents (Freud) 102
Clark, H. C. 63, 180–1, 182
classical conditioning 40
Cole, L. 181
collective unconscious 189–90
commercial societies 161–3
conscience 58–9
conscious defenses 116
consciousness 190–1
Cramer, P. 108
Cropsy, J. 161
cultural unconscious 190

Darwall, S. 23, 37
defenses: adaptive 79–80, 122–4, 200; analysis in TMS 81–94, 106–8; conscious 116; in contemporary psychoanalysis 113–15; duty and 89–91; merit and demerit 86–9; preliminary stages of 78; propriety of action and 83–6; psychoanalytic concept of 78–81; self-judgment and 89–91; splitting 96; in superego development 108–10; "two-person" analysis of 79; unconscious 116; virtue 91–4
Deity: benevolence of 73–5; as the designer of universe 72; general rules 57–8, 72–3; invisible hand of 69; moral laws and 104–5; role in moral system 67–75; rules of morality and 62, 68; self-love and 71
delayed gratification 6, 121, 129–30, 132–3
demerit 62, 82, 86–9
dependence: personal 146–53, 201; social relations and 144–5
direct association 40
division of labor: dependence and 139–41; of the principle which gives occasion to 141–4
domination 144–5
Douglas, J. 147
Douglas, M. 8, 146–7
Dunn, J. 44–5
duty 82, 89–91

Easterbrooks, M. A. 39
ego 102, 124, 191–2
"Ego and the Id, The" (Freud) 100, 101, 109
Einstein, A. 96
Eisenberg, N. 41
Elliot, G. 59
Emde, R. 39

For Product Safety Concerns and Information please contact our
EU representative GPSR@taylorandfrancis.com in line with Taylor & Francis
Verlag GmbH, Kaufingerstraße 24, 80331 München, Germany